POLICE

POLICE

Practices, Perspectives, Problems

Steven M. Cox
Western Illinois University

Allyn and Bacon
Boston • London • Toronto • Sydney • Tokyo • Singapore

Executive Editor: Karen Hanson
Vice President and Publisher: Susan Badger
Marketing Manager: Joyce Nilsen
Editorial-Production Administrator: Donna Simons
Editorial-Production Service: Shepherd, Inc.
Composition and Prepress Buyer: Linda Cox
Manufacturing Buyer: Megan Cochran
Cover Administrator: Suzanne Harbison

Library of Congress Cataloging-in-Publication Data

Cox, Steven M.
    Police : practices, perspectives, problems / Steven M. Cox.
        p. cm.
    Includes bibliographical references and index.
    ISBN 0–205–16198–7
    1. Police—United States.   2. Law enforcement—United States.
I. Title.
HV8138.C672   1995   95–684
363.2'0973—dc20   CIP

Printed in the United States of America

10 9 8 7 6 5 4 3 2 1   00 99 98 97 96 95

Photo Credits: p. 1, p. 17, p. 31, p. 45, p. 61, p. 95, p. 121, p. 141, p. 163, p. 181,
p. 205, p. 225: James L. Shaffer

For Matthew and Melissa

CONTENTS

PREFACE

The U.S. municipal police are the most studied, and perhaps most criticized, police in the world. Still, a great deal of confusion exists among prospective police officers, citizens other than police officers, and even among police officers themselves concerning the police role.

In this book, I have attempted to present a realistic, practical view of the police as they interact with other citizens. It is my belief that much of the current criticism of the police and dissatisfaction among the police results from confusion over the appropriate role of the police and the misleading and sometimes unreasonable expectations that arise as a result.

It is also my belief that Sir Robert Peel developed and promoted a model for municipal police that has often been ignored in our society, but has recently been resurrected in the form of community-oriented policing. That is, the basic requirement for an effective, efficient, civil police is a meaningful partnership between the police and other citizens. Only when such a partnership exists can the police perform (or be expected to perform) their tasks as service providers and occasional law enforcers, because only then will the public provide the support and resources necessary for the successful performance of these tasks.

This partnership must be based on open, two-way communication between the police and other citizens in the joint venture of order maintenance and law enforcement. This brings us back to the importance of understanding the police role in our society.

Although I have discussed police discretion, functions, organization, recruitment, training, and a variety of other topics separately, it is important to recognize that they are all interrelated and must be considered as part of the network of policing. Stresses and strains in any one area will have repercussions in others and the relationships between the various parts must be considered if policing is to make sense.

It is also important to note from the outset that the terms policing and law enforcement are not synonymous. The latter constitutes only a small, though critical, part of the former. The basic task of the police in any society is not law enforcement, but order maintenance, which may or may not include, in any given encounter, law enforcement.

A good deal of what follows is based on my own observations and interactions with municipal police officers over the past twenty-five years.

S.M.C.

ACKNOWLEDGMENTS

A number of individuals contributed to the writing of this book. I would like to thank Professor William E. Johnson, Western Illinois University, John Broderick, Stonehill College, Herbert C. Friese, Burlington County College, Donald J. Melisi, Middlesex Community College, Victor E. Kappeler, Eastern Kentucky University, and Robert G. Huckabee, Indiana State University, for reviewing and commenting on the manuscript during its development. For substantive comments and encouragement along the way I would also like to thank Professors John Wade, John J. Conrad, Michael Hazlett, William McCamey, Dennis Bliss, and Stan Cunningham, Western Illinois University, and Jack Fitzgerald, Knox College.

A special thanks to Professor Giri Raj Gupta, who encouraged me along the way, reviewed the entire manuscript, and suggested changes to improve the work.

Numerous police administrators have contributed their insights to the work as well. Thanks to Chiefs Jerry Bratcher, O.J. Clark, John Wilson, and Don Cundiff among others. Special thanks to Director General Yu-Jiun Lu of the National Police Administration of the Republic of China.

Without the input of the dozens of officers who have allowed me to observe them in the course of their work or who have shared their perceptions in the classroom, this book would have been impossible.

I owe a debt of gratitude to the works of David Bayley, Egon Bittner, Jerome Skolnick, James Q. Wilson, Jonathan Rubinstein, Herman Goldstein, Peter Manning, John P. Clark, Albert J. Reiss, Jr., George Kirkham, Anthony Bouza, the late Robert Trojanowicz, and countless others who have provided the foundation for the work which follows.

Finally, thanks to Karen Hanson of Allyn and Bacon who believed in the project and to the editorial production and marketing staff of Allyn and Bacon.

1

HISTORICAL DEVELOPMENT OF THE UNITED STATES MUNICIPAL POLICE

Introduction

U.S. police are employed at the international, national, state, county, and municipal levels in both public and private agencies. Some 700,000 police personnel are employed in public agencies, ranging in size from one officer to some 25,000 officers. More than 90,000 sworn officers and civilians work in the ten largest departments, but there are more than 10,000 departments with ten or fewer employees (Dunham and Alpert, 1993:2). Some utilize the most modern technological equipment available; some have difficulty even obtaining good radios. Some are highly trained; others receive very little training. Some routinely intervene in the daily lives of their fellow citizens; others do not. Some are held in high regard by their fellow citizens; others are not (see Highlight 1.1). Any attempt to discuss this heterogeneous group as a whole is likely to be confusing, inaccurate, or both.

In order to help avoid such confusion and inaccuracy, we will focus this book on municipal police. A great deal of what we say also applies to county police, some to state police, and somewhat less to federal and international police. We have not attempted to deal with private police in detail here, although their relationship with municipal police is discussed in several places. As you read this book, then, please keep in mind that we are discussing municipal police unless otherwise noted. Before turning our attention to municipal policing, a very brief look at the composition of state and federal police might be helpful in order to distinguish them from local police.

State and Federal Police

Prior to 1900, federal and state governments played very limited roles in policing. In fact, only two states, Texas (1823) and Massachusetts (1865), had some type of state police at the turn of the century (Johnson, 1981; Roberg and Kuykendall, 1993). The Pennsylvania State Police was established in 1905 to deal with ethnic and labor disputes, but its duties eventually expanded to include general police functions throughout the state. Over the next twenty years, numerous other states adopted the Pennsylvania model of state police.

As the number of highways increased, state police agencies took on the responsibility for traffic enforcement on these thoroughfares, particularly in areas outside corporate limits of cities and towns. Eventually a bifurcation occurred: some agencies (twenty-five states) focused almost exclusively on traffic control (highway patrol departments), while others (twenty-four states) maintained more general enforcement powers (state police departments) (Barker, Hunter, and Rush, 1994: 70). All states except Hawaii now have some type of state police agency. In addition to their basic tasks, many of these agencies provide statewide communications/computer systems, assist in crime-scene analysis and multi-jurisdictional investigations, provide training for other police agencies, and collect, analyze, and disseminate information on crime patterns in the state. Most state police agencies are also responsible for security of state parks (park police or rangers), security of state property and state officials, and regulation of liquor- and gambling-related activities. These

---

HIGHLIGHT 1.1   Policing in America

"Dirty Harry" Comes to Illinois Town; Citizens Freak Out

Tough Police Chief Is Hired to Clean Up Collinsville; Trouble Is, He Is Doing It

COLLINSVILLE, ILL.—When this St. Louis suburb wanted a crackdown on crime, it hired a new police chief: David Niebur, a tough Minneapolis cop.

That was two years ago. Now, felony arrests are up 40%, traffic citations have soared 50%, and felony convictions have doubled. But something else is soaring here: The tempers of town leaders. Some call their new chief, a Midwestern Dirty Harry and his force "Niebur's Nazis."

"He's turned this town into a police state," grouses Alverna Wrigley, a perennial mayoral candidate and among those who have launched petitions and other legal efforts to unseat him. Hiring Chief Niebur, says Michael Fischer, the former police commissioner, was "one of the worst mistakes I ever made."

For angered residents of this town of 22,000, recent events are a bitter reminder of an old saw: Be careful what you wish for, you just might get it. "Everybody wants to get tough on crime, but they expect it to be the other guy who gets affected by the crackdown," says Darrell Sanders, the Frankfort, Ill., police chief and a finalist for the Collinsville job.

Law enforcement was far more relaxed under former chief Nick Mamino, a well-liked Andy Griffith type. "Under Chief Mamino, you would actually get chewed out for making too many arrests," says Sgt. Edward Delmore.

And the local elite expected police to use a liberal dose of discretion with them. "Every town has its haves and have nots, and in a community the size of Collinsville, I'm not sure a little good-old-boyism is a bad thing," says former city commissioner, Fred Krietemeyer.

But Mr. Mamino, now the bookkeeper at his mother's topless bar outside town, denies he gave special treatment to local VIPs, and adds that under his leadership "enforcement was aggressive when it needed to be."

Still, crime was rising in Collinsville, which abuts East St. Louis, Ill.—a rough, crime-ridden city. In 1988, Collinsville was jarred awake by a drug-linked double homicide at the Thrifty Inn.

When Chief Mamino announced plans to retire, city leaders, for the first time, went outside the department for a successor. Mr. Niebur, a top administrator on the Minneapolis force, came with a master's degree from Harvard and a reputation as a tough street-cop. He received a dozen decorations in his 18 years with the Minneapolis P.D., including a medal of valor for fatally shooting an armed man threatening a child.

But he also ranked near the top of his department in the number of complaints brought against him by civilians—"Police officers who don't generate any complaints are the ones who don't do anything," he says—and had a reputation for openly rating his superiors. Once, outraged by a fatal shooting of a Minneapolis policeman, then-Sgt. Niebur publicly branded his boss, Minneapolis Police Chief Tony Bouza, a "murderer" for requiring officers to be alone in patrol cars.

It didn't take Chief Niebur long to make waves in Collinsville. Just days after taking over, he refused to let Mr. Fischer, the civilian police commissioner, select sites for traffic speed traps. "I think I know more about police work than a guy who sells trucks," the chief told reporters—after Mr. Fischer ordered him to stop making unapproved comments to the press. Mr. Fischer suspended the chief, but the city council reinstated him.

Continued

The chief also embarrassed city commissioners by publicly declaring that the department he inherited was as technologically backward as the Mayberry P.D. He cited an antiquated squad-car radio system that shared its only frequency with the Missouri penal system. "We had an officer calling for an ambulance get drowned out by a call for a hundred pounds of potatoes in the prison commissary," he said.

To spur arrests, Chief Niebur ordered his 30 officers to stop suspicious-looking cars to check IDs and cruise local bars for people with outstanding warrants. One recent night, six officers stopped a performance by a local band at Patti's Pub and arrested the lead guitarist, who failed to appear in court on a drunken-driving charge. Such tactics are "wrecking our business," complains Tony Koste, who runs Eagles, a private club.

Motorists are also upset. Since Chief Niebur took over, Collinsville has shot ahead of two larger cities to lead the county in traffic fines. "If the light above your license plate is dim—you'll get a ticket here," grumbles William Evers III, a local lawyer.

Rushing Retirement

And prominent citizens no longer can make those tickets disappear, says Chief Niebur. He recalls that soon after he arrived, a local businessman "walked into my office believing it would be an automatic thing that I'd fix his traffic ticket." When Chief Niebur refused, the man "told me it was a sad state of affairs when somebody as important as he was couldn't get a ticket fixed," the chief says.

The new ways came as quite a shock to Marvin Rushing, a Collinsville cop for 23 years. As Officer Rushing watched a tow truck pull a car from a ditch early one morning, Sgt. Delmore, now one of the chief's Young Turks, drove up and asked if the driver of the car—a young woman standing nearby—was drunk. Officer Rushing replied that he didn't believe so. Sgt. Delmore ordered the woman tested anyway, and she had a blood-alcohol level almost twice the legal limit. Afterwards, Chief Niebur brought disciplinary charges against Officer Rushing, prompting him to retire.

Complains Mr. Rushing: "Niebur treats people like machines."

Fear and Loathing

Many in Collinsville yearn for the days when crime wasn't much talked about here, let alone attacked. Petition drives aimed at dismissing Chief Niebur have gained hundreds of signatures, but organizers say fear of retribution has quelled progress. "People are afraid of being harassed," says Roy Conger, a baker and leader of one effort. Mr. Conger, 22, has been arrested four times on misdemeanors since the chief took over, including improper use of traffic lanes, to which he pleaded guilty; the remaining charges are outstanding. (Mr. Conger was arrested twice before Chief Niebur arrived, on an armed-robbery charge, which was dismissed, and on a charge of criminal damage to property, to which he pleaded guilty.)

A leading Collinsville attorney says he is preparing a lawsuit on behalf of residents he says have been wrongly arrested. Mr. Fischer, the former police commissioner, has petitioned a state court here to uphold his suspension of Chief Niebur. A new city council and city manager have expressed support for the chief, but declined to renew his two-year contract in July. "It means I can be fired at the will of the city manager, which isn't the best position to be in," Chief Niebur says.

But he isn't backing off. He recently spent thousands of dollars making Collinsville one of the smallest cities anywhere to boast its own SWAT team. After the local paper ran a photo of the team practicing on a flight of stairs recently, many residents laughed, says Michael Meurer, executive director of the Chamber of Commerce, because "we've only got about two buildings in Collinsville tall enough to have flights of stairs, and one of them's a retirement center."

Indeed, even admirers such as Mr. Meurer question whether Collinsville is big enough for Chief Niebur's ambitions. "He's done a tremendous job of turning our police into an elite force," says Mr. Meurer, "but I just worry that sooner or later we're going to run out of crime, and then what?" (Helliker, 1991) agencies employ about 110,000 personnel, or about 15 percent of all police personnel in the United States (Maguire, Pastore, and Flanagan, 1993: 23).

United States Marshals were the first federal police, established in 1789 for the purpose of enforcing directives of the federal courts. There are currently over sixty federal agencies that exercise police powers, including the Secret Service, the Federal Bureau of Investigation (FBI), the Drug Enforcement Administration (DEA), the U.S. Customs Service, the Immigration and Naturalization Service, the Internal Revenue Service (IRS), and the Bureau of Alcohol, Tobacco, and Firearms (ATF). These agencies employ more than 65,000 personnel or about 8.2 percent of all police personnel in the United States (Maguire, Pastore, and Flanagan, 1993: 23). While each agency has a set of specific duties, there is a good deal of overlap and duplication among them. They do not, for the most part, engage in those activities normally provided by local and county police, such as patrol, provision of services, and maintenance of order (Langworthy and Travis, 1994). Relatively few federal officers, usually referred to as "agents," are uniformed; their primary duties center around investigation and control of federal crimes, such as bank robberies and crimes that involve the crossing of state lines. They are also responsible for protecting federal property and federal officials. Finally, federal agencies provide training and logistic support for state and local police, and the FBI collects and disseminates national crime statistics.

Municipal Police

Municipal policing is a relatively recent phenomenon. In the Western world, it began for all practical purposes in 1829 in London as a result of the efforts of Sir Robert Peel, who was then Home Secretary. Peel believed that the police should be organized along military lines, under government control. He also thought police officers should be men of quiet demeanor and good appearance, and be familiar with the neighborhoods in which they were to police. Finally, he supported a territorial strategy of policing in which officers would walk prescribed beats in order to prevent and deal with crime. By 1870, Peel's territorial strategy had spread to every major city in the United States (Lane, 1992: 6–7).

Municipal police in the United States have always provided an extremely wide range of services, many of which, as we shall see, have little to do with crime or law enforcement. Each municipal department exists in its own context. Policing in a metropolitan area may be considerably different from that in a small rural community in terms of the frequency of certain types of activities and the degree of specialization within the department, although the types of services provided are basically the same. Within any given police agency, each officer has considerable discretion with respect to the way in which he or she provides services. The diversity in American municipal police organizations makes them unique, and is thereby often confusing to foreign visitors familiar with more centralized police services.

What are the origins of municipal police? Why and how did we decide that it is necessary to specially designate certain individuals to provide the services associated with the police? What are these services? What are the special characteristics of municipal police? These and other questions will be addressed in the remainder of this chapter and in Chapter 2.

The Concept of Police

As we interact with other people, we develop expectations concerning actions and reactions of one another. These expectations depend to some extent on the characteristics of the particular individuals involved in the interaction, but they also come to be associated with the positions occupied by the participants. Thus, we expect certain types of behavior from priests, physicians, teachers, and police officers; and, while these expectations may be modified depending on what we know about a particular priest or physician, the basic elements of our expectations remain much the same regardless of who occupies the position or fills the role. Some of these expectations are based on actual interaction with people in various positions, while others are based on hearsay, rumor, and/or media reports that may lead us to anticipate the content of future interactions with people in various roles long before they occur.

Through this process, we come to regard certain behaviors as "normal" for people in certain roles. Behaviors that fail to meet our expectations are regarded as "abnormal" or "deviant." Since we organize our lives in terms of our perceptions of how others will react to us, those who behave in deviant fashion cause us concern. To help maximize the probability that others will behave as we expect them to, we try to provide positive feedback to them for behaving in this fashion and punish them for behaving in alternate fashion. In small, homogeneous groups, behavior is controlled informally through the use of group pressure. Violations of customs, traditions, or moral standards are punished in a variety of ways ranging from gossip to excommunication.

As the size of the group increases and people become more dispersed, homogeneity gives way to heterogeneity, and specialization and differentiation become the rule. As different groups or segments of the community pursue their own ends, different value systems emerge. Community consensus no longer exists to the same extent as in smaller, more homogeneous groups, and conflict between groups becomes commonplace.

Still, each specialized group depends to a greater or lesser extent on every other group. Farmers depend on soldiers for protection, and soldiers on farmers for food. Failure to provide expected goods and services makes life difficult. Without some assurance that intergroup obligations will be met (contracts fulfilled), life would become highly unpredictable, and disorder would characterize society. Traditional, customary, and moral obligations may not be honored voluntarily, so it becomes necessary to formalize these normative expectations (that is, to pass laws in the interest of maintaining some degree of order in the society). To ensure that such agreements are kept, certain individuals are designated to watch for violations and to provide mediation and/or arbitration services for conflicting parties. If mediation and arbitration fail, these specially designated persons are charged with apprehending the offending party and bringing him or her before other specially designated persons (prosecutors, judges) who have further authority to sanction the undesirable behavior.

The conflicting demands of various groups must all be accommodated (at least to the point of being heard) in a democratic society, and virtually guarantee that not all parties can be satisfied at the same time. Those responsible for policing the society, then, occupy inherently problematic positions.

Historical Development of the United States Municipal Police—The Early Years

English settlers (about 90 percent of all early settlers) in America brought with them a night watch system that required able-bodied males to donate their time to help protect the cities. As was the case in England, those who could afford it often hired others to serve their tours, and those who served were not particularly effective. Voluntary citizen participation in law enforcement was not very effective, and something was needed to replace it. In 1749, residents of Philadelphia convinced legislators to pass a law creating the position of warden. Each warden was authorized to hire as many watchmen as needed, the powers of the watchmen were increased, and their salaries were paid from taxes. Other cities soon adopted similar plans (Johnson, 1981: 7).

By the 1800s, with the rapid growth of cities, crime and mob violence had become problems in both British and U.S. cities. In England, Sir Robert Peel was finally successful in establishing the London Metropolitan Police in 1829. Shortly thereafter, day watch systems in the United States were established (Philadelphia—1833; Boston—1838; New York—1844; San Francisco—1850; Los Angeles—1851). By the 1850s, day and night watch systems were consolidated to provide 24-hour protection to city dwellers (Berg, 1992: 31). By the middle of the nineteenth century, the main structural elements of U.S. municipal policing had emerged. Watch and ward systems had been replaced, in the cities at least, by centralized, government-supported police agencies whose tasks included crime prevention, provision of a wide variety of services to the public, enforcement of morality, and apprehension of criminals. These tasks were performed by municipal police, and supplemented by county sheriffs in rural areas. Over time, these police agencies were further supplemented by the development of state and federal agencies (Sweatman and Cross, 1989: 12).

Although they adopted many practices from their British counterparts, U.S. police lacked the central authority of the Crown to establish a legitimate mandate for their actions. Small departments acted independently within their jurisdictions. Large departments were divided into precincts, which often operated more as small individual departments than as branches of the same organization (Kelling and Moore, 1988: 3). Colonists feared government intervention into their daily lives and thus disliked the idea of a centralized police force. Police officers represented the local political party in power rather than the legal system (Roberg and Kuykendall, 1993: 59).

As a result of the political heterogeneity, officers were often required to enforce unpopular laws in immigrant ethnic neighborhoods. Because of their intimacy with the neighborhoods, they were vulnerable to bribes for lax enforcement or nonenforcement (Kelling and Moore, 1988: 4). In addition, the police found themselves in frequent conflict with rioters, union workers and their management counterparts, looters, and others. "Expectations that the police would be disinterested public servants . . . ran afoul of the realities of urban social and political life. Heterogeneity made it more difficult to determine what was acceptable and what was deviant behavior. Moreover, urban diversity encouraged a political life based upon racial and ethnic cleavages as well as clashes of economic interests. Democratic control of police assured that heterogeneous cities would have constant conflicts over police organization and shifts of emphasis depending upon which groups controlled the political machinery at any one time" (Richardson, 1974: 33–34).

In some cities, such as New York, political corruption and manipulation were built into policing. New York police officers in the 1830s were hired and fired by elected officials—who expected those they hired to support them politically, and who fired those who did not. "The late nineteenth century policeman had a difficult job. He had to maintain order, cope with vice and crime, provide service to people in trouble, and keep his nose clean politically" (Richardson, 1974: 47). The police became involved in party politics, including granting immunity from arrest to those in power (Lane, 1992: 12). Corruption and extortion became traditions in many departments, and discipline and professional pride were largely absent from many departments.

According to Johnson (1981: i) the United States' brand of local self-government gives both citizens and professional politicians considerable influence in policing. "The need to respond to the diverse, often conflicting demands of various constituencies has given American policing a unique character which affects its efficiency as well as its reputation. However one views the police today, it is essential to understand how the theory and practice of politics influenced the nature, successes, and problems of law enforcement."

Policing During the Nineteenth and Early Twentieth Centuries

Attempts at reform, including the Pendleton Act (1883), which extended civil service protection to first federal and later state and local employees, led to some improvement; however, old traditions and perceptions died hard and, in some cases, not at all. An excellent illustration of the complex intermingling of politics and policing is the office of sheriff. The sheriff was and remains a political figure charged with police duties. In America, rural policing was, almost from the beginning, in the hands of the sheriff (Virginia, 1634).

By the middle of the nineteenth century, as a result of the not infrequent killing of unarmed officers by armed offenders, many American police officers had purchased and carried their own firearms. "However unhappy the critics of an armed police might be, they had to face one unavoidable fact. U.S. citizens, unlike the British, had a long tradition that every citizen had the right, even the duty, to own firearms. Guns were part of the American culture. . . . Beginning in the 1840s, people in cities began to use firearms against one another systematically for the first time. . . . The problem facing the police had now become critical. Patrolmen never could be sure when a rowdy might have a gun, yet the officer knew he had to intervene in disorder quickly or risk having a small dispute between a small number of people grow into a serious problem. . . . The public accepted an armed police because there appeared to be no other alternative at the time" (Johnson, 1981: 29–30).

In the United States, many citizens were opposed to the idea of centralized police forces because they feared that such forces might become instruments of government repression. The desire to protect individual rights was strong, yet the need to ensure some degree of order in the society was also apparent. In order to both maintain order and enforce the law, municipal police had to be granted the right to intervene in the daily affairs of private citizens. Regulation of morals, enforcement of traffic laws, mediation of domestic disputes, involvement with juveniles, and other police activities require such intervention. Yet, many of the early settlers in America had come precisely because they did not want government intervention in and regulation of their daily activities. Predictably, then, police intervention in areas that citizens generally regarded as private has generated suspicion and hostility toward the police. Nonetheless, with increasing demands for public order comes increasing intolerance of criminality, violence, and riotous behavior. Citizens want the police to address their concerns and to solve the problems they have brought to the attention of the police, but otherwise to leave them to their own pursuits (Toch and Grant, 1991: 3).

This was certainly the case in the United States beginning in the late 1800s and early 1900s, when technological advances such as the call box, telephone, two-way radio, and patrol car led the police to believe that they could make great strides in eliminating urban crime. Promises to cut response time, apprehend more criminals, and prevent more crimes led to an increasing number of requests from citizens to produce such results (Reiss, 1992: 53).

As the police continued to be involved in areas having little to do with law enforcement/crime, the public came to expect the police to respond to almost any request for assistance; and, particularly during the hours between 5:00 PM and 8:00 AM, did not hesitate to call the police for assistance normally provided by some other agency. Fighting crime and enforcing laws were duties of the police, but the proportion of time devoted to these activities was and remains very small in comparison to the proportion of time spent providing other services.

Throughout most of the nineteenth and into the twentieth century, the basic qualification for becoming a police officer was a political connection (Roberg and Kuykendall, 1992: 61–66). Basic literacy and good physical health were not among the prerequisites (Richardson, 1974: 27), although sheer physical size was often a consideration. Officers were expected to "handle" whatever problems they encountered while patrolling their beats, not simply to enforce the law. "For the patrolman, unless he was exceptionally stubborn or a notoriously slow learner, the moral was clear: if you want to get along, go along" (Richardson, 1974: 57).

To be promoted to the rank of captain or above in many big city departments, an officer needed political support and, in some cases, a great deal of money. The police were a part of the political machinery, and politicians were seldom interested in impartial justice.

Beginning in the 1870s, attempts to reform the government in general and the police in particular emerged. Examinations were recommended for those seeking public employment or promotion in an attempt to remove direct political influence and to recruit better-qualified personnel. While some improvements resulted, political motivations continued to plague the selection of both officers and chiefs. "Too many chiefs were simply fifty-five-year-old patrolmen" (Richardson, 1974: 70).

This tradition continued into the twentieth century and is, indeed, still deep-rooted in policing. The hiring and firing of police chiefs accompanying changes in the political leadership of communities continues today, as do attempts on behalf of politicians to influence the daily activity of police officers and chiefs.

While the mixture of politics and policing has created numerous problems for the police, there is another side to this issue. In a democratic society, how are the police to be controlled? If the police are to be accountable and responsive to the citizens they serve, through what procedures are their needs and desires to be made known to the police? "The suggestion that police agencies be directly supervised by elected municipal executives conjures up the image of police administrators beholden to various interests—including criminal elements—on whose continued support the elected mayor, their boss, may depend . . . is this not one of the costs of operating under our system of government?" (Goldstein, 1977: 151,152).

In short, our system operates with the use of elected representatives, and while their representation may not always satisfy us, we depend on them to convey our needs and desires to the institutions over which they preside. In our society politics and policing are inevitably interwoven and, while we must be constantly alert to potential problems that result from this relationship, this is both necessary and desirable in a democratic society.

In the early 1930s, movements to professionalize the police began to materialize (although police professionalization was recognized as an important issue at least as early as 1909 by August Vollmer, Chief of Police in Berkeley, California, from 1905 to 1932 and the father of modern police management systems). In part because of the Depression, policing became more attractive to young men who in better times might have sought other employment, thus making it possible to recruit and select better-qualified police officers. Vollmer, Arthur Neiderhoffer, William Parker, and O. W. Wilson, among others, promoted professionalism and higher education for police officers, coupled with the impact of various reform movements, began to show positive results.

The onset of World War II and the Korean War, however, made recruitment of well-qualified officers more difficult during the 1940s and 1950s, and the riots and civil disorders of the late 1960s and early 1970s made policing less attractive to some. During this period, observers of the police, and sometimes the police themselves, seemed to equate technological advances with professionalism. While technological advances did occur, changes in standards, development of ethical codes, education of police officers by those outside the field, and other indicators of professionalism were basically lacking. Still, some important changes had occurred: reformers had identified inappropriate political involvement as a major problem in U.S. policing; civil service successfully removed some of the patronage and ward influences on police officers; and law and professionalism were established as the basis of police legitimacy. Under these circumstances, policing became a legal and technical matter left to the discretion of professional police executives. "Political influence of any kind on a police department came to be seen as not merely a failure of police leadership but as corruption in policing" (Kelling and Moore, 1988: 5).

Contemporary Policing

In the 1960s and early 1970s there was a rapid development of two-year and four-year college degree programs in law enforcement, and an increased emphasis on training. These changes were in large part due to the 1967 report of the President's Commission on Law Enforcement and Administration of Justice, which helped induce Congress to pass the Omnibus Crime Control and Safe Streets Act of 1968. This act established the Law Enforcement Assistance Administration (LEAA) and provided one billion dollars a year to improve and strengthen criminal justice agencies. Federal and state funding were available to police officers seeking to further their educations, and potential police officers began to see some advantage in taking at least some college-level courses (Weiner, 1981: 61). Although there were vast differences in the quality of these programs, they did create a pool of relatively well-qualified applicants for both supervisory and entry-level positions.

This development, coupled with improvements in police training, salaries and benefits, and equipment, helped create a more professional image of the police. At the same time, however, police came under increasing scrutiny as a result of their roles in the urban disorders of the late 1960s and early 1970s. Challenges to both authority and procedure were common, and criticism from the outside continued into the 1980s. The police are still viewed by some as at least partly responsible for continued high crime rates and civil unrest, and the number of complaints and civil actions brought against the police has skyrocketed. As we entered the 1990s, Bouza (1990: 270–271) notes, "It is becoming ever clearer that underlying social and economic conditions are spawning crime and that society's unwillingness to do anything meaningful about them has really sealed the fate of the police effort to cope with the symptoms. Society wants to fight crime with more cops, tougher judges, and bigger jails, not through such scorned 'liberal' schemes as social welfare programs. . . . Police executives believe that today's unattended problems, concentrated in our urban centers, will only get worse, eventually resulting in riots and heightened violence."

There is clearly a discrepancy between what the public assumes the police can accomplish (based on media presentations, etc.) and what the police can actually accomplish. While the expectation may be that more police will solve the problems referred to by Bouza, the reality is that no increase in the numbers of police officers, in and of itself, will produce the desired result. The discrepancy is highly problematic, impacting not only police administrators's decisions concerning operations, but also on the type of personnel who apply for police positions and the type of job preparation they receive.

At the same time, collective bargaining and unionization in police departments have changed considerably the complexion of relationships between police administrators and rank-and-file officers. While police unions have undoubtedly helped improve police salaries and working conditions, they remain controversial because of their emphasis on seniority and perceived opposition to reform. According to Gaines, Southerland, and Angell (1991), police unions have gained better financial packages for their members, forced police organizations to change, and helped bring about participatory management, orderly grievance procedures, and well-regulated disciplinary hearings. They have also, however, often opposed advanced education for all officers, transfers between departments, changes in recruitment standards, and civilian review boards. Alpert and Dunham (1992: 86–88) indicate that many of these issues remain alive in the mid-1990s. There is little doubt, however, that collective bargaining in police agencies is here to stay.

A noteworthy development in policing occurred in 1979. In response to repeated calls for police professionalization, the Commission on Accreditation for Law Enforcement Agencies was established. The commission was formed through the efforts of the International Chiefs of Police Association, the National Organization of Black Law Enforcement Executives, the National Sheriffs Association, and the Police Executive Research Forum. The commission became operational in 1983 and since then has been accepting applications for accreditation, conducting evaluations based on some 924 standards for law enforcement agencies, and granting accreditation. By 1994, some three-hundred police agencies had been accredited, with another five-hundred or so awaiting accreditation. In fact, those agencies originally accredited were beginning to apply for reaccreditation.

The amount and quality of research on the police improved dramatically beginning in the 1960s. The 1967 Presidential Commission on Law Enforcement and the Administration of Justice, the National Advisory Commission on Civil Disorders in the same year, and the 1973 National Advisory Commission on Criminal Justice Standards and Goals represented major efforts to better understand styles of policing, police-community relations, and police selection and training (Alpert and Dunham, 1992). Many other privately and government-funded research projects further contributed to our knowledge in these and other areas relating to the police.

Yet today, municipal police reflect 150 years of conflict and attempts at reform. Most chiefs continue to be selected against a backdrop of party politics, which may be good or bad, as we have seen. There have been some consolidation and standardization of services, but not a great deal. The police appear to have become more concerned about social responsibility, but still have difficulties interacting with some segments of society. Diversity remains the main characteristic of municipal police, with local control the key to such diversity. Progress in policing has been made on many fronts. Progressive police chiefs such as Jerry Bratcher (Palatine, IL), Lee Brown (formerly Houston and New York City), Anthony Bouza (formerly Minneapolis), and Fred Rice (formerly Chicago), to name just a few, have pushed the boundaries of traditional policing and have shared their thoughts and findings at both national and international levels by publishing and promoting exchange programs. Research on and by the police has increased dramatically in the past several years. As Petersilia (1993: 220) points out, ". . . Police leaders have been under considerable pressure to manage personnel and operations as efficiently as possible. This pressure may help explain why police administrators have apparently been even more willing than leadership in other criminal justice areas to question traditional assumptions and methods, to entertain the conclusions of research, and to test research recommendations."

The Community-Policing Era

Throughout the history of U.S. policing, community control of the police has been a major concern. When police administrators attempted to maximize the advantages of speed and mobility through the use of patrol cars, they created social distance between the officers and the other citizens they served; many citizens preferred to have police officers walking the beat. Furthermore, research on foot patrol suggested that it contributed to city life, reduced fear, increased citizen satisfaction with the police, improved police attitudes toward citizens, and increased the morale and job satisfaction of police officers (Kelling and Moore, 1988: 10).

Unfortunately, the promised advantages of speed and mobility have had little positive effect on crime. As police departments became more technologically sophisticated, citizens' expectations increased; using traditional means, the police have been unable to meet these expectations. By the mid 1980s it was clear that the police by themselves were unable to deal with increasing crime and violence. Recognizing that only with public cooperation could their performance in the areas of crime control and order maintenance be improved, progressive police administrators turned to community-oriented or community-based policing as a possible solution to their problems (see Chapter 3 for a detailed discussion of community policing).

At the same time, problem-oriented policing was the subject of research in several communities. This approach to policing emphasizes the interrelationships among what might otherwise appear to be disparate events. For example, in one major city, for any given year, 60 percent of the calls for police assistance originated from 10 percent of the households calling the police (Pierce, 1987). Rather than dealing with all of these calls as separate incidents to be "handled" before clearing the calls and going on to other calls, problem-oriented policing focuses attention on the underlying difficulties that create patterns of incidents. This focus allows officers to take a holistic approach, working with other citizens and other agency representatives to find more permanent solutions to a variety of police problems (see Highlight 1.2).

These two approaches to policing (community-oriented and problem-oriented) emphasize the importance of the police-community relationship, so clearly recognized by Peel over 150 years ago. Further, they recognize the fact, discussed in the following chapters, that police work is largely order maintenance performed through the use of negotiations. In fact, Sherman (1978: 4), in proposing changes to improve education for future police officers, recommends that in addition to familiarizing students with the criminal justice sys-

---

HIGHLIGHT 1.2   Police Citizen Cooperation Important

FBI Director William Sessions recently made the following observations in connection with National Crime Prevention Month:

Most people believe that law enforcement professionals should be the sole preventers of crime; however, we cannot manage this responsibility alone.

To understand this, all we need to do is to look at the crime statistics for 1989, which reveal that crime is up all over the United States. Both violent and property crimes rose last year. In fact, the FBI's annual Crime Index total for 1989 showed an increase for the fifth consecutive year.

The challenge to those of us in law enforcement is to fight crime harder and to cooperate more closely with citizens and volunteer groups in our shared struggle against crime. And the key to our success will be crime prevention—forming strong partnerships with citizens of the community as we confront the challenges of crime in the 1990s and into the next century.

Of course, crime prevention is not a new concept. In the early days of our Nation, private citizens kept the peace in their communities through respect for the law and through voluntary involvement in peace-keeping efforts. For the most part, the church, the family, and the community imposed social sanctions that were the primary controls in preventing and controlling crime.

Unfortunately, as cities grew and the populations changed, this community support for law enforcement broke down. As a result, the responsibility for crime prevention shifted. Law enforcement officers, not citizens, became society's first line of defense against crime.

But as today's statistics remind us, law enforcement cannot prevent, or reduce, crime without enlisting broad-based citizen participation, cooperation, and support. Moreover, our resources and manpower are shrinking, while our responsibilities are growing and the criminal element is becoming more sophisticated. So, we must get back to the basics and use community-based efforts to help control crime.

In the war on crime, we must build better educational systems for the public so that instead of fearing crime, they will take measures to prevent it. Indeed, every time a citizen becomes involved in crime prevention, our neighborhoods, our communities, and our Nation are improved (Sessions, 1990: 1).

Reprinted with permission from the *FBI Law Enforcement Bulletin*, 59(10), 1.

tem, all police education programs should emphasize the consideration of value choices and ethical dilemmas in policing, and should "include comprehensive treatment of the most commonly performed police work, which falls outside of the criminal justice system."

While it is difficult to generalize about the future of the police in the United States because of their diversity, Alpert and Dunham (1992: 32) have pinpointed four continuing dilemmas for the police, each of which has its roots in the historical issues discussed above. These issues are:

1. fiscal crises resulting from inflation, poor management, tax revolts, increased salary demands, and higher crime rates;
2. the research "revolution," which has shown us what doesn't work with respect to policing, but has not yet provided insight into what does work;
3. problems of police corruption, which continue to exist;
4. conflict between the police and the community.

In the remainder of this book we will explore the issues raised here, along with the variety of ways in which the American police attempt to define and fulfill their obligations and responsibilities (realistic and unrealistic), and the consequences of their attempts.

Discussion Questions

1. Why is it so difficult to discuss and generalize about the police in the United States?

2. Briefly discuss the history of U.S. police and the problems they currently face that are part of this history.

3. How, in the conduct of human interaction, did the need for a police arise?

4. What problems confronting the police are inherent in democratic societies?

5. What are the positive and negative effects of the interaction between politics and the police in our society?

References

Alpert, G.P. and Dunham, R.G. 1992. *Policing Urban America* 2 ed. Prospect Heights, IL: Waveland Press.

Barker, T., Hunter, R.D., and Rush, J.P. 1994. *Police Systems & Practices*. Englewood Cliffs, NJ: Prentice Hall.

Berg, B.L. 1992. *Law Enforcement: An Introduction to Police in Society*. Boston: Allyn & Bacon.

Bouza, A. V. 1990. *The Police Mystique*. New York: Plenum.

Dunham, R.G. and Alpert, G.P. 1993. *Critical Issues in Policing: Contemporary Readings* 2 ed. Prospect Heights, IL: Waveland Press.

Gaines, L.K., Southerland, M.D., and Angell, J.E. 1991. *Police Administration*. New York: McGraw-Hill.

Goldstein, H. 1977. *Policing a Free Society*. Cambridge, MA: Ballinger Publishing Co.

Helliker, K. 1991. "'Dirty Harry' Comes to Illinois Town; Citizens Freak Out." *The Wall Street Journal* (10 September), p. A1.

Johnson, D.R. 1981. *American Law Enforcement: A History.* St. Louis: Forum Press.

Kelling, G.L. and Moore, M.H. 1988. "The Evolving Strategy of Policing." *Perspectives on Policing.* (November) U.S. Department of Justice. Washington, DC: U.S. Government Printing Office.

Lane, R. 1992. "Urban Police and Crime." In Tonry, M. and Morris, N. (eds.), *Modern Policing.* Chicago: University of Chicago Press, 1–50.

Langworthy, R.H. and Travis, L.F. III. 1994. *Policing in America.* New York: Macmillan.

Maguire, K., Pastore, A.L., and Flanagan, T.J. 1993. *Sourcebook of Criminal Justice Statistics—1992.* Washington, DC: U.S. Government Printing Office.

Petersilia, J. 1993. "Influence of Research on Policing." In Dunham, R.G. and Alpert, G.P. (eds.), *Critical Issues In Policing: Contemporary Readings.* Prospect Heights, IL: Waveland Press.

Pierce, G. et al. 1987. "Evaluation of an Experiment in Proactive Police Intervention in the Field of Domestic Violence Using Repeat Call Analysis." Boston: The Boston Fenway Project.

Reiss, A.J., Jr. 1992. "Police Organization in the Twentieth Century." In Tonry, M. and Morris, N. (eds.), *Modern Policing.* Chicago: University of Chicago Press, 51–97.

Richardson, J.F. 1974. *Urban Police in the United States.* Port Washington, NY: Kennikat Press.

Roberg, R.R. and Kuykendall, J. 1993. *Police in Society.* Belmont, CA: Wadsworth.

Rubinstein, J. 1973. *City Police.* New York: Farrar, Straus and Giroux.

Sessions, W. S. 1990. "Director's Message: Police and Citizens Working Together." *FBI Law Enforcement Bulletin* 59(10), 1.

Sherman, L.W. 1978. *The Quality of Police Education.* San Francisco: Jossey-Bass.

Sweatman, B. and Cross, A. 1989. "The Police in the United States." *C.J. International* 5(1), 11–18.

Toch, H. and Grant, J.D. 1991. *Police as Problem Solvers.* New York: Plenum.

2

THE ROLE OF THE UNITED STATES MUNICIPAL POLICE

Municipal police in the United States are expected to perform a multitude of tasks, as we shall see shortly. In order to perform these tasks, the police must intervene in the daily lives of other citizens, many of whom would prefer to be let alone. The issue of the proper extent and nature of police intervention into the lives of other citizens is a constant source of controversy. Goldstein (1977: 1) noted that the police, because of their function, are an anomaly in free society. They have a great deal of authority under a system of government in which authority is reluctantly granted and sharply curtailed when it is granted. Still, a democracy is dependent on its police to maintain the degree of order that makes a free society possible. In a democracy, the police are expected to prevent people from preying on one another; to provide a sense of security; to facilitate movement; to resolve conflicts; and to protect the very processes and rights—free elections, freedom of speech, and freedom of assembly—on which continuation of a free society depends.

The Police Role

Reiss (1971: 1) viewed the police as the fundamental mediators between the community and the legal system and as the major representatives of that legal system: "At the same time that the police enforce the law and keep the peace, they adapt the universal standards of the law to the requirements of citizens and public officials in the community."

Similarly, Wilson (1968) discussed two basic functions of the police— order maintenance (peace keeping) and law enforcement—and three distinctive styles of performing these functions. Gaines, Kappeler, and Vaughn (1994) further detailed police functions by adding provision of miscellaneous services and enforcement of convenience norms (traffic regulations, for example) to law enforcement and order maintenance.

Who defines the police role for working police officers? Private citizens obviously influence the nature of the role by their contacts with the police, through memberships in various organizations that support or monitor the police, and through the election of public officials who appoint police administrators. Legislative bodies influence the role of the police by enacting statutes that govern the police as well as statutes that the police use to govern others. In addition, legislative bodies determine the budgetary resources available to police agencies. The courts in our society have been actively involved in "policing the police" by handing down decisions that regulate police conduct concerning due process requirements. Executives such as city managers and prosecutors also help define the police role by determining the types of cooperative agreements and the types of evidence necessary for a prosecutable case, respectively. Of course, police officers themselves are actively involved in defining their roles as well by choosing to intervene in some incidents while ignoring others within the general guidelines provided by those persons previously discussed (Langworthy and Travis, 1994: 150–157). Together, these facts indicate that the role of the police will differ with time and place. Most law enforcement agencies do not determine which problems they address; rather, they respond to those problems that citizens feel are important, even though the police themselves would not define them as priority matters. Citizens often fail to notify the police about matters the police consider important, and they often require assistance for matters that many officers would characterize as trivial.

In our society, a good deal of emphasis has been placed on the traditional role of police as law enforcers/crime fighters. Unfortunately, because the major emphasis in policing has been on crime control, no matter how effectiveness is measured, the police do not fully meet the standard. In spite of increasing expenditures for new forms of equipment (911 systems, computer-aided dispatch, etc.), police often fail to meet their own or public expectations in the areas of crime control and prevention (Kelling and Moore, 1988: 8). In the 1980s it became apparent that in emphasizing the crime-control model and slighting the order-maintenance function, the police had contributed to an increase in public fear of crime, which caused them to abandon neighborhoods and public places (parks, parking garages, etc).

The importance of the relationship between the people and their police, expressed by Sir Robert Peel more than a century and a half ago—but ignored in many U.S. police departments—once again began to receive attention. The duties assigned to citizen-watchmen almost a thousand years ago included many that helped citizens feel secure in their homes and on the street.

When the police once again recognized that these functions are at least as important as crime fighting, the cycle had come full circle and a once very familiar model of policing began to receive attention again (see Highlight 2.1). Community policing returned the focus to order maintenance and provision of other services in addition to crime control and police-community partnerships; these preventive activities are important means of maintaining order, increasing citizen satisfaction with police, and controlling crime.

Contemporary Police Functions

For numerous reasons, it is extremely important to be explicit about the various police functions. First, we can recruit and select competent police personnel only if we have a clear notion of what these personnel are to accomplish once hired. Second, evaluation for retention and promotion is useful only to the extent that we evaluate in terms of what the police actually do. Third, budgetary decisions should be based on an accurate analysis of police roles. Fourth, efficiency and effectiveness in organizational structure depends on accurate task description. Fifth, public cooperation with the police

---

HIGHLIGHT 2.1   Police Role Comes Full Circle

The memory of a stabbing across the street from her dry cleaning business earlier this summer is still fresh in Fanny Kraus' mind.

"Since that happened, I'm scared to death," Kraus says, standing in the store she has owned for years. "But when I see Frank, I feel safe."

"Frank" is Frank Conklin, an Evanston patrol officer who walks a beat that covers the city's Main Street business district. "He watches over us," Kraus says.

Such a friendly relationship, and similar ones along Conklin's beat, might never have occurred if he patrolled in a squad car, maybe with his windows rolled up, the air conditioner running and the police radio on.

Evanston re-established foot patrols five years ago to make police more visible and more approachable. The decision, officials say, was a good one.

So good, in fact, that the same decision is now being made by an increasing number of suburban police departments—in communities as diverse as Naperville, Arlington Heights, Aurora, Joliet, Waukegan and Wheaton—as they look to the origins of

police work and find that a cop walking a beat is an idea whose time has come again.

And the officers' roles are as varied as the communities themselves.

In Naperville, foot patrol officers watch for trouble along the city's River Walk, an often-crowded place on warm summer evenings. In Arlington Heights and Wheaton, they patrol the business districts, dealing with parking problems, shoplifting or security concerns.

In Aurora and Waukegan, they walk beats in high-crime neighborhoods.

Big cities, Chicago among them, have always had foot patrols, though their duties have largely shifted to squad cars over the years. But in the suburbs, foot patrols often were abandoned—if ever used.

Joliet, for example, stopped foot patrols more than 20 years ago. It began again this summer when two officers were assigned to walk the downtown business district. The officers are encouraged to talk to merchants, and anyone else they meet downtown, and listen to their concerns, said Captain David Gerdes (Lucadamo, 1990).

depends on developing reasonable expectations with respect to the relative roles of the police and the public in policing a free society.

Perhaps Skolnick (1966: 1) put it best:

> *For what social purpose do the police exist? What values do the police serve in a democratic society? Are the police to be principally an agency of social control, with their chief value the efficient enforcement of the prohibitive norms of substantive criminal law? Or are the police to be an institution falling under the hegemony of the legal system, with a basic commitment to the rule of law, even if this obligation may result in a reduction in social order? How does this dilemma of democratic society hamper the capacity of the police, institutionally and individually, to respond to legal standards of law enforcement?*

All authorities agree that the police perform the basic functions of order maintenance and law enforcement, but the order of importance frequently has been questioned. How are the two functions related? Are the police better at one than the other? What are the specific functions of the police in the United States?

The Police as Public Servants

U.S. police, by virtue of their service role, operate under conditions similar to those of social workers, probation officers, and teachers. Moore (1992: 123) points out that in community policing, the police are not only expected to reduce crime and violence within constitutional limits and at a reasonable cost, but also to meet the needs and desires of the community. Community satisfaction and harmony are important goals. "Politics, in the sense of community responsiveness and accountability, reemerges as a virtue and an explicit basis of police legitimacy" (Moore, 1992: 123).

Roberg and Kuykendall (1993: 47) note that some police officers consider themselves social service workers. These officers believe that crime is a result of a number of factors and that making an arrest is only one alternative (and often not the most desirable) available to them.

The police are first and foremost public servants with a mandate to maintain order. They go about the business of maintaining order by the more or less judicious exercise of discretion (individual judgment), utilizing the processes of negotiation, mediation, and arbitration (Cox, 1986: 116). In short, they interpret and selectively enforce law with a view toward maintaining order. Regardless of the alternative selected by the police officer, it is important to recognize that there are numerous different public groups observing the police at any given time and that the police are, as public servants, accountable and responsible to each of these individuals. In order to be accountable and responsible as service providers, the police have made—and will have to make more—structural and ideological changes. Some of these changes include long-term assignment of officers to beats, use of police officers in school-liaison programs, and a wide variety of police-initiated positive encounters with other citizens and organizations.

The role of the police as service providers is not without problems. It is difficult for those who try to be all things to all people to build a professional image. The training required to be an expert in many areas is not readily available and is costly. Thus, police officers frequently try to provide services for which they have little if any training; this may result in poor performance, thereby further damaging the image of the police as professionals. Finally, the costs of providing a wide variety of services may considerably escalate the costs of policing.

There are times when the law-enforcement and order-maintenance functions are incompatible and police officers must decide which function is more important. Their decisions in such cases (which are relatively common), depend upon how they view their role, which depends on both organizational and public expectations. For example, a police agency that adopts an aggressive tactical orientation typically espouses a different set of values from one that carefully engages neighborhood residents in planning for crime-control activities. The values of agencies that adopted aggressive policies over the last half-century, include the following:

1. Police authority based solely in the law.
2. Communities can assist the police best by providing information.
3. Response time is the most important measure of police effectiveness.
4. Social problems are not a primary concern of the police.
5. Police, as experts in crime control, should develop their strategies internally.

These values may be compared with those of a community-oriented department, typified by the value statement of the Houston Police Department:

1. The community is to be involved in all policing activities.
2. Police strategies must preserve and advance democratic values.
3. Police services should reinforce the strengths of the city's neighborhoods.
4. The public should have input into policies that directly affect them.
5. The department will seek input from employees on matters relating to job satisfaction and effectiveness (Wasserman and Moore, 1988: 4).

The Order Maintenance Function

If we divide police activities into those directly related to law enforcement and those not law-enforcement oriented, it is clear that the vast majority of police time is spent on the latter. Wilson (1968), Reiss (1971), Bercal (1970), and Bouza (1990) all note that fewer than 20 percent of the calls responded to by the police relate directly to crime control/law enforcement.

As Cox and Fitzgerald (1991: 195) note, much of an officer's time is spent on service functions such as traffic control, routine patrol, responding to community citizens' health or other personal emergencies, summoning help for stranded motorists, picking up drunks off the streets, and the countless other tasks that the community expects its police to perform. Many of the situations in which the police intervene are not (or are not interpreted by the police as), criminal situations and do not call for arrest or its possible consequences.

In short, most police activity is not related directly to enforcement and in some cases the police deliberately avoid enforcing the law in an attempt to maintain order. Thus, on a street between a city and outlying factories, the police may not set up speed traps during rush hours—even though they know a good deal of speeding occurs at shift changes—because it disrupts the flow of traffic and may lead those who are cited to believe they have been singled out because hundreds of other drivers engaging in the same behavior are not cited.

For reasons that will become clear shortly, the police are undoubtedly far better at order maintenance than law enforcement. First, however, let us explore how the police go about maintaining order and why they are relatively effective in doing so.

Strangely enough, it may be that the capacity of the police to use force, coupled with the fact that they rarely use it, accounts for their ability to maintain order in the vast majority of cases in which they are involved.

U.S. police maintain a virtual monopoly on the legitimate use of force in our society. Bittner (1970) views the police as a mechanism for the distribution of situationally justified, non-negotiable force. In other words, when the situation justifies the use of force, and the police have decided to arbitrate instead of negotiate, the police, onlookers, those who called the police, and those against whom the police are about to proceed understand that force is likely to be used if all other alternatives fail. It may well be that these expectations alone are enough to keep a great many potentially hostile situations civil. The arrival of the police officer in uniform, complete with weapons and colleagues, conveys the message, in most situations, that the definition of the situation arrived at by the police will dictate ensuing actions.

It is interesting to note that when the police are dealing with mobs or large groups of demonstrators, the threat of force against individuals is less strongly perceived and the police are likely to have a more difficult time maintaining and/or establishing order. Since these instances are relatively rare, the police are usually very good at order maintenance. In fact, they are far better at order maintenance than law enforcement, although they often fail to publicize this fact or to evaluate personnel in terms of their contributions in this area.

The Law-Enforcement Function

How good are the police at law enforcement? What, realistically, can the police be expected to accomplish in this area? Can and do the police enforce all of the laws all of the time—or even most of the time? Can they reasonably be expected to prevent most crimes or apprehend most offenders?

U.S. municipal police are not now nor have they ever been very effective at preventing most kinds of crime or apprehending criminals. This is due, in large measure, to societal constraints that prevent them from intervening at will in a variety of circumstances and to the unwillingness of other citizens to assist them in crime control. For example, the police may know that a certain couple is routinely involved in domestic violence, but unless one of the spouses or a neighbor calls on them to intervene, or they see the violence occurring themselves (unlikely since it probably occurs in the privacy of the couple's home), they cannot intervene.

There are also numerous crimes with which the municipal police seldom deal. White collar crimes, for example, are not typically investigated by local police departments even though such crimes cost U.S. citizens more than all street crimes combined. Studies have repeatedly shown that fewer than half of all major crimes are reported to the police. It is unrealistic to expect that the police will routinely solve crimes about which they are uninformed (although they sometimes do, of course, when arresting an offender for a known offense).

Further, the police annually make arrests in only 20 to 25 percent of the serious cases about which they do have knowledge. This statistic, too, may be attributed to factors largely beyond the control of the police (e.g., unwillingness of the public to provide information leading to prosecution or to serve as witnesses, and so on). We must also keep in mind the number of police officers relative to the size of the population (about 700,000 of the former and about 255,000,000 of the latter). Consequently, police cannot effectively control the public on their own, whatever techniques they employ. The police infrequently discover situations requiring their intervention except when they are traffic related.

We need to be clear about the nature of the argument we are making with respect to the police role in law enforcement. Law enforcement is a critical element of policing. When the police actually enforce the law, their behavior and intervention are critical: They are the largest group of criminal justice practitioners and their role in this activity largely determines whether the remainder of the criminal justice network will go into operation (illegal searches and seizures make prosecution extremely problematic, for example). Nonetheless, law-enforcement activities do not account for the major portion of police time and, if the police are held solely responsible for law enforcement, they will continue to be inadequate to the task.

We will examine briefly what the police can reasonably be expected to accomplish in the area of law enforcement (see Table 2.1). For the moment, we will exclude traffic enforcement and concentrate on law enforcement as it relates to crime. Expectations of the police with respect to crime control can be roughly divided into two areas—preventing violations and apprehending offenders. We can also divide crimes into those that involve property and those that involve the person. Finally, we can develop categories based on the relationship of victim and offender, that is, whether they are acquaintances or strangers. Table 2.1 indicates the likelihood that the police can prevent or apprehend offenders based on these characteristics.

Keep in mind that we are considering only police action with respect to crime in this analysis. Can the police alone successfully prevent crimes between acquaintances? Since most such crime occurs in private or semiprivate settings, prevention would require that the police have prior knowledge that such offenses might occur and that police be present in these settings before or at the time of such crimes. Typically, this situation requires that one

TABLE 2.1   Potential Effectiveness of Police in Crime-Related Law Enforcement

	Type of Crime and Relationship Between Offender and Victim			
	Personal		Property	
Police Action	Acquaintance	Stranger	Acquaintance	Stranger
Prevention	Very Limited	Possible	Very Limited	Possible
Apprehension	Very Limited	Possible	Very Limited	Possible

of the parties involved call the police prior to the occurrence of the crime and this does, of course, happen. The effectiveness of the police in preventing such incidents, then, depends largely on the civilians involved rather than on the police themselves.

While admitting that the physical presence of the police during such encounters is problematic, some observers would maintain that the police might effectively deter such offenses by making and publicizing arrests. The evidence on the effects of legal coercion, however, suggests that, in and of itself, legal coercion is not a particularly effective means of inducing conformity to norms (Zimring and Hawkins, 1971; Livingston, 1992: 432–434). If deterrence is to occur, offenders must be convinced that apprehension is a realistic possibility; given current odds, it seems unlikely for most crimes committed in private or semiprivate settings. Additionally, many crimes against the person in particular are committed in the "heat of passion," without rational consideration of sanctions, making it unlikely that prior police action would deter the offenders. In short, whether police are aware of crimes committed in private or semiprivate settings is largely beyond their control, making prevention and apprehension difficult at best.

If we focus on crimes committed by strangers, it is possible, though still unlikely, that the police may be able to prevent such crimes and/or apprehend offenders. When such crimes occur in private or semiprivate places, the police are unlikely to be involved in prevention. It may well be, though, that victims are more willing to report crimes committed by strangers, and this may aid in apprehension. Once again, whether the police are successful depends not on their direct efforts (though it may depend on their community-relations efforts), but on the willingness of victims to report.

Some would suggest that to the extent that crimes are committed by either strangers or acquaintances in public places, the police should be considerably more effective in prevention and apprehension. The typical police strategy in this regard is routine patrol or some variation of it. The Kansas City preventive patrol study (Kelling et al., 1974) and others have demonstrated that increasing police patrols has no direct relationship to decreasing crime rates. Klockars and Mastrofski (1991: 131) conclude that it makes about as much sense to have police patrol routinely in cars as it would to have firefighters patrol in fire trucks. When one calculates the likelihood that a police officer on patrol will happen upon a crime in progress, these results are not surprising. While it may be that directed or targeted patrol procedures will produce better results, we cannot realistically expect that the police will have sufficient resources to assign police officers to high-risk areas (parking garages, parks, bars, etc.) on a continual basis. As a result, it is unlikely that the police will be able to improve apprehension rates significantly (Spelman and Brown, 1981). The growing use of private security guards in high-risk areas supports the argument that the municipal police are not effective in keeping such areas free of crime.

One clear illustration of the law-enforcement capabilities of the police comes from racial demonstrations and political protests occurring over the past three decades. During the racial demonstrations of the 1960s—the vast majority of which were sparked (not necessarily caused) by police encounters with minority group members—U.S. citizens watched on television as the police stood helplessly by while hundreds of violators committed thousands of serious violations. The police, of course, made many arrests, but numerous violators escaped apprehension. In some instances, the police were powerless to prevent repetition of such demonstrations and the National Guard had to be called in to bring a halt to the unlawful behavior.

In 1980, another incident with racial overtones, again involving a police encounter with a minority group member, occurred in Miami, Florida. Some seven thousand police and military personnel were deployed in this case. Nonetheless, eighteen people were killed, four hundred were injured, 150 buildings were destroyed, and damages were estimated at four million dollars (Thomas, 1980). In 1992, the acquittal of police officers accused of brutally assaulting Rodney King was cited as a precipitating factor in the even more costly riots in South Central Los Angeles. In these riots, sixty people were killed, 2,400 injured, over 5,000 buildings were destroyed or damaged, some 15,000 people were arrested, and damages were estimated at one billion dollars (Calhoun, Light, and Keller, 1994). Clearly, when called upon to enforce the law in the face of a large volume of crime occurring in a short period of time, the police alone are inadequate to the task.

The police don't seem to be any better at enforcing traffic laws. One needs only to drive the highways of the United States or city streets leading to and from factories and industrial parks during rush hours to note that attempts to control speed are ineffective. For every violator the police apprehend, a large number of others escape. When a police officer apprehends a speeder, the officer typically writes a traffic citation. While the citation is being written, other motorists speed by without much fear of apprehension because the officer involved usually cannot utilize speed-measuring devices while occupied with the citation. Some police agencies stop several violators at one time by utilizing several police officers and vehicles, but their resources are finite while the number of violators is infinite. The fact that the actual number of violators remains high indicates that deterrence is short lived.

We might also consider the effectiveness of the police in enforcing laws dealing with crimes without complainants (prostitution, narcotics, gambling). Since these crimes involve goods or services for which there is a demand, one could expect that the police would be largely ineffective in preventing such offenses and in apprehending offenders. Government estimates suggest that less than 10 percent of the narcotics entering or produced in the United States are confiscated, the police themselves indicate that the best they can do with respect to prostitution is to move it from one locale to another, and enforcing laws against gambling is difficult at best.

Police at the municipal level do not deal regularly with white collar crimes. A recent attempt to locate an expert in computer crimes, for example, disclosed no local officers with such expertise in a five-state area and only a small number of state officers who considered themselves experts in this area. Gosseaux and Curran (1988: 60) note that the scope and sophistication of many white collar offenses overwhelm the resources available to most local and state enforcement authorities. As a result, it is typical that white collar investigations and prosecutions are given low priority in relation to street crime.

Finally, the police themselves cannot actually enforce the law. Prosecution and judgment rest with other components of the criminal justice network. Whether offenders apprehended by the police are actually prosecuted and fined or imprisoned is beyond the control of the police except in cases involving relatively minor offenses.

Order Maintenance and Law Enforcement: Interdependent Roles

We have discussed the order-maintenance and law-enforcement roles of the police separately, but they are very much interdependent. When the police arrest violators, they typically (though not always, as we have seen) contribute to order maintenance. Similarly, as they go about the business of maintaining order by providing nonenforcement services, they are building a foundation for their roles as enforcers. When we assess the effectiveness and efficiency of the police, then, we must keep in mind that law enforcement is not their primary task, and that the ability to be effective in this role depends on factors that are not under direct police control.

Evaluation of the law-enforcement role is important but should be placed in proper perspective (see Highlight 2.2). Education and training of police officers should be oriented toward helping them learn to perform the tasks they actually perform. These tasks most often involve intervention in troublesome situations in that the primary skills required are communication skills which enable the officer to negotiate, mediate, or arbitrate (Sykes and Brent, 1983; Cox and Fitzgerald, 1991). The police officers' role as communicators is fundamental to their function as enforcers because the better they communicate, the more effective they are likely to be in enforcement.

HIGHLIGHT 2.2   Conclusions Based on Studies of Traditional Policing

1. Increasing the number of police officers doesn't necessarily reduce crime rates or lead to the solution of more crimes.
2. Routine patrol doesn't reduce crime or increase chances of apprehending offenders.
3. Saturation patrol reduces crime temporarily by displacing it to other areas.
4. Police rarely encounter serious crimes against the person while patrolling.

5. Improving response time doesn't affect the likelihood of arresting offenders or satisfying callers.
6. Only a small proportion of crimes solved are solved as a result of the work of police criminal investigators

(Adapted from Skolnick and Bayley, 1986: 4–5).

Progressive police administrators recognize that effectiveness in law enforcement can best be improved by concentrating on the public-service or order-maintenance function, including educating the public on the needs of the police as well as listening to the needs of the public. Hiring more police officers and improving police technology are likely to be less important to the law enforcement effort than convincing the public to share in this effort.

The discussion above is not intended to devalue the police, but rather to place in proper perspective the role they are able to fulfill. It is clear from our discussion that relying on traditional police approaches has led to limited success in the law-enforcement arena and less than complete success in order maintenance. Are there more effective ways of policing? If the police alone are not able to curb crime, maintain order, and provide all of the services demanded by the public, can they form partnerships with others to improve performance in these areas? Chapter 3 discusses community policing, believed by many to be the most promising solution to many of the problems just discussed.

Discussion Questions

1. What are the basic roles of municipal police in the United States?

2. Why is it important to clarify the roles of the police?

3. In what ways are U.S. police like teachers and social workers?

4. Identify and discuss differences among several of the different public groups to whom the police are accountable and responsible in our society.

5. Why are the police as effective as they are at order maintenance?

6. How can the police enforce all of the laws all of the time? If they cannot enforce all of the laws all of the time, how do they decide which ones to enforce when?

7. Is law enforcement a critical part of policing? If so, in what ways?

8. Discuss the connection between police effectiveness at preventing crime and apprehending criminals and the setting in which the crime occurs; the relationship between victim and offender; and the type of crime involved.

9. How important, and in what ways, are communication skills to police officers?

References

Bercal, T. 1970. "Calls for Police Assistance." *American Behavioral Scientist, 13.*

Bittner, E. 1970. *The Functions of the Police in Modern Society: A Review of Background Factors, Current Practices, and Possible Role Models.* Rockville, MD: National Institute of Mental Health DHEW Pub. no. (ADM) 75-260.

Bouza, A.V. 1990. *The Police Mystique.* New York: Plenum.

Calhoun, C., Light, D., and Keller, S. 1994. *Sociology.* New York: McGraw-Hill.

Cox, S. 1986. "The Role of the Police in Law Enforcement." Papers Presented at the Chinese-American Police Conference, Taipei, Taiwan.

Cox, S. and Fitzgerald, J. 1991. *Police in Community: Critical Issues* 2 ed. Dubuque, IA: Wm. C. Brown.

Gaines, L.K., Kappeler, V.E., and Vaughn, J.B. 1994. *Policing in America.* Cincinnati: Anderson.

Goldstein, H. 1977. *Policing a Free Society.* Cambridge, MA: Ballinger.

Gosseaux, J.S. and Curran, D.J. 1988. "The Team Approach to Curtailing White-Collar Crime." *The Police Chief* (August), 60–68.

Kelling, G.L. and Moore, M.H. 1988. "The Evolving Strategy of Policing." *Perspectives on Policing.* U.S. Department of Justice. Washington, DC: U.S. Government Printing Office.

Kelling, B., Pate, T., Dieckman, D., and Brown, C. 1974. *The Kansas City Preventive Patrol Experiment: A Summary Report.* Washington, DC: Police Foundation.

Klockars, C. and Mastrofski, S. 1991. *Thinking About Police: Contemporary Readings.* New York: McGraw-Hill.

Langworthy, R.H. and Travis, L.F. III. 1994. *Policing in America: A Balance of Forces.* New York: Macmillan.

Livingston, J. 1992. *Crime and Criminology.* Englewood Cliffs, NJ: Prentice Hall.

Lucadamo, J. 1990. "Cop's Feet are Back on the Beat." *Chicago Tribune* (16 September), sec. 1, p. 15.

Moore, M. H. 1992. "Community Policing." In Tonry, M. and Morris, N. (eds.), *Modern Policing.* Chicago: University of Chicago Press, 99–158.

Reiss, A. 1971. *The Police and the Public.* New Haven, CT: Yale University Press.

Roberg, R.R. and Kuykendall, J. 1993. *Police in Society.* Belmont, CA: Wadsworth.

Skolnick, J. 1966. *Justice Without Trial.* New York: Wiley.

Skolnick, J.H. and Bayley, D.H. 1986. *The New Blue Line: Police Innovation in Six American Cities.* New York: The Free Press.

Spelman, W. and Brown, D. 1981. "Response Time." In Klockars, (ed.), *Thinking About Police: Contemporary Readings.* New York: McGraw-Hill.

Sykes, R.E. and Brent, E.E. 1983. *Policing: A Social Behaviorist Perspective.* New Brunswick, NJ: Rutgers University Press.

Thomas, J. 1980. "5 Officers Shot in Miami Unrest; 15 Persons Hurt." *The New York Times.* (16 July), 10.

Wasserman, R. and Moore, M. 1988. "Values in Policing." *Perspectives on Policing.* U.S. Department of Justice. Washington, DC: U.S. Government Printing Office.

Wilson, J.Q. 1968. *Varieties of Police Behavior.* Cambridge, MA: Harvard University Press.

Zimring, F. and Hawkins, G. 1971. "The Legal Threat as an Instrument of Social Change." *Journal of Social Issues* 27(2).

3

COMMUNITY POLICING

It is apparent that American municipal police are far better staffed, educated, trained, and equipped than ever before. Yet, examples of excessive force, police corruption, and inefficiency appear frequently in the media. As indicated in Chapter 2, the police are unable to prevent most crimes or to apprehend most offenders. For these and other reasons, various segments of the public remain highly dissatisfied with the police. In this chapter we will discuss the latest in a series of attempts to deal with these problems.

Problematic Issues for the Police

As we have seen, corruption and inefficiency have been problems in U.S. policing from its beginnings and they continue to tarnish the police image. Scandals involving theft, use and sale of drugs by officers, police brutality, and other serious violations are far too common (Campbell, 1991; Frankel, 1993; Lacayo, 1993; Sharn, 1993; Ferguson, 1993).

It appears that many of the programs developed by the police in an attempt to adapt to a rapidly changing society have resulted in or continued a cycle of isolation and alienation. Specialization, for example, was viewed as one way of providing better service to the public. As a result, numerous specialized units (internal affairs, community relations, juvenile, robbery, homicide, drug, sex crimes, and traffic) were developed. In many cases, the outcome of such development has been little cross training, an it's-not-my-job attitude, tight-knit, highly secretive units, and little effective communication between patrol officers and the officers who staff these specialized units. If and when scandals arise in such units, the confidence of both the general public and noninvolved officers within the police ranks is understandably shaken.

In the last decade gangs, drugs, and increasingly violent encounters involving automatic weapons and the willingness to use them have become focal points. The increasing visibility of immigrants and a small number of terrorist incidents within the borders of our country have led to a rebirth of concern about racial and ethnic differences and the reemergence of extreme right-wing groups. Meanwhile, relationships between the police and members of racial/ethnic minorities continue to be less than civil in many cases and downright unpleasant in some. All of the new police technology and all of the old police traditions have failed to provide answers to these apparently different but very much related questions.

These limitations have led to a search for new ways of addressing these issues and to the emergence (some would argue reemergence) of community-oriented policing. As we look at community policing, we should keep in mind that it does not require that all traditional policing strategies be replaced. "Traditional police methods are not, as many fear, incompatible with community policing. Community policing is not just a joint problem-solving process. It can also involve arrest-oriented, get tough solutions. The difference is that under community policing, the 'tough' police action is not a surprise to the law-abiding community. In fact, it may have been requested by residents and citizens working with the police" (*NIJ Research in Brief*, 1992: 9).

Community Policing

There is a good deal of confusion about what community policing means, what it might be expected to accomplish, and how and why it might be expected to work where other strategies have failed. In fact, many believe that community-oriented policing (COP) simply retreads shop-worn elements of police-community relations programs; others believe it is little more than the latest "buzzword" or passing fad that will soon disappear like similar previous strategies. (Trojanowicz, 1990). This belief is perhaps especially prevalent in traditional police agencies, which are highly resistant to change as a result of their paramilitary organizational structure, civil services regulations, and unionization (Skolnick and Bayley, 1986).

Skolnick and Bayley (1986) studied police innovation that focused on involving the public in the police mission in six U.S. cities. They concluded that these innovative programs, designated as community-oriented policing, took a number of different forms. Still, the researchers identified a number of elements common to all of the programs. These elements included police-community reciprocity, areal decentralization of command, reorientation of patrol, and civilianization (Skolnick and Bayley, 1986: 212–220). A brief discussion of each of these elements will help create a foundation for understanding community policing.

Police-community reciprocity refers to a genuine feeling on the part of the police that the public it serves has something to contribute to policing. Further, the police communicate this feeling to the public, learn from public input, and consider themselves accountable to the community in which they serve. The police and the public become "co-producers of crime prevention" (Skolnick and Bayley, 1986: 212–213).

Areal decentralization of command refers to the establishment of substations, ministations, and other attempts to increase interaction between police officers and the public they serve in a particular geographic area.

Reorientation of patrol involves moving from car to foot patrol in order to increase police interaction with other citizens. This shift may involve permanently assigning certain officers to walking beats or may be accomplished by having officers park their cars while they get out and talk to residents. Positive contacts between officers and other citizens are thought to be one result of foot patrol, crime prevention another.

Civilianization refers to introducing civilians to an increasing number of positions with police agencies. For example, more civilians are being employed in research and training divisions, in forensics, and as community-service officers who handle many noncrime-related tasks. Skolnick and Bayley (1986: 219) concluded that civilianization was related to successfully introducing and carrying out programs and policies related to community mobilization and crime prevention.

In reality, then, community-oriented policing is much more than community relations. Community-oriented policing requires adopting both philosophical and operational changes, and to a great extent, turns traditional policing practices upside down. It is, after all, "not easy to transform blue knights into community organizers" (Skolnick and Bayley, 1986: 211).

Trojanowicz and Bucqueroux (1990: xiii–xv) have elaborated some of the principles on which this transformation from traditional to community policing is based. They include:

1. Community policing is a philosophy based on the belief that law-abiding citizens should have input with respect to policing, provided they are willing to participate in and support the effort.
2. Community policing is an organizational strategy requiring that all police personnel (civilian and sworn) explore ways to turn the philosophy into practice.
3. Police departments implementing community policing must develop "Community Policing Officers" (CPOs) to act as links between the police and community residents.
4. CPOs must have continuous, sustained contact with law-abiding citizens.
5. Community policing implies a contract between the police and other citizens that helps overcome apathy while curbing vigilantism.
6. Community policing is proactive.
7. Community policing helps improve quality of life for those who are most vulnerable (poor, elderly, homeless).
8. While community policing utilizes technology, it relies on human ingenuity and interaction.
9. Community policing must be fully integrated into the department.
10. Community policing provides personalized police service on a decentralized basis.

Trojanowicz and Bucqueroux (1990) also point out what community policing is not (20–35):

1. Community policing is not a technique to be applied only to specific problems, but is a new way of thinking about the police role in the community.
2. Community policing is not public relations. The latter is a by-product of the former.
3. Community policing is not "anti-technology," but utilizes technology in a different framework.
4. Community policing is not soft on crime.
5. Community policing is not an independent program from a police department. It must involve the entire department.

6. Community policing is not cosmetic. It requires substantive changes in the relationship between the policed and other citizens.
7. Community policing is not a top-down approach, but seeks to learn about the concerns of average citizens.
8. Community policing is not simply social work renamed. It incorporates traditional policing responses.
9. Community policing is not a quick fix; it cannot immediately solve all of the crime problems in a community.
10. Community policing is not "safe," but requires risk-taking and experimentation.

Put in other terms (Overman, 1994: 20): "Traditionally, we in law enforcement have set our own priorities with little regard to community input. . . .We must begin to listen to the people we serve and prioritize our efforts based on quality of life issues. This is where community policing begins. . . .We must go beyond the traditional approaches and begin to judge our effectiveness by the condition of the [street] corner rather than by the number of arrests [on it]."

Carey (1994: 24) notes that community policing is not just directed at addressing problems that cannot be addressed by traditional policing methods. It can also be used by suburban and low-crime communities to address the specific needs and problems of their citizens. In short, the community-policing philosophy recognizes that patrol officers are the government representatives best positioned to address a number of social problems and enforcing the law is only one of several strategies the police can employ to cope with such problems.

The basic concerns of COP are, then, empowerment of both police officers and other citizens and cooperation between the police and the public in an attempt to improve the quality of life in a given community (Kane, 1993: 1). COP requires a philosophical commitment by the police to cooperate with other citizens in the process of controlling crime, drugs, fear of crime, and neighborhood decay. Further, COP mandates that all police personnel, sworn and nonsworn, reevaluate their positions to seek better ways of reaching their goals.

There is also a requirement that at least part of the police force be deployed as community officers who maintain direct, regular ties with the citizens they police. These community officers must provide a full range of services to those in their areas of responsibility, serving as "mini-chiefs" within these areas (Trojanowicz, 1990: 8). Long-term interaction between police officers and neighborhood residents fosters the development of relationships based on mutual trust and cooperation. It also encourages the exchange of information between citizens and police officers, including mutual input concerning policing priorities and tactics for specific neighborhoods (Walters, 1993: 220). As Trojanowicz and Bucqueroux (1990: 1) put it: "By challenging people to work as partners in making their communities better and safer places, Community Policing produces a subtle but profound shift in the role and responsibility of the police. No longer are they the experts with all the

answers, the "thin blue line" that protects the good people from the bad—
"us" versus "them." Community officers are part of the community, generalists who do whatever it takes to help people help themselves."

Kelling and Stewart (1989) discuss a number of things that neighborhood
residents can do to help the police protect their neighborhoods. First, they
can call the police when they see untoward behavior and come forward to
testify as witnesses in criminal court. Second, each individual can take
actions to help reduce fear, disorder, and crime. Such actions include buying
and using locks, assisting neighbors who need help, hiring private security
guards to supplement police protection, and avoiding dangerous areas.
Third, they can work with the police to organize neighborhood-watch
groups, patrol their neighborhoods, and organize neighborhood "safe
houses" for children. Fourth, those who belong to private organizations can
encourage them to implement programs for youth in the neighborhoods in
question. Fifth, commercial firms can hire private security firms to help protect their businesses. By cooperating with the police and other criminal justice agencies in these ways, citizens can improve the safety of their neighborhoods and fulfill their roles as part of the police-community partnership.

In COP, patrol officers become liaisons, ombudsmen, problem solvers,
and mobilizers of community resources. They seek to obtain community or
neighborhood cooperation to identify and resolve problems rather than simply handling individual incidents. They look for patterns that are indicative
of problems that may best be addressed by resources other than or in cooperation with the police. In short, they practice problem-oriented policing as
a part of the overall COP strategy.

Community policing may be viewed as addressing the following issues
(adapted from Trojanowicz, 1990: 10):

1. Goal—problem solving
2. Line Function—regular contact between officers and other citizens
3. Addressing problems pointed out by citizens who cooperate in setting the
   police agenda
4. Police accountability to citizens who receive services
5. Managed change and restructuring within the department with respect to
   selection, training, evaluation, and promotion
6. Department-wide acceptance of COP philosophy
7. Influence from the bottom up—citizens and patrol personnel help establish priorities and policies
8. Continuously accessible officers in decentralized offices
9. Police encouragement of other citizens to solve many of their own problems
10. Reduction of citizen fear, crime, and neighborhood disorder as determi-
    nants of success

Implementing COP requires a number of concrete changes in most police
organizations. Cox (1992: 2–3) has summarized these changes as follows:

1. Redefining the department's role
2. Training all officers in COP
3. Evaluating employees according to different criteria
4. Assigning specific patrol areas
5. Prioritizing calls
6. Tailoring police work to community needs.

A community police officer's day is illustrated in Highlight 3.1

Problem-Oriented Policing as a Component of COP

The concept of problem-oriented policing (POP) originated in 1979 in the works of Herman Goldstein. Goldstein (1979) noted many of the difficulties discussed in the first section of this chapter and added that while many police agencies give the appearance of being efficient, this appearance fails to translate into benefits for the communities served. He looked carefully at public expectations of the police and determined that they center around problem solving. Goldstein concluded that if the police were expected to solve problems, they could not be evaluated accurately by focusing only on crime statistics. Instead, evaluation would have to focus on the problems encountered and the effectiveness of the police response to such problems.

Problem-oriented police officers, then, need to define the problems they encounter, gather information concerning these problems (frequency, seriousness, duration, location), and develop creative solutions to them. Such solutions, in many cases, require the cooperation of the public and/or other service agencies.

Problem-oriented policing represents a dramatic shift from traditional policing, which is incident driven: police typically receive a complaint or call, respond to it, and clear the incident. While the specific situation is addressed, the underlying conditions are not addressed and so more calls are likely to be

---

HIGHLIGHT 3.1   A Community Police Officer's Day

In addition to traditional law enforcement activities, such as patrol and responding to calls for service, the day might include:

- Operating neighborhood substations.
- Meeting with community groups.
- Analyzing and solving neighborhood problems.
- Working with citizens on crime prevention programs.

- Conducting door-to-door surveys of residents.
- Talking with students in school.
- Meeting with local merchants.
- Making security checks of businesses.
- Dealing with disorderly people.

(Mastrofski, 1992: 23–24)

made, requiring further responses to similar incidents. POP regards these incidents as symptoms of underlying conditions that must be addressed to keep the incidents from proliferating (Toch and Grant, 1991: 6).

Patterns of incidents that are similar, then, represent problems that must be attended to by the police. Problems, rather than crimes, calls, or incidents, become the basic unit of police work (Toch and Grant, 1991: 18). Line officers become problem identifiers and solvers. Identifying and solving community problems requires input from those who live in the community, as well as from other service providers. Thus, POP and COP share concerns with community involvement and the conditions underlying crime and disruption of order.

Criticisms of Community Policing

While there is little doubt that community policing is heralded as the major trend in U.S. policing, some have raised questions about its worth. One common criticism is that many police departments embrace the rhetoric of community policing rather than the philosophy. Indeed there are police administrators who institute foot-patrol programs or establish neighborhood-watch programs and claim to have initiated community policing. As Offer (1993: 8) correctly notes, the considerable enthusiasm for community policing has led to its introduction as an organizational objective with little substance in many police departments. While Offer's observations are accurate, they are not a criticism of community policing itself, but of those who claim the title without developing the substance.

Another criticism aimed at those who adopt community policing strategies concerns the fact that there is little empirical evidence to suggest that community policing is effective in reducing serious crime. Indeed, available evidence seems to indicate that, while people involved in community policing efforts feel more secure, crime is not significantly reduced. It may be, however, that people who feel more secure will use the streets and other public places more frequently, thus eventually making it more difficult for criminals to ply their trades. On the other hand, it also may be that people who feel more secure, but are not in fact more secure, are more likely to engage in activities that make them available as victims, thus increasing the risk of crime. Brown (1992b: 4) indicates that the only way that police can have an impact on violent crime is by forming partnerships with the residents of high-crime areas and making police officers "permanent, highly visible fixtures in the neighborhood." In any case, further and careful evaluation of community policing programs is clearly in order.

The third major criticism of community policing has to do with its costs. Implementing COP may decrease the mobility and availability of the officers involved because the officers are out of their vehicles a good deal of the time and involved in community-organization activities; thus, they are sometimes unavailable to respond to calls. In fact, in many programs, COP officers no longer perform routine motorized patrol and other officers must take over this duty if it is to continue. It has been suggested, in addition, that the money spent on community policing might be better spent on improving social and economic conditions (Pisani, 1992).

In fairness, it must be noted that community policing is seldom touted as a money-saving approach. While it costs money to implement any new program, there are various ways of measuring costs. Departmental budgets may have to be increased initially to support COP. If the strategy succeeds in improving cooperation between the police and other citizens, however, how do we measure the savings in crimes prevented or solved as a result of this increased cooperation? Further, some departments have found that by rearranging priorities, eliminating services for nonemergency calls, and providing reporting alternatives (telephone, fax, letters) for the public, costs can be managed (Burgreen and McPherson, 1992).

A fourth criticism of community policing focuses on the possibility that permanent assignment of police officers who have a good deal of independence in operations enhances the possibility of corruption. This criticism is based primarily on historical accounts of corruption by police officers who walked beats, who were not subject to routine supervision, and who frightened neighborhood business persons (legitimate and illegitimate) into paying them for not enforcing the law and/or for protecting them from other predators. Trojanowicz (1992: 2) argues, however, that the very nature of COP works against such corruption; that is, COP officers are known by name to everyone in the neighborhood and have every reason to believe that they cannot "cross the line undetected."

Finally, some critics argue that the time is simply not right to change from traditional policing strategies to COP. There are always crises to be faced and numerous reasons for not changing strategies at any given time. Burgreen and McPherson (1992: 31) recognized this fact: "If we don't risk changing when the time is right, we will be forced to change when we are not prepared. If we are afraid to change because we are comfortable, we may be holding on just to prove that certainty is better than taking a risk. No one benefits in this scenario. Not the police, and certainly not the community."

After considering the various criticisms of COP, Brown (1992a: 11) concludes, "I've talked to people all over the country about community policing and no one has been able to punch a hole in it. It's logical. It's just a better way of using police resources."

Some Examples of Community Policing

Operation Cul-de-Sac (OCDS)

Operation Cul-de-Sac, sponsored by the Los Angeles Police Department (LAPD), began in 1990. OCDS was an attempt to examine the potential for COP in high-crime areas and to determine which initiatives designed to build police-citizen partnerships worked best in order to use such initiatives as models for the future (Vernon and Lasley, 1992).

In order to create a "community" in which COP could be implemented, LAPD, with the agreement of the residents involved, placed iron gates on streets marking the outer boundaries of the OCDS area. Foot, bicycle, and horse patrols were implemented for a short time in order to increase inter-personal contacts between the police and other citizens. Next, six officers were permanently assigned to the area. These officers joined forces with com-munity groups to clean up graffiti and develop neighborhood-watch pro-grams while maximizing positive contacts with residents.

Within a short time, residents began to take their neighborhood back from gangs. They began to use the streets and parks again. Part I crimes decreased and remained lower than they were prior to OCDS. Drive-by shootings also decreased significantly. With respect to inner-city neighborhoods, OCDS demonstrated that "Police agencies engaging in community-based policing efforts would be well advised to focus their efforts on the quality rather than the quantity of police/citizen interactions. In other words, expressions of help-fulness and understanding on the part of officers toward citizens appear to be many times more important to the overall effectiveness of community polic-ing programs than such factors as visual presence, frequency of contact, or even officer politeness and helpfulness" (Vernon and Lasley, 1992: 22).

Community Policing in Seattle

Beginning in 1987, citizens living in South Seattle began expressing concerns over police services. After meeting with police and elected officials, a com-munity group decided they would have to supply the "vision and imagina-tion" necessary to solve a number of problems. The group was viewed as advi-sory by the police but saw themselves as involved in a partnership with the police. In 1988, the South Seattle Crime Prevention Council (SSCPC) was formed and the members met regularly with police officials who discussed police plans and tactics with them. SSCPC served as an umbrella group, bring-ing other neighborhood groups into cooperative efforts with the police and increasing the geographic area covered (*NIJ Research in Brief*, 1992).

Other city agencies, such as the housing authority, soon became involved in the program. These agencies, involved citizen groups, and the police worked together to define problems, select targets, and develop strategies to deal with existing problems. Shared responsibility became a guiding principle and all parties benefited. Police experienced more community support and other citizens felt more secure. "Over time the partnership has developed into an effective means of increasing community security by expanding its focus to encompass a range of issues that affect the quality of neighborhood life. It has demonstrated that crime prevention, broadly defined, benefits from the joint attention of police and community" (*NIJ Research in Brief*, 1992: 11).

Neighborhood Oriented Policing (NOP) in Joliet, Illinois

Joliet's program began in 1992 with the development of specialized units con-sisting of volunteers assigned full-time to NOP (Vlasak, 1992). Initially, these officers went door to door introducing themselves, passing out information about the program, and providing residents with cellular phone numbers where they could be reached while on duty.

Officers attended neighborhood-watch meetings and promoted after-school opportunities for young people. They spent time with school children during recess and on their lunch hours and served as guest readers for younger children.

Signs of success have begun to appear. Some new businesses have been established in the NOP area and graffiti is less prevalent than it was before the program began. Crime and calls for service have decreased, as have complaints against the police. Local media have also been supportive. There have been some setbacks related to a death sentence handed down for a gang member who murdered a police officer, but overall, Chief Nowicki of the Joliet Police Department believes that "Joliet's citizens are reacting positively and starting to treat the officers as a part of, and a partner of, their communities" (Vlasak, 1992: 15).

Operation CLEAN

Operation CLEAN (Community and Law Enforcement Against Narcotics) was initiated by the Dallas Police Department in 1989 in order to help citizens reclaim their neighborhoods from drug dealers (Hatler, 1990). The series of programs involves concerned citizens and numerous city departments including the police, fire, streets and sanitation, housing and neighborhood services, and the city attorney.

Each operation involves a number of phases, beginning with target area selection, moving to intensive police involvement in investigation and arrests, and finally to reducing the level of police services from its peak and returning control of the neighborhood to its residents.

Results of CLEAN operations show a reduction in calls for police services in the target areas, decreases in serious crime, the establishment of citizen crime-watch programs, and improved fire safety and sanitation. Police planners in Dallas conclude that local law enforcement agencies can work with other city departments and concerned citizens to improve quality of life in their city (Hatler, 1990: 25).

Community Policing: The Houston Experience

Brown, in implementing COP in Houston, found that programs may be roughly divided into two phases (Brown, 1989). In Phase I, programs are implemented that provide the public with meaningful opportunities to participate in police efforts. Phase II involves changing the style, organization, and mission of the police department and other city agencies.

Brown reports that in Houston, the evolution from Phase I to Phase II took five years. During that evolution, several things occurred:

1. Barriers to change were broken down.
2. Leaders and rank-and-file officers were educated about the merits of community policing.
3. Department personnel came to see community policing as their creation, not something imported from the outside.

4. The benefits of community policing were discussed with and demonstrated to the public and elected officials.
5. Training in community-policing strategies and techniques was instituted.
6. A willingness to experiment with new ideas was demonstrated (Brown, 1989: 5).

Based on his experiences, Brown (1989: 10) concludes:

Because community policing is a relatively new style of policing, questions have been raised about its effectiveness. Any doubts, however, should be put to rest. Experience has shown that community policing as a dominant policing style is a better, more efficient, and more cost-effective means of using police resources. In the final analysis, community policing is emerging as the most appropriate means of using police resources to improve the quality of life in neighborhoods throughout the country.

Dolan (1994: 28) puts it in somewhat different terms, stating that community policing makes sense today. Over the years the police have lost touch with their communities and now find themselves interacting primarily with criminals or people in crisis. Burnout and frustration are results of these interactions. Community policing, however, offers the police a means to become professionally healthy. Officers of all ranks are encouraged to spend time outside the patrol car, interacting with law-abiding citizens. The end result should be a greater sense of accomplishment for the officers and greater appreciation from the community.

In spite of the numerous endorsements, not all departments have embraced community policing. Dolan (1994) discusses the nature of resistance to community policing among officers who have come to consider themselves the experts in crime control and order maintenance. Those who have found their niches in specialty areas also are often resistant to the idea that they may be back on the streets as generalists or that others may be permitted to utilize some of "their" techniques. This resistance must be overcome through recruiting and training techniques, managerial demonstration of long-term commitment to COP, slow "selling" of the philosophy to all levels of the department, and involvement of all concerned parties from the initial stages of development. In addition, "We must open up the police fraternity for scrutiny and help shed the mystique surrounding law enforcement" (Overman, 1994: 20).

Overcoming the obstacles to community policing will not be an easy task. Nonetheless, the effort appears to be worthwhile when we consider traditional policing's lack of success in many areas. "The arguments for change are obviously linked to our past. The first question we must ask ourselves is, 'Are the streets safer than they were 20 years ago?' The obvious answer to this question is 'No.' 'Have we won the war on drugs?' Again the answer is 'No.' " (Overman, 1994: 20) It is clearly time, then, to carefully consider alternatives to our traditional efforts.

Discussion Questions

1. List and discuss some of the problems characterizing traditional policing. Do you believe community policing can successfully address these problems? Why or why not?

2. What is community policing? Why is it believed to be a better approach than traditional policing?

3. Discuss problem-oriented policing and its relationship with community policing.

4. What are some of the criticisms of community policing? In your opinion, are these criticisms justified? Why or why not?

5. Are there any COP programs in your area? If so, discuss them. If not, why do you think they are not being attempted?

6. Why is there often resistance to community policing within police departments? How can such resistance be overcome?

7. What evidence exists that we need to consider alternatives to traditional policing? Is it reasonable to expect that community policing will solve all quality of life issues in the short-term? Why or why not?

References

Brown, L. 1989. "Community Policing: A Practical Guide for Police Officials." *Perspectives on Policing*. (September) U.S. Department of Justice. Washington, DC U.S. Government Printing Office.

Brown, L. 1992a. "An Interview with Commissioner Lee P. Brown of New York." *Law Enforcement News* 18(358), 10–14.

Brown, L. 1992b. "Violent Crime and Community Involvement." *FBI Law Enforcement Bulletin* (May), 2–5.

Burgreen, B. and McPherson, N. 1992. "Neighborhood Policing Without a Budget Increase." *The Police Chief* 59(12), 31–33.

Campbell, L.P. 1991. "Police Brutality Triggers Many Complaints, Little Data." *Chicago Tribune* (24 March), sec. 1, pp. 10–11.

Carey, L.R. 1994. "Community Policing for the Suburban Department." *Police Chief* 61(3), 24–26.

Cox, J.F. 1992. "Small Departments and Community Policing." *FBI Law Enforcement Bulletin* 61(12), 1–4.

Dolan, H.P. 1994. "Community Policing: Coping with Internal Backlash." *The Police Chief* 61(3), 28–32.

Ferguson, C. 1993. "Cops Get Long Terms for Beating." *USA TODAY* (13 October), p. 1A.

Frankel, B. 1993. "Ex-NYC Officer Tells Stark Tale of Cops Gone Bad." *USA TODAY* (28 September), p. 3A.

Goldstein, H. 1979. "Improving Policing: A Problem Oriented Approach." *Crime and Delinquency* 25, 236–258.

Hatler, R.W. 1990. "Operation CLEAN: Reclaiming City Neighborhoods." *FBI Law Enforcement Bulletin* (October), 23–25.

Kane, C. 1993. "Community Policing: Forging Police-Citizen Partnerships." *The Compiler* 13(2), 1.

Kelling, G.L. and Stewart. J.K. 1989. "Neighborhoods and Police: The Maintenance of Civil Authority." *Perspective on the Police* (May) U.S. Department of Justice. Washington, DC: U.S. Government Printing Office.

Lacayo, R. 1993. "Cops and Robber." *Time* (11 October), 43–44.

Mastrofski, S.D. 1992. "What Does Community Policing Mean for Daily Police Work?" *National Institute of Justice Journal* no. 225, 23–27.

NIJ Research in Brief. 1992. "Community Policing in Seattle: A Model Partnership Between Citizens and the Police." (August) National Institute of Justice. Washington, DC: U.S. Government Printing Office.

Offer, C. 1993. "C-OP Fads and Emperors Without Clothes." *Law Enforcement News* 19(376), 8.

Overman, R. 1994. "The Case for Community Policing." *Police Chief* 61(3), 20–23.

Pisani, A.L. 1992. "Dissecting Community Policing—Part 1." *Law Enforcement News* 18(358), 13.

Sharn, L. 1993. "'20 Years and It's Not Over,' Serpico Says." *USA TODAY* (30 September), p. 2A.

Skolnick, J.H. and Bayley, D.H. 1986. *The New Blue Line: Police Innovation in Six American Cities.* New York: The Free Press.

Toch, H. and Grant, J.D. 1991. *Police as Problem Solvers.* New York: Plenum.

Trojanowicz, R.C. 1990. "Community Policing Is Not Police-Community Relations." *FBI Law Enforcement Bulletin* 59(10), 6–11.

Trojanowicz, R.C. 1992. "Preventing Individual and Systemic Corruption." *Footprints* 4(1), 1–3.

Trojanowicz, R.C. and Bucqueroux, B. 1990. *Community Policing: A Contemporary Perspective.* Cincinnati: Anderson.

Vernon, R.L. and Lasley, J.R. 1992. "Police/Citizen Partnerships in the Inner City." *FBI Law Enforcement Bulletin* (May), 18–22.

Vlasak, T. 1992. "Walking the Beat in Joliet, Illinois." *The Complier* 11(4), 13–15.

Walters, P.M. 1993. "Community-Oriented Policing: A Blend of Strategies." *FBI Law Enforcement Bulletin* 62(11), 20–23.

4

POLICE DISCRETION AND POLICE ETHICS

How do the police go about filling the requirements of their various roles? The answer to this question lies to a great extent in the exercise of discretion by individual officers. As we noted in Chapter 2, the movement toward community policing has placed increasing demands on street officers to make decisions previously made only by supervisors and to be innovative and creative in making these decisions. We are asking these officers to exercise their discretion as police officers to help solve community problems. Administrative agencies, such as the police, play a critical role in the legal process because they have a good deal of flexibility in implementing formal legal rules. While much of this flexibility accrues to such agencies because of the vagueness of legal rules and limited resources, another source of latitude is the recognized need to deal with concrete situations in which law must be adjusted to social realities.

The Exercise of Police Discretion

Police discretion involves the use of individual judgment by officers in making decisions as to which of several behavioral responses is appropriate in specific situations. According to Sykes, Fox, and Clark (1985: 172), police "discretion exists whenever an officer is free to choose from two or more task-relevant, alternative interpretations of the events reported, inferred, or observed in a police-civilian encounter."

Discretion is a normal, desirable, and unavoidable part of policing that exists at all levels within the police department. Administrative discretion involves decisions to selectively enforce laws and establish role priorities. Supervisory discretion involves decisions by supervisors to allocate resources in specific ways at specific times in response to specific requests for services.

Such discretionary behavior is required because the code of criminal law, to say nothing of departmental policies, is expressed in terms that often make a clear interpretation of the writer's intentions difficult. In addition, police resources are limited; the police simply cannot be everywhere at once. Further, policing, like many other occupations, consists of a number of specializations and not all departments have the specialized personnel to investigate all types of crime or provide all types of services. Finally, other components of the criminal justice network also have limited resources (jail cells, prison cells, time available on court calendars) and the police are well aware of these limitations.

Of course, all other components of the criminal justice network are also involved with discretionary activities. Many of these activities, however, are less visible than those of the police. As a result, the police are sometimes perceived by the public as being responsible for decisions that are actually made elsewhere in the network, over which they have little or no control.

Factors Influencing Police Discretion

While police officers are not, in the strictest sense of the words, judges or jurors, they must and do perform the functions of both on certain occasions. That is, they must decide what the facts are in any given encounter, what the law has to say with respect to the encounter, and how best to bring the encounter to a successful conclusion. They also consider matters in extenuation and mitigation because each individual wants to provide his or her own account of the circumstances leading up to the encounter.

The extent to which police officers are encouraged to exercise discretion varies from department to department, from shift to shift, and between divisions within the same department, but the exercise of discretion is routine in all police agencies (Reiss, 1992: 74). This is true because the police simply cannot enforce all of the laws all of the time or perform all of the services demanded at the same time. Thus, both law enforcement and policing are selective processes in which some laws are enforced and some services are provided most of the time while others are not. The determination of which and when services are provided rests to some extent with police administrators, the general public, prosecutors, judges, and other politicians, but police officers do not typically operate under immediate, direct supervision. Therefore, they are relatively free to determine their own actions at any given time. Their decisions are typically influenced by the following factors:

1. The law
2. Departmental policy
3. Political expectations
4. Public expectations
5. The situation/setting
6. The occupational culture in which they operate

For example, most states prohibit some forms of gambling. Official departmental policy may also call for official action against illegal gamblers. The prosecutor, however, may not want to invest the resources of his or her office in prosecuting small-time gamblers and there may be public demand for the opportunity to bet on horse races, play punch or tip boards, or play cards for money in the back rooms of local fraternal organizations. The occupational culture of the police may lead to a view of social gambling as relatively harmless and even something to be participated in when the opportunity arises (see Highlight 4.1). Needless to say, unless pressure is exerted by members of the community and/or the media, gambling laws are not likely to be strictly enforced. In fact, Davis (1971: 162) notes that one outstanding characteristic of the American legal system is the prevalence of the discretionary power of police officers to refrain from enforcement even when enforcement is clearly appropriate.

HIGHLIGHT 4.1   Factors Affecting Police Discretion

Police Use of Discretion

Research Conducted by Hal Hugh Nees, II

A Comparison of Community, System, and Officer Expectations

Police officers display significant levels of discretion in how they handle various law enforcement scenarios, according to a research study conducted in conjunction with a doctoral thesis in Public Administration at the University of Colorado. For purposes of the study, the available choices were limited to the following: Take no action, warn the offender, refer to a social agency, issue a summons, or arrest an individual. The study also examines the officer's age, sex ethnicity, education, geographic residence, marital status, and political orientation.

The study entails the review of 20 incidents covering traffic violations, disturbances, drug and alcohol violations, prostitution, juvenile status crimes, vandalism, and gambling. All were misdemeanor offenses, with the exception of one involving the cultivation of marijuana. The sample groups of respondents included 1,077 police officers, probation officers, prosecuting attorneys, defense attorneys, judges, community leaders, and ordinary citizens in and around Colorado.

The comparison of police officer to all other groups shows that officers tend to treat individuals more harshly when dealing with curfew violations, drugs and alcohol, prostitution, and vandalism. The survey groups generally thought that the officers need to act more harshly when handling traffic violators and gambling offenses. The study also points out that even members within each group do not always agree with each other.

Officers handle intoxicated individuals differently, depending upon the suspect's attitude and demographics. It is more likely that cooperative individuals would be allowed to return home, while "outsiders" would be taken to jail.

Educational level and the experience of officers have an impact on their decision making process. Generally, the higher the officer's education, the fewer sanctions the officer would impose on an individual. However, the study implies that during the early years of police service, officers tend to act more harshly, tapering off during their mid-level years, and then gradually escalating their choice of sanctions in the final years of their careers.

The results of this study recommend that law enforcement agencies can take significant steps in the area of "discretion management"—the ability of a jurisdiction to uniformly and fairly exercise levels of discretion by their officers. This research reinforces previous studies that show that boundaries of discretion are defined too generally by many law enforcement agencies. The study also questions whether law enforcement agencies reflect the priorities within their individual communities (Icove, 1990).

Reprinted with permission from the *FBI Law Enforcement Bulletin,* 59(10), 21.

Thus, the police actually make policy about what laws to enforce, the extent to which they should be enforced, against whom, and on what occasions (Davis, 1975: 1). If this is true with respect to the law enforcement role of the police, is it not also likely to be true in terms of the other services they provide?

According to Manning (1978: 11–12), the police occupational subculture emphasizes the following assumptions:

1. People are not to be trusted and are potentially dangerous.
2. Personal experience is a better action guide than abstract rules.
3. Officers must make the public respect them.
4. Everyone hates a cop.
5. The legal system is untrustworthy; police officers make the best decisions about innocence or guilt.
6. People must be controlled or they will break laws.
7. Police officers must appear respectable and be effective.
8. Police officers can most accurately identify crime and criminals.
9. The basic jobs of the police are to prevent crime and enforce laws.
10. More severe punishment will deter crime.

The consequences of these assumptions, if carried over to the realm of police discretion, might (and in fact quite often do) lead to the following behaviors on behalf of police officers:

1. Ignoring abstract rules and principles (including laws)
2. Resorting to the threat or use of force to make the public show respect for police officers
3. Paranoid behavior
4. Street justice
5. Efficiency instead of effectiveness
6. Regarding nonenforcement tasks as less than real police work
7. Adding charges when making arrests in order to try to insure that some punishment or more severe punishment will result

Further, as Van Maanen (1978: 221–223) points out, the police develop stereotypes with respect to those they police. Thus, certain types of people are regarded as suspicious characters, outsiders, "dirt bags," or "assholes" and may be singled out for differential (discretionary) treatment. Perceived lack of respect on the part of representatives of any of these categories is likely to be regarded as a serious violation by the police, even when no other violation has occurred (Chevigny, 1969; Reiss, 1992). Similarly, members of these groups may be perceived as less deserving of police services than members of "respectable" groups. Consequently, racial and ethnic minority group members, homosexuals, or known criminals may receive fewer or less timely services than those not belonging to such groups.

For example, reports of crimes occurring in high-crime minority areas may not be taken seriously by officers who come to perceive both that certain types of offenses are typical in such areas and that prospects for solving these crimes are minimal. Attitudes and opinions formed within the context of the police culture are, then, an important variable in the exercise of officer discretion.

The police subculture, although important, is not the only determinant of police discretion, nor are street-level officers the only police personnel who exercise such discretion. Among other important considerations in the exercise of discretion are the law, the seriousness of the offense in question, departmental policy, personal characteristics of those involved in a given encounter, the safety of the officer involved, and the visibility of the decision (Sykes, Fox, and Clark, 1985; Reiss, 1992; Gaines, Kappeler, and Vaughn, 1994: 195–202). One study of police response to drunk drivers in Maine found that officers sometimes fail to stop vehicles when they suspect the drivers may be drunk. Factors associated with such decisions included length of police service, rank, attitudes toward drunk driving laws, and level of frustration with failure to prosecute such drivers and low conviction rates (Meyers et al., 1987).

Further, the education, training, and length of service of the officer and the wishes of the complainant have been shown to affect decisions rendered by police officers (Brooks, 1993). A department involved in community policing may provide more education and training in the exercise of discretion as well as more encouragement to use discretion than a traditional department. Still, the department's policy will have differential impact on officers with different lengths of service and different levels of education who may be assigned to vastly different neighborhoods.

Consequences of Police Discretion

There are a number of interrelated problems related to the use of discretion by the police. They include:

1. Inconsistency
2. Unpredictability
3. Lack of accountability (Feldberg, 1989)

Inconsistency may result in differential treatment by officers of different types of individuals. As indicated previously, such treatment may be based on membership in a specific racial, ethnic, or age group and when one or more of these is the cause of differential treatment, discrimination is the result. "American society proclaims its citizens equal before the law, but discretion may give rise to situations in which, it appears, some individuals have less to fear from the law than others" (Feldberg, 1989: 148).

Thus, Hispanics may be stopped and questioned more frequently by the police than whites, or politically prominent persons may be given a verbal warning while others less prominent may receive a citation for the same violation. The police may respond more slowly to calls involving violence in a ghetto than to similar calls originating elsewhere; giving rise to the often-heard complaint from ghetto dwellers that the police are less concerned about them than about white, middle-class citizens. Such complaints, real or imagined, may lead to diminished willingness on behalf of those residing in the inner city to cooperate with the police when they do arrive, which may lead to increased suspicion and hostility on behalf of the police, and so on.

Unpredictability may lead to problems because it makes it difficult for citizens to conform their behavior to police requirements. Thus, one police officer may allow "rolling stops" at a stop sign while another may require complete cessation of forward motion. An individual practicing rolling stops may continue to do so because under police observation he or she has done so without difficulty, or because he or she has seen police officers practice such stops. When the next rolling stop leads to a traffic citation, the driver finds it difficult to understand how one officer approves of his or her driving practices while another member of the same department regards them as serious violations.

Clearly, inconsistency and unpredictability may be problematic not only with respect to officers employed in the same department, but across departments as well. Driving 60 miles per hour in a 55-mile-per-hour zone may be acceptable in one jurisdiction, but may lead to a citation in the next, causing the driver to have difficulty in predicting police response. The facts that the driver was in violation in both instances, could have been cited in both jurisdictions, and the officer who wrote the citation was perfectly justified in doing so often do little to comfort the driver who may continue to believe that the officer writing the citation was "out to get" him or her.

Accountability is a key to building mutual trust and respect between the police and other citizens. Some lack of accountability inevitably accompanies the exercise of officer discretion, creating potential difficulties not only for the public but for police supervisors and administrators as well. It is difficult to plan and distribute police resources when one officer believes in taking half an hour to settle a domestic dispute while another handles such calls in a matter of minutes. Similarly, the amount of time devoted by one investigator to a burglary case may greatly exceed that devoted by another. At what point is an officer simply wasting time, leading to low productivity, as opposed to making a genuine effort to find a solution to the problem at hand?

Yet another concern with lack of accountability resulting from police discretion has to do with the cultivation and utilization of informants. There is little doubt that certain types of police investigations depend heavily on the information supplied by police informants. How far should the police go in paying for such information when they know the money they provide is being used for illegal goods or services, and how far should they go in overlooking crime committed by informants in order to gain or sustain their cooperation? Further, the exercise of discretion may enhance the potential for corruption among police officers. In one instance, for example, a police supervisor received an anonymous phone call requesting that he ensure that no patrol vehicles would be in the area of a certain airport on the outskirts of town between the hours of 10 and 11 P.M. on certain nights. In exchange for this service, he was to receive one thousand dollars per week in small bills left at a mutually agreed-upon location.

While the request itself was clearly illegal, the behavior requested was not and the officer was faced with three discretionary decisions. First, he had to decide whether or not to report the incident to his supervisors. Second, if he chose not to report the incident, should he or should he not arrange to patrol the designated area at the specified time? Third, if he chose not to have the area patrolled, should he accept the money with all the attendant risks? While proper decisions may be made easily by most police officers in such cases, media stories concerning officers who become involved in the protection of drug-related activities or distribution of drugs occur frequently; they remind us that under the right circumstances, for a large enough sum of money, such offers can be extremely attractive. As a result, police agencies heavily involved in drug investigations face the added burden of having to police the officers who are conducting the investigations in order to increase the visibility of their activities to supervisors.

The same problems that characterize officer discretion occur at administrative and supervisory levels as well. The selective enforcement policies implemented by police administrators may be inconsistent and unpredictable and lead to a lack of accountability. How is it that officers are available to suppress traffic violations on a street today, but none were available yesterday and none will be available tomorrow? The answer, of course, lies in determinations made by police administrators or supervisors (or those elected officials for whom they work) about proper distribution of personnel at specific times in response to specific problems; members of the public may not understand (or approve of) how such determinations are made.

There are also a number of positive consequences of police discretion. At the administrative and supervisory levels, the very ability to move personnel from one location to another to deal with current problems is a plus for both the public and the police department. At the level of the patrol officer, extenuating and mitigating circumstances related to violations probably should be taken into account. For example, the officer who issues a traffic citation to a husband rushing his pregnant wife to the hospital is within his or her rights, but the circumstances would probably lead most of us to excuse the behavior if there is no accident. In such cases, most of us would prefer to have the officer not adhere to the formal aspects of the law but to consider the substance of the case in point.

A number of years ago, Bittner (1967) pointed out the advantages of discretionary activities on the part of police assigned to skid-row. He noted that in order to keep the peace (maintain order) on skid-row, the police often avoided making arrests even when they were clearly possible; that they intervened, at the request of certain types of citizens, in matters that contained no criminal or legal aspects; and that they accorded special treatment to individuals they defined as "not normal," even when such treatment was questionable on legal grounds. In fact, Bittner noted, officers often acted on the basis of perceived risk rather than culpability and were more interested in reducing the aggregate of troubles in the area than in the merits of each individual case. He concluded that there is a belief that patrol work on skid-row requires a good deal of discretionary freedom to allow officers to "play by ear" in keeping the peace.

Twenty-five years later, Meehan (1992: 475), in analyzing police encounters with juveniles, concluded: "Police officers must juggle and balance their response to accommodate the conflicting demands of the citizenry, the law, and the formal police organization, and all of these with their own sense of working (policing) the streets. In the face of these conflicting demands, officers adopt ad hoc methods and develop a set of shared assumptions about juvenile behavior in order to draw inferences for controlling groups, making decisions, and taking action."

There are special populations dealt with by the police that often require considerable discretion because the lifestyle in which they are entrenched differs significantly from that of other populations. Among these populations are people with mental disorders and the homeless. In most (perhaps 75 percent) situations involving the mentally ill, the police use informal dispositions such as calming the person down or taking him or her home, while arrests are made in about 17 percent of the cases and hospitalization occurs in about 12 percent of such encounters (Finn and Sullivan, 1988). Similarly, the police are often called to remove the homeless from a particular area because they hurt business or frighten passersby. In other cases, the homeless are a danger to themselves, particularly in freezing weather. Options available to the police are limited because many shelters are either full or refuse to admit homeless persons who are mentally ill or alcoholic. Innovative dispositions are sometimes made by the police or by teams of helping professionals who provide a network of services to attempt to assist the homeless.

In other cases, the police simply choose to ignore the behavior in question. For example, in a recent visit to a large city, an individual was observed walking along the very edge of the sidewalk next to a busy thoroughfare, talking to himself, and occasionally shouting at passersby. He appeared to be imagining himself walking a tightrope and was shouting at others to gain their attention and to get them to applaud his "feat." Two police officers were standing nearby and they clearly observed both his behavior and the fact that many pedestrians were crossing the street to avoid coming close to the person in question. For more than twenty minutes, the officers observed the behavior, taking no action and ignoring comments by others that something should be done. Finally, the tightrope walker moved on and when questioned the officers indicated that he was well known to them and their colleagues, but that he seldom caused any "real" trouble.

Of course, the positive exercise of discretion is precisely what we are encouraging officers to demonstrate in community policing. Finding innovative solutions to problems without necessarily arresting people for "incidents" and encouraging other service agencies and the public to assist in this enterprise are at the heart of COP.

Controlling Police Discretion

Should the exercise of police discretion be subject to greater control? Davis (1975: 140) pointed out some time ago that, "Police discretion is absolutely essential. It cannot be eliminated. Any effort to eliminate it would be ridiculous. Discretion is the essence of police work, both in law enforcement and in service activities. Police work without discretion would be something like a human torso without legs, arms, or head."

Still, discretion is sometimes misused and often denied. Powell (1990) found that lack of guidelines in police agencies gave individual officers ample opportunity to inject their own prejudices and legal interpretations into their job performance.

Failure to recognize and communicate the importance of discretion at all levels in policing may lead to a pretense of full enforcement and equal treatment in similar conditions when the reality is selective enforcement and unequal treatment. Thus, a necessary first step in dealing with discretion is to recognize its existence and importance. Once we admit that discretion exists in police work, we can talk about its proper and improper uses. We can stop attempting to deceive the public and we can provide training with respect to the appropriate uses of discretion (see Highlight 4.2).

For example, we agree that a driver who is exceeding the speed limit by three or four miles per hour should not be subject to arrest. We might thus establish a "tolerance limit" of five miles per hour, instruct officers that those driving over the speed limit, but within the tolerance, need not be arrested. While this does not guarantee absolute control over officers' behavior (they could, for example, still cite a driver for driving two or three miles per hour over the speed limit), it does let them know that it is permissible to ignore or warn those who are marginally speeding (Langworthy and Travis, 1994: 294–295).

Similarly, we might agree that an officer who decides to render service or enforce the law based solely on the gender, race, or physical appearance of the other citizen involved is exercising discretion inappropriately (based on personal characteristics). Supervisors could then discourage such behavior and explain why decisions based solely on personal characteristics of subjects are unacceptable. In effect, we would be enhancing the value of police discretion by providing the officer with appropriate education and training.

Since the police are a public service agency, honesty and accountability to the public are particularly important. Admitting that selective enforcement occurs and that not all police officers respond in the same way to similar situations (already "open secrets") are steps in the right direction. While a comprehensive set of guidelines for the exercise of police discretion may not be possible, improvement of current guidelines is clearly possible. Such clarification will not only assist the community in understanding police actions, it might also remove some of the confusion among police officers as to how much and what types of discretion are available to and expected of them. Simply telling an officer to exercise his or her discretion, in the traditional police world, is likely to have little effect because there are other indicators that innovation is seldom rewarded and mistakes seldom go unpunished.

For this very reason, implementation of COP is difficult because it requires officers to do what they have been told not to do over time. Successful programs must convince officers that failure is acceptable in the course of experimentation and will not be regarded in negative fashion. Unfortunately, a typical response to controlling police discretion has often been to use negative sanctions to prevent or correct discretionary behavior.

HIGHLIGHT 4.2   Training in Police Discretion

Training in Discretion

How, then, can the concept of discretionary powers be incorporated into practical departmental life? We believe that agencies should address discretion during recruit and inservice training in order to institutionalize and legitimize its acceptable uses.

Several teaching methodologies can be employed to present key discretion concepts. For example, case studies which describe actual situations, where officers relied on their experience and judgment to resolve potentially explosive situations, are excellent teaching aids. Ideally, the officers involved in the incident would participate with the training staff and the class. Additionally, case studies could be developed to highlight specific policy points regarding acceptable practices.

One of the most important training goals should be to provide officers with a clear notion of when and where to apply discretionary behavior. Guidelines and checklists can assist officers with these critical questions. Also, by clearly specifying the types of situations where discretion would be unacceptable or perhaps illegal, departments can clearly demonstrate the bounds of acceptable behavior.

Role playing provides an excellent technique to frame problems of discretion. Elements of realism and immediacy can be injected into many role-playing scenarios. Videotaping these scenarios has the added benefit of letting officers criticize their own actions. A common exclamation of officers after viewing a tape is: "I wouldn't have believed I did that unless I had seen it!"

Practical problems are also appropriate vehicles for discussing discretion. Whenever officers are required to participate physically in an exercise, they are more likely to remember the teaching objective.

In the field of management and leadership training, there are a variety of situational and contingency models that can be employed. Certainly a situational-type model could be developed to present ideas with a discretionary dimension. Possible dimensions of such a model might be order maintenance and law enforcement.

All in all, the methods by which departments discuss and teach discretion are not nearly as important as the fact that the topic is formally presented. Leaders have an obligation to their subordinates to guide and train them in their duties. Until policing openly faces the issue of discretion, it will not provide officers with the appropriate support they need (Witham and Gladis, 1986).

Reprinted with permission from the *FBI Law Enforcement Bulletin,* 55(11), 16–20.

A number of consequences are likely to accompany the punitive approach. These include temporary rather than permanent change, inappropriate emotional behavior, inflexibility, possible changes in desirable behavior, and fear or distrust of those administering the negative sanctions. Further, the stigma accompanying punishment may have negative effects on self-esteem and status as well, which may lead to anger and hostility in those punished.

A better approach to controlling discretion is the use of incentives to promote voluntary compliance with policies concerning discretion. Such incentives include officer participation in policy formulation, establishment of specialized units to deal with specific tasks, positive disciplinary practices (aimed at correcting the aberrant behavior without humiliating the officer involved), and more and better training with respect to the exercise of discretion and the social and historical context that require the police to be accountable to several audiences (public, administration, colleagues) for their behavior. Similarly, training and education dealing with police ethics may provide the foundation for making appropriate discretionary decisions in a variety of different situations (Brooks, 1993; Gaines, Kappeler, and Vaughn, 1994: 221–230).

Police Ethics

The term *ethics*, in its most general sense, refers to the moral obligation of human beings to act in ways that are just and proper. People who work in different fields develop and formalize ethics in the performance of their occupations/professions. This is the case with medical doctors and lawyers, for example, and has been the case with the police as well.

The International Association of Chiefs of Police adopted the original "Law Enforcement Code of Ethics" in 1957. Over the years, the relevancy of the original code was called into question and so it was revised and renamed the "Police Code of Conduct" in 1989 (*The Police Chief*, 1992: 14). A copy of the 1989 Code appears in Highlight 4.3.

A special code of ethics or conduct is required for the police because of two special ethical problems confronting police officers. First, they are entitled to use coercive force. Second, they are entitled to lie to and otherwise deceive others in the course of their duties (while conducting undercover operations or interrogating suspects, for example). Further, special standards of conduct appear to be necessary in policing because police officers over the years have engaged in activities that have offended the moral sensibilities of a good number of people. Finally, the need for special ethical standards arises whenever certain types of conduct are not subject to control by other means, usually when practitioners exercise considerable discretion and those affected must trust them to be ethical. As noted earlier in this chapter, this is clearly the case with respect to the police.

Kleinig (1990) and Delattre (1989), among others, note that training related to values is deficient in many police academies. There is widespread agreement that the teaching of ethics is essential in recruit training, yet such training often gets slighted. In Florida, for example, the academy is a minimum of 520 hours, but specific instruction in ethics is limited to one hour (Braunstein and Tyre, 1992: 31). How, then, are new police officers to learn the ethical parameters within which they should exercise discretion?

The teaching of ethics may be done by field training officers and police supervisors. In fact, since academies are not involved in teaching ethics to any great extent, police supervisors and trainers or outsiders invited in by supervisors and trainers must fill the gap. As Payne (1993: 5) notes, police managers must be sure that their officers make ethical decisions on a daily basis or risk losing the public's trust. When citizens mistrust the police, they will attempt to exert control by lodging complaints, filing lawsuits, or demanding external police review boards or new legislation.

HIGHLIGHT 4.3   Police Code of Conduct

All law enforcement officers must be fully aware of the ethical responsibilities of their position and must strive constantly to live up to the highest possible standards of professional policing.

The International Association of Chiefs of Police believes it important that police officers have clear advice and counsel available to assist them in performing their duties consistent with these standards, and has adopted the following ethical mandates as guidelines to meet these ends.

Primary Responsibilities of a Police Officer

A police officer acts as an official representative of government who is required and trusted to work within the law. The officer's powers and duties are conferred by statue. The fundamental duties of a police officer include serving the community, safeguarding lives and property, protecting the innocent, keeping the peace and ensuring the rights of all to liberty, equality and justice.

Performance of the Duties of a Police Officer

A police officer shall perform all duties impartially, without favor or affection or ill will and without regard to status, sex, race, religion, political belief or aspiration. All citizens will be treated equally with courtesy, consideration and dignity.

Officers will never allow personal feelings, animosities or friendships to influence official conduct. Laws will be enforced appropriately and courteously and, in carrying out their responsibilities, officer's will strive to obtain maximum cooperation from the public. They will conduct themselves in appearance and deportment in such a manner as to inspire confidence and respect for the position of public trust they hold.

Discretion

A police officer will use responsibly the discretion vested in his position and exercise it within the law. The principle of reasonableness will guide the officer's determinations, and the officer will consider all surrounding circumstances in determining whether any legal action will be taken.

Consistent and wise use of discretion, based on professional policing competence, will do much to preserve good relationships and retain the confidence of the public. There can be difficulty in choosing between conflicting courses of action. It is important to remember that a timely word of advice rather than arrest—which may be correct in appropriate circumstances—can be a more effective means of achieving a desired end.

Use of Force

A police officer will never employ unnecessary force or violence and will use only such force in the discharge of duty as is reasonable in all circumstances.

The use of force should be used only with the greatest restraint and only after discussion, negotiation and persuasion have been found to be inappropriate or ineffective. While the use of force is occasionally unavoidable, every police officer will refrain from unnecessary infliction of pain or suffering and will never engage in cruel, degrading or inhuman treatment of any person.

Confidentiality

Whatever a police officer sees, hears or learns of that is of a confidential nature will be kept secret unless the performance of duty or legal provision requires otherwise.

Members of the public have a right to security and privacy, and information obtained about them must not be improperly divulged.

Integrity

A police officer will not engage in acts of corruption or bribery, nor will an officer condone such acts by other police officers.

Continued

The public demands that the integrity of police officers be above reproach. Police officers must, therefore, avoid any conduct that might compromise integrity and thus undercut the public confidence in a law enforcement agency. Officers will refuse to accept any gifts, presents, subscriptions, favors, gratuities or promises that could be interpreted as seeking to cause the officer to refrain from performing official responsibilities honestly and within the law. Police officers must not receive private or special advantage from their official status. Respect from the public cannot be bought; it can only be earned and cultivated.

Cooperation with Other Police Officers and Agencies

Police officers will cooperate with all legally authorized agencies and their representatives in the pursuit of justice.

An officer or agency may be one among many organizations that may provide law enforcement services to a jurisdiction. It is imperative that a police officer assist colleagues fully and completely with respect and consideration at all times.

Personal-Professional Capabilities

Police officers will be responsible for their own standard of professional performance and will take every reasonable opportunity to enhance and improve their level of knowledge and competence.

Through study and experience, a police officer can acquire the high level of knowledge and competence that is essential for the efficient and effective performance of duty. The acquisition of knowledge is a never-ending process of personal and professional development that should be pursued constantly.

Private Life

Police officers will behave in a manner that does not bring discredit to their agencies or themselves.

A police officer's character and conduct while off duty must always be exemplary, thus maintaining a position of respect in the community in which he or she lives and serves. The officer's personal behavior must be beyond reproach.

(International Association of Chiefs of Police, 1990)

Myron (1992) observes that many have claimed that policing has so many gray areas that providing clear-cut ethical guidelines is impossible. Still, Myron argues, there are a number of police behaviors that are absolutely unethical. Among these are theft (of found property, for example), brutal violation of human and civil rights, planting evidence, obtaining retroactive search warrants, and forcing people to sign disclaimers. Also included are lying on official reports, in court, or to supervisors. Finally, Myron (1992: 26–27) concludes there is no offender so important that the police should violate the Constitution or statutory law to arrest him or her. All of these ethical considerations—and many others as well—should influence the exercise of police discretion.

Clearly, the exercise of discretion is intimately related to other aspects of police work. To some extent, the police role is shaped and determined by the exercise of discretion and by ethical considerations. In what kinds of situations do the police have the authority to intervene? What kinds of services will they provide in different situations? Under what circumstances can they give "breaks" to other citizens? How much attention do they pay to what other citizens say? Similarly, the extent and nature of discretion encouraged among officers is determined to some extent by the organizational character-istics and selection and promotional procedures of the department. Of course, community policing also depends on judicious exercise of discretion. The National Commission on Causes and Prevention of Violence (1968: 312) rec-ognized long ago that the way in which discretion is exercised in police agen-cies is one of the critical areas in police-community relations. "How a police-man handles day-to-day contacts with citizens will, to a large extent, shape the relationships between the police and the community. These contacts involve considerable discretion. Improper exercise of such discretion can needlessly create tension and contribute to community grievances."

Police discretion, then, is a consideration in most areas of police activity and should be recognized as an important aspect of policing. Bouza (1990: 6) sums it up best when he notes that there is a constant struggle between the police supervisor's need to control and direct officers' actions on the street and the officer's fight to retain autonomy. "One of the comic opera aspects of this invisible battle is the administration's imposition of endless restrictive regulations (of the well-known Mickey Mouse variety) that have nothing to do with performance (like the length of mustaches and the color and state of the uniform) but that lend a semblance of sovereignty over the process." Bouza goes on to point out that another hidden truth about policing is that, while supervisors can decide the general direction of the department, street officers retain the power to work their wills in countless ways. "The result is that guidelines become rough limits, within which a great deal of indepen-dent action can be exercised" (Bouza, 1990: 6).

Discussion Questions

1. What is police discretion? How extensive is its use?

2. Why is the police subculture important in understanding discretion?

3. What are some possible negative consequences of the exercise of discretion? Positive consequences?

4. What factors besides the police subculture affect the exercise of police discretion?

5. Can we eliminate the exercise of police discretion? How might we gain more control over it?

6. What are some differences between traditional and community-oriented police agencies with respect to the use of discretion by rank-and-file officers?

7. Discretion is exercised by police administrators and supervisors as well as by line officers. Discuss some of the discretionary prerogatives of police managers.

8. Discuss the evolution of the police code of ethics/conduct. Why are ethics espe-cially important for the police?

9. How effective are police academies at teaching ethics? Where and how do most officers learn police ethics?

10. Why are police ethics especially important in community policing?

References

Bittner, E. 1967. "The Police on Skid-Row: A Study of Peacekeeping." *American Sociological Review,* 32(5), 699–715.

Bouza, A.V. 1990. *The Police Mystique: An Insider's Look at Cops, Crime, and the Criminal Justice System.* New York: Plenum.

Braunstein, S. and Tyre, M. 1992. "Building a More Ethical Police Department." *The Police Chief* 59(1), 30–36.

Brooks, L.W. 1993. "Police Discretionary Behavior: A Study of Style." In Dunham, R. G. and Alpert, G. P. (eds.), *Critical Issues in Policing: Contemporary Readings* 2 ed. Prospect Heights, IL: Waveland Press, 140–164.

Chevigny, P. 1969. *Police Power: Police Abuses in New York City.* New York: Vintage Press.

Davis, K.C. 1971. *Discretionary Justice: A Preliminary Inquiry.* Chicago: University of Chicago Press.

Davis, K.C. 1975. *Police Discretion.* St. Paul, MN: West.

Delattre, E. 1989. *Character and Cops: Ethics in Policing.* Washington, D.C. American Enterprise Institute for Public Policy Research.

Feldberg, M. 1989. "Discretion." In Bailey, W.G. (ed.), *The Encyclopedia of Police Science.* New York: Garland Press, 146–151.

Finn, P.E. and Sullivan, M. 1988. "Police Response to Special Populations: Handling the Mentally Ill, Public Inebriate, and the Homeless." *Research in Action.* (January) National Institute of Justice Washington, DC: U.S. Government Printing Office.

Gaines, L.K., Kappeler, V.E., and Vaughn, J.B. 1994. *Policing in America.* Cincinnati: Anderson.

Icove, D.J. 1990. "Research Review: Police Use of Discretion." *FBI Law Enforcement Bulletin* 59(10), 21.

International Association of Chiefs of Police. 1990. *Police Chief* (January), 18.

Kleinig, J. 1990. "Teaching and Learning Police Ethics: Competing and Complementary Approaches." *Journal of Criminal Justice* 18, 1–18.

Langworthy, R.H. and Travis, L.F. 1994. *Policing in America: A Balance of Forces.* New York: Macmillan.

Manning, P. 1978. "The Police: Mandate, Strategies, and Appearances." In Manning, P. and Van Maanen, J. (eds.), *Policing: A View from the Street.* Santa Monica, CA: Goodyear, 7–13.

Meehan, A.J. 1992. "'I Don't Prevent Crime, I Prevent Calls': Policing as a Negotiated Order." *Symbolic Interaction* 15(4), 455–480.

Meyers, A.R., Heere, T., Kovenock, D., and Hingson, R. 1987. "Cops and Drivers: Police Discretion in the Enforcement of Maine's 1981 OUI Law." *Journal of Criminal Justice* 15(5), 361–368.

Myron, P. 1992. "Crooks or Cops: We Can't Be Both." *The Police Chief* 59(1), 23–29.

National Commission on the Causes and Prevention of Violence: Report of the Commission. 1968. *Rights in Conflict: The Violent Confrontation of Demonstrators and the Police in the Parks and Streets of Chicago During the Week of the Democratic National Convention of 1968.* New York: Bantam Books.

Payne, D.M. 1993. "Ethics in Police Decision making: Modeling the Corporate Methods." *FBI Law Enforcement Bulletin* 62(8), 5–8.

Powell, D.D. 1990. "A Study of Police Discretion in Six Southern Cities." *Journal of Police Science and Administration* 17(1), 1–7.

Reiss, A.J. 1992. "Police Organization in the Twentieth Century." In Tonry, M. and Morris, N. (eds.), *Modern Policing.* Chicago: University of Chicago Press, 51–98.

Sykes, R., Fox, J., and Clark, J. 1985. "A Socio-Legal Theory of Police Discretion." In Blumberg, A. and Niederhoffer, E. (eds.), *The Ambivalent Force: Perspectives on the Police.* New York: Holt, Rinehart & Winston, 171–183.

The Police Chief. 1992. "The Evolution of the Law enforcement Code of Ethics." 59(1), 14.

Van Maanen, J. 1978. "The Asshole." In Manning, P. and Van Maanen, J. (eds.), *Policing: A View from the Street.* Santa Monica, CA: Goodyear, 221–238.

Witham, D.C. and Gladis, S.D. 1986. "The Nature of Police Authority." *FBI Law Enforcement Bulletin* 55(11): 16–20.

5

POLICE ADMINISTRATION AND OPERATIONS

The functions of the U.S. police are extremely diverse as is the manner in which such functions are performed. U.S. police officers are expected to regulate public manners and morals, prevent crime through territorial patrol, apprehend criminals, recover stolen property, bring an end to domestic disputes, and accomplish dozens of other tasks as well. Police performance in these and other areas is generally governed by the Constitution and related statutes and court decisions, which outline the *federal* powers, duties, and limitations of police officers. Their performance is further governed by state constitutions and related statutes and court decisions, which outline the *state* powers, duties, and limitations of police officers. Municipal charters and ordinances govern their operations at the municipal level.

At the state level, for example, the Illinois Compiled Statutes (1993) state that the corporate authorities of each municipality may pass and enforce all necessary police ordinances (24: 11–1–1) and prescribe the duties and powers of all police officers (24: 11–1–2). Police officers are described as "conservators of the peace" with powers to: "(1) arrest or cause to be arrested, with or without process, all persons who break the peace, or are found violating any municipal ordinance or any criminal law of the state; (2) to commit arrested persons for examination; (3) if necessary, to detain arrested persons in custody overnight or Sunday in any safe place, or until they can be brought before the proper court; (4) to exercise all other powers as conservators of the peace that the corporate authorities may prescribe" (24: 3–9–4).

Further, "it shall be the duty of every sheriff, coroner, and every marshal, policeman, or other officer of any incorporated city, town, or village, having the power of a sheriff, when any criminal offense or breach is committed or attempted in his or her presence, forthwith to apprehend the offender and bring him or her before a judge, to be dealt with according to law; to suppress all riots and unlawful assemblies; and to keep the peace, and without delay to serve and execute all warrants and other process to him or her lawfully directed" (125: 82).

Other states, of course, have similar statutes, which, like those cited here, serve to indicate some of the specific functions of the police (serving warrants, detaining persons) as well as some of the general ones (keeping the peace). In addition, the Bill of Rights and civil rights legislation restrict police behavior by establishing, defining, and guaranteeing certain freedoms for all U.S. citizens. Basically, this means that police powers and actions cannot conflict with the rights of the individual to freedom of speech, religion, press, assembly, and security from unreasonable searches and seizures.

U.S. police, as we have noted throughout this text, are primarily public servants whose foremost duty is to maintain order, whose powers are established and defined by federal, state, and local laws and court decisions, and whose actions are tailored to and by the communities in which they police.

Basic Police Functions

The cover of a major news magazine shows two policemen reaching for their guns as they burst through the doors of an apartment in a housing project.

In the background is a police car with flashing red lights. A less dramatic scene on another page shows a policewoman talking to a grateful mother whose lost child was returned. Which one of these illustrations most accurately describes the police role? How frequently do the events depicted by these illustrations occur? What percentage of police activity is violent and dangerous? What do police officers really do?

The answer to the final question is that they spend a good deal of their time on routine matters, including coffee breaks, meals, taking reports, running errands, and attending court. Traffic, social service, police-initiated events, and crimes against property account for most of the rest of patrol officers' time. Only a small percentage of the officers' time is spent on "serious crime."

Police officers give advice on repossession, insurance matters, commercial fraud, and how to help children with school problems. They spend part of their time helping to protect alcoholics from being rolled and helping citizens find shelter for the mentally ill and the retarded (Bittner, 1967; Toch and Grant, 1991; Bowker, 1994). Langworthy and Travis (1994) indicate that the police, like welfare and health departments, are responsible for the general safety and security of the community. Bouza (1990) describes police functions that include dealing with "the human animal's dark underside," consisting of people who are out of control, nasty, and generally in trouble or disarray.

Of course, the way in which the police view their role helps determine the nature of the functions they perform and, as we shall see shortly, the manner in which they organize to perform these functions. Thus, it is apparent that any list of police functions must be arbitrary and incomplete; however, the following police functions have been suggested in the literature:

1. To prevent and control serious crime that threatens life and/or property
2. To assist individuals in danger of physical harm
3. To protect constitutional guarantees
4. To facilitate pedestrian and vehicle traffic
5. To assist those who cannot care for themselves
6. To resolve conflict
7. To prevent problem situations from escalating
8. To distribute situationally justified, nonnegotiable force when necessary to accomplish any of the other functions
9. To generate feelings of security among citizens (American Bar Association, 1973; Goldstein, 1977; Sparrow, Moore, and Kennedy, 1990; Cox and Fitzgerald, 1991)

Perhaps some specific examples of police responses in the areas of both order maintenance and law enforcement will help illustrate the many and varied tasks the police are called on to perform. A National Institute of Justice Report (1988) discusses the need for police to respond to special populations including the mentally ill, the public inebriate, and the homeless. In dealing with the mentally ill, a task that involves as many as 5 to 10 percent of police encounters in some cities, the police typically handle cases informally by calming the person down or taking him or her home with only about 12 percent of such encounters resulting in hospitalization and about 17 percent resulting in arrests.

Interestingly enough, the police often find themselves with the sole responsibility of dealing with mentally ill persons whose behavior warrants some form of intervention. The same holds true for public inebriates who become the responsibility of the police because limited bed space and selective admission practices at detoxification centers hinder their attempts to place those who are publicly intoxicated. At the same time, of course, the use of jails to house public inebriates is deemed inappropriate, placing further restrictions on the alternatives available to the police. The police are also frequently called to remove the homeless from streets and parks because they have a negative impact on business, create an appearance of community neglect, and are often a danger to themselves (especially in cold weather). What options are available to the police in these cases? Shelter facilities have limited space and many refuse to admit those who are mentally ill or alcoholic. Thus, finding a suitable alternative for the homeless often becomes a task for the police.

The functions listed above are to be performed through the processes of arrest and detention, investigation, and police-community relations programs. In order to help ensure that these processes will be carried out successfully, the police must recruit, select, train, educate, evaluate, and promote officers capable of fulfilling these functions. The selection and training procedures used by the police result in the hiring of officers capable of performing the functions listed using the processes outlined. However, there is tremendous variation in the manner in which these officers perform their tasks—even on the same shift in the same division in the same department. As we have seen, the exercise of discretion by police officers plays an important role in their encounters with other citizens. So, too, does the manner in which the police organize in order to perform their tasks.

Styles of Policing

James Q. Wilson (1968) has identified three relatively distinct types of policing. The first type, referred to as the "watchman style," involves police organizations in which the principle function is order maintenance rather than law enforcement in cases that do not involve serious crime. The police use the law more as a means of maintaining order than to regulate conduct and judge the seriousness of infractions less by what the law says about them than by their immediate and personal consequences. In other words, circumstances of person and situation are taken into account. Police officers are encouraged to follow the path of least resistance in carrying out their daily duties. "Little stuff" is to be ignored, but officers are to be "tough" when serious matters arise. This style of policing often occurs in departments with low-level educational requirements (high school education or less), relatively low wages, little formal training, considerable on-the-job training, and few formal policies. Such departments have few specialized personnel, thus departmental transfers are rare. Officers are encouraged to take personal differences into account when enforcing the law and addressing citizens. Other than in serious cases, who the citizen is is as important as what he or she has done (Wilson, 1968: 140–171).

The second style of policing is the "legalistic style." In such police organizations, officers are encouraged to handle commonplace situations as if they were matters of law enforcement as opposed to order maintenance. Traffic tickets are frequently issued, juveniles are often detained and arrested, misdemeanor arrests are common, and the police take action against illicit enterprises on a regular basis. Patrol officers are under pressure to "produce" arrests and tickets and are expected to simply "do their jobs" as defined by the administration, which views a high volume of traffic and other stops as simply a means to discovering more serious crimes. Technical efficiency is highly valued and promotions are based on such efficiency. Middle-class officers with high school educations are recruited and professional image (new buildings and equipment) is viewed as important. The law is used to punish those perceived as deserving. Orders are issued by supervisory personnel and are expected to be followed whether or not officers deem them appropriate (Wilson, 1968: 172–199).

The third policing style is the "service style." Service-style police intervene frequently but not formally, take seriously all requests for service, and often find alternatives to arrest and other formal sanctions. Officers are encouraged to be consumer oriented and to perform a function that meets community needs. Officers are expected to be neat, courteous, and professional. Authority is less centralized and community relations and public education are viewed as important aspects of policing. College education is valued, salaries are reasonably good, and specialized expertise is encouraged (Wilson, 1968: 200–226).

While most police organizations have characteristics of all three styles of policing, tendencies to emphasize one style over the other two are often easily discernible. In fact, particular communities sometimes become known for their emphasis on a specific style of policing ("don't speed in that town, they ticket everybody—the town lives off income from traffic citations" or "you can get anything you want in that town as long as you don't rock the boat"). While many watchman and legalistic departments exist, service-style organizations appear to represent the current trend in policing. Given the emphases on community policing and cooperation between the police and other citizens in maintaining order and enforcing the law, this trend is not surprising.

Police Organizations

One way of looking at organizations is to view them as arenas in which tasks are performed. The dynamic nature of organizations can easily be seen in the comparison with a sports arena in which the major focus of attention is on the playing field, people are constantly changing positions, entering, and leaving, some spectators and participants are happy while others are unhappy, and many secondary activities are occurring at any given time (concession-stand sales, souvenir sales, business conversations, etc.). All of these activities in the arena (organization) require planning, organizing, staffing, directing, and controlling; they are performed in varying degrees by personnel occupying positions at different levels within the organization.

For example, planning and organizing are tasks that involve more time from upper-level management than from field supervisors, while the opposite is true of directing and controlling (Halloran and Frunzi, 1986; More and Wegener, 1992: 29–30). In terms of police organizations, the chief of police and his or her immediate staff are likely to be involved in budgeting and policy making while the shift and field supervisors are more concerned with day-to-day operations (directing and controlling personnel). In short, we can analyze organizations in terms of the tasks (functions) they perform, recognizing that organizations are in a constant state of change brought about by both internal (e.g., number, quality, dedication of personnel) and external (e.g., legal, financial) factors.

It is obvious that the types of functions performed by police officers depend to a considerable extent on the type of organization in which they are employed. The organizational structures of police departments vary considerably depending on the style of policing involved, the sizes of the community and the police force, the resources available, and so on—and these variables are, of course, interdependent. Organizational structures range from the small, one-person department in which the officer (chief, marshal, constable) performs all police functions to those involving thousands of police personnel and dozens of specializations. Nonetheless, most police organizations share some common characteristics. Most have traditionally been paramilitary organizations with characteristics such as the following:

1. Centralized command structure and chain of command
2. Control exerted through the issuance of commands, directives, and orders
3. Vertical communications going from top to bottom
4. Coercion as the method of employee motivation
5. Initiative neither sought nor encouraged
6. Authoritarian leadership
7. Low tolerance for nonconformists
8. Lack of flexibility in confronting novel situations (Hernandez, 1989; Toch and Grant, 1991; Roberg and Kuykendall, 1993)

If these traits were ever conducive to effective police work, they are considerably less so with the transition to better-educated, better-trained officers. Some police chiefs reflect on the "good old days" when officers simply did what they were told by an officer of superior rank and seldom questioned the orders and directives they received. Most realize, however, that current conditions require officers who can think on their feet, question, understand, and explain the rationale for the directives they follow, and exercise discretion wisely. Proactive police work in contemporary society calls for organizations that:

1. Support the exercise of initiative and discretion at all levels
2. Exert control through the use of guidance techniques, coaching, and counseling
3. Are characterized by communications that flow both vertically and horizontally in both directions
4. Use positive reinforcement as opposed to punishment to motivate personnel
5. Promote flexibility in operations
6. Are more decentralized
7. Encourage decision making at the lowest possible level
8. Emphasize participative management
9. View change as an indicator of organizational health
10. Develop and distribute guidelines delineating organizational expectations and evaluate personnel in terms of these guidelines (Skolnick and Bayley, 1986; Sparrow, Moore, and Kennedy, 1990; Toch and Grant, 1991; Fitzgerald and Cox, 1991)

People-Processing Organizations

As noted previously, organizations may be viewed as interpersonal networks that focus on the performance of certain tasks or functions. Police organizations are "people-processing" networks in which the raw material processed (people) is nonuniform (Perrow, 1967). In such organizations, individual staff are responsible for the actions of other people and, in general, have a great deal of personal responsibility (discretion) for the effectiveness (success in achieving goals) and efficiency (judicious use of resources) of the organization. The importance of both formal and informal, horizontal and vertical, and internal and external lines of communication is emphasized in such organizations. Also emphasized is the importance of specialized personnel with expertise in handling various types of nonuniform raw material (clients). For example, it may be difficult for the same person to expertly deal with patrol, investigations, juveniles, elderly, mentally ill, hardened criminals, those involved in domestic disputes, and so on. Difficult or not, however, police personnel in small agencies must attempt to provide all types of services to all types of clientele. Thus, the same person may answer the phone, respond to a crime scene, conduct an investigation, prepare charge sheets and written reports, secure evidence, interrogate suspects, interview witnesses, and appear in court to testify. In larger departments, many of these tasks are performed by different divisions/personnel.

Officers in small departments are often expected to be adept in all aspects of policing. Except in very small departments, there is typically some attempt to designate certain officers as specialists in investigations while others are viewed as performing basic patrol, supervisory, or administrative functions.

Most departments with a sufficient number of personnel tend to organize into at least two divisions with distinct if somewhat overlapping responsibilities: operations and administrative services. Each of these is often divided into several subdivisions as we shall see.

Operations Division

Patrol

Patrol operations have long been regarded as the backbone of the police organization. This division is typically the largest in a department in terms of personnel, often accounting for 60 percent of the department's personnel (Berg, 1992: 58). It is generally responsible for providing continuous police service and some degree of visibility.

The patrol division is typically divided into three *watches*, *tours*, or *shifts* to provide twenty-four-hour coverage. The day shift often operates from 8 A.M. to 4 P.M., the afternoon or evening shift from 4 P.M. to 12 midnight, and the night shift from 12 midnight until 8 A.M. Some departments employ power shifts, which typically involve assigning additional personnel to cover part of the evening and part of the night shift (for example, adding additional personnel who work from 8 P.M. until 4 A.M.). Officers have traditionally worked eight-hour shifts five days per week with two days off, but some departments now schedule officers for ten-hour shifts for four days with the following three days off (Moore and Morrow, 1987).

In addition to providing twenty-four-hour coverage, patrol divisions are also responsible for all geographic areas within the limits of the municipality. The city is typically divided into *beats*, *zones*, or *areas*, with each beat having coverage on all three shifts. Patrol officers perform their basic duties within their assigned beats, but sometimes leave the beat to assist officers in other beats. In larger cities, beats may be combined to form "sectors," which are administered by a sergeant, lieutenant, or both. In the largest cities, sectors may be combined to form "precincts."

In the past, patrol operations were assumed to deter crime and many police administrators continue to believe that patrol serves a deterrent function and enhances citizen satisfaction. A number of patrol studies suggest that routine patrol does not perform either of these functions (Kelling et al., 1974; Skolnick and Bayley, 1986; Toch and Grant, 1991), but many police administrators continue to operate as if it did. In any case, there is little doubt that the influence of patrol officers on other citizens is considerable.

Most patrol officers respond to calls for service in their zones, beats, or districts and patrol the streets in the area while not on a call. Thus, the majority of patrol work is reactive, although occasionally patrol officers do come upon a crime in progress, and they often use patrol to initiate contact based on traffic violations. In addition, patrol officers are generally responsible for securing crime scenes and conducting preliminary investigations as first responders. Once the crime scene has been secured, patrol officers often turn further investigatory responsibilities over to the investigative or detective division, although in some departments patrol officers maintain responsibility for such investigations.

An increasing number of police administrators, recognizing that routine patrol may not be effective, are experimenting with other types of patrol. These new tactics include directed or targeted patrol in which cars and officers are assigned to areas based on crime analyses in the hopes of catching, deterring, or moving offenders, split patrol in which part of the force is involved in directed or targeted patrol while the remainder of the patrol officers answer calls for service, and foot patrol (often used in congested areas), which is intended to increase citizen contact and deter and prevent crime. This use of patrol personnel has become increasingly common under the community-policing model.

In some departments, boat, air, bicycle, and canine-assisted patrol are employed and in still others volunteers are used to patrol specific areas under the supervision of police officers (Wrobleski and Hess, 1990; Berg, 1992).

Directed patrol strategies appear to make far more sense than routine patrol in which we simply send officers out at the beginning of their shift with little or no direction. In many cases, these officers simply drive around waiting for a call for service with no apparent goal other than to be seen. When this occurs, the net result may be a loss of worker hours that could be used far more wisely and wear and tear on the vehicles involved. In addition to their involvement in crime control, patrol officers are also responsible, in smaller departments, for traffic control and investigating traffic accidents. Larger departments are likely to have separate traffic- and accident-investigation units in the operations division.

Over the years, working in the patrol division for a prolonged period of time has taken on negative connotations. In the words of one young patrol officer, "Everyone knows you have to get out of patrol if you want to go anywhere in the police world." In fact, patrol officers with twenty-five years of service are often held in low regard by those with higher aspirations in policing. This view fails to recognize that some police officers like working the streets and the type of interaction it entails. Many have a wealth of experience to share about the beats and/or communities in which they patrol, but much of this experience is lost when they retire. To some extent, community policing has returned respectability to patrol work by emphasizing the importance of mutual recognition and understanding on the part of police officers and the citizens they serve. Still, many young officers seek their police fortunes elsewhere—often in the investigations bureau.

Investigations

The investigations bureau, a subdivision of the operations division, is responsible for obtaining and processing evidence and making arrests based on such evidence. The evidence involved may be tangible (physical evidence collected at a crime scene or at the residence of a suspect) or intangible (accounts from witnesses or informants). While this division is often regarded as the "glamour division" because it is thought to involve "real police work," evidence indicates that investigators are not particularly likely to solve crimes unless a witness steps forward to identify the offender (Greenwood, Chaiken, and Petersilia, 1977; William and Snortum, 1984; Bouza, 1990).

Nonetheless, investigators spend a good deal of time photographing and sketching crime scenes, interviewing and interrogating suspects and witnesses, collecting and analyzing fingerprints, and sifting through records, reports, and other materials that may contain some leads relevant to specific crimes. In some instances, evidence is processed in the departmental crime laboratory, in others such evidence is sent to state crime laboratories for processing. Once evidence has been obtained, investigators are responsible for establishing a custody chain, which governs storage and protection of the evidence. Case preparation and testifying in court are additional responsibilities of investigators.

Investigators are also responsible for conducting undercover operations and developing informants (though many patrol officers have informants as well), often in connection with investigations related to vice or drugs.

Juvenile or youth officers are frequently found in the investigations bureau as well. Among these officers are specialists in gang intelligence, physical/sexual abuse of children, crime prevention among youth, and school liaison officers who serve as counselors, facilitators, and coordinators for youth along with representatives of other service agencies and schools. Included here are D.A.R.E. (Drug Abuse Resistance Education) officers who teach in the school system. In an increasing number of states, youth officers must be specially trained or certified because they deal with laws relating to juvenile or family court acts, which are often considerably different from criminal statutes in terms of procedural requirements.

Administrative/Staff Services Division

The administrative services division may include several subdivisions:

1. Personnel
2. Research and planning
3. Budgeting
4. Data collection/crime analysis/computer section
5. Training
6. Counseling services
7. Maintenance
8. Communications/records
9. Civilian employees
10. Legal advisors
11. Internal affairs (Thibault, Lynch, McBride, 1985)

Personnel employed in this division are often, as you can see from the previous list, specialists. They are not typically in the chain of command, although the rank structure in the division may be the same as in other divisions. These staff personnel provide information and advice to the chief and other supervisors concerning a wide variety of topics and either create or process the mass of paperwork characteristic of police organizations.

While there are certainly other types of organizational structures, some of which are much more decentralized for purposes of team or community policing, a typical organizational chart for a small department would appear as shown in Figure 5.1. In larger police organizations the number of specializations within each division increases, leading to an organizational structure such as that shown in Figure 5.2.

In departments of the size and complexity illustrated in Figure 5.2, officers may not even know all the officers who work on their shifts or in their divisions. In fact, the various precinct houses are geographically distributed and each may be viewed, to some extent, as a separate department with ties to central headquarters. Further, only designated officers may be permitted to handle cases in their specialization; that is, an officer working in burglary may not handle a robbery or some other type of theft. Officers may become so specialized that they handle only one particular type of crime, such as computer theft. Patrol personnel may be limited by departmental policy as to their involvement in investigations.

In some departments, for instance, patrol officers responding to a crime scene are only to secure the scene and complete a preliminary report, which is then given to the investigative division for follow-up. In many instances the patrol officer never learns the final outcome of the case he or she initiated. As might be expected, this division of labor sometimes leads to intradepartmental rivalries and occasionally to open hostility between divisions in the same department. It is not uncommon to find investigators and patrol officers working for the same agency who seldom speak or share information with one another. This lack of communication is also present when looking at the broader picture, which involves cooperation among different police agencies working on the same case. This lack of communication, often based on territorial jealousy, seriously impairs the ability of the police organization to perform its functions and has been a major problem in contemporary policing.

As you can see from Figures 5.1 and 5.2, police departments employ both sworn and nonsworn (civilian) personnel. One of the major trends accompanying community policing in the last decade has been to increase the number of civilians employed.

Although police organizations have traditionally employed paramilitary paradigms, such organizational structures are typically resistant to change and are not ideally suited to meet the rapidly changing needs of a public-service agency. As we have seen, they fail to promote communication both horizontally and from the bottom up and frequently fail to encourage employee commitment through participation. To be sure, there are times in policing when a highly centralized, authoritarian command structure is an advantage. When

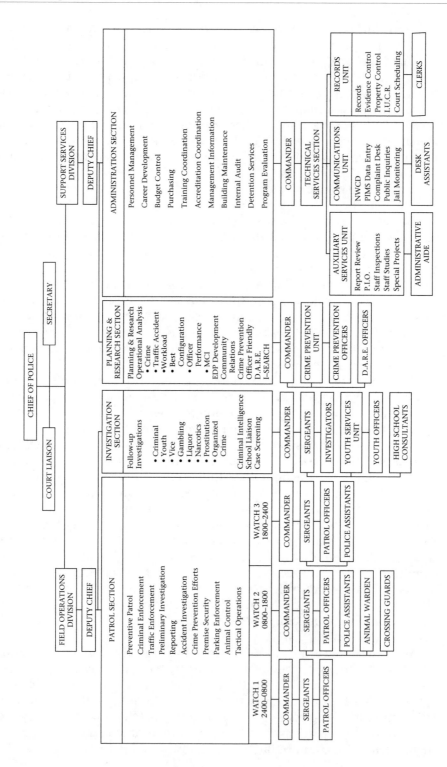

FIGURE 5.1   Palatine Police Department Organizational Structure

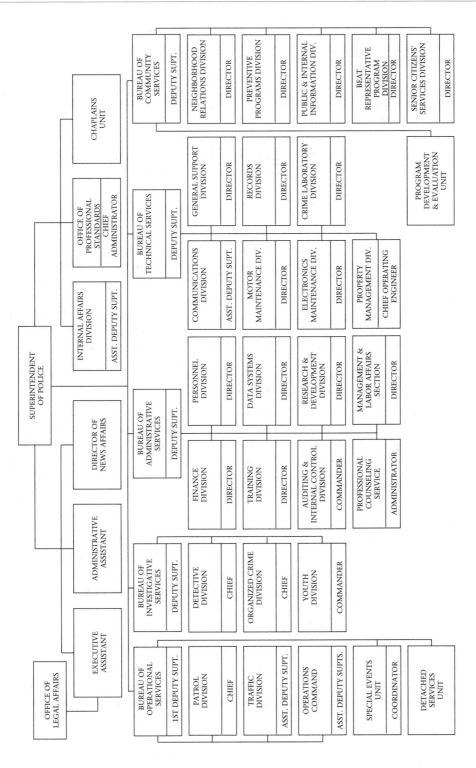

FIGURE 5.2   Chicago Police Department Organization for Command

the station house is being threatened by riotous protesters or when a police officer responds to an armed robbery in progress, there is little time to call a committee meeting to decide what to do. Most police work, however, is not of this nature; even when it is, prior planning can often provide for effective action. In addition, with the many functions to be performed, it is doubtful that any chief executive officer has all of the skills and knowledge required to make wise decisions in all types of circumstances.

Last, but not least, police officers today are very likely to want explanations from their superiors when orders or directives are issued. Research (Franz and Jones, 1987: 161) has demonstrated that paramilitary police organizations are characterized by greater communications problems and amounts of distrust and lower levels of morale and perceived levels of organizational performance than other types of organizations. These authors and others (Gaines, Southerland, and Angell, 1991: 104–107) question the capacity of the quasi-military police organizational model to meet today's policing needs.

For these reasons and others, many police departments have experimented with more decentralized structures. Neighborhood policing and community policing are concepts based on the notion of less-centralized control. Here, teams of police officers are responsible for certain geographic areas and, while they continue to be coordinated and directed in general terms from police headquarters, make many of the day-to-day decisions confronting the police.

Staffing in Police Organizations

In spite of current experimentation, most police departments maintain a common organizational structure in terms of personnel positions. Agencies are headed by a chief of police who is responsible to city administrators for organizing and distributing police resources. The chief's job is basically administrative, but he or she also serves as a figurehead for the agency. Some departments employ a deputy chief to assist the chief in his or her duties, but this position is perhaps less popular today than in the past. Typically, the functional divisions of the department are headed by officers with the rank of commander or captain who are responsible for ensuring that their units function in accordance with the goals established by the chief in consultation with city administrators. These positions, too, are basically administrative. Watch commanders, usually lieutenants, are responsible for providing police services for the chronological periods of the day in which their watches or shifts operate.

Other lieutenants may occupy staff positions supervising specific programs or areas of operation within the department (research and planning, for example). Sergeants typically serve as field-level supervisors; they are responsible for supervising specific groups of personnel while acting as a liaison with the shift commander. This position includes some administrative work but often requires working the streets or handling cases as well. Those with the rank of sergeant may also serve in staff functions such as those described for staff lieutenants. Sample job descriptions for some of the positions discussed here can be found in the appendix at the end this book.

Police Organizations in Context

It is important to note that police organizations do not exist in a vacuum, nor are police functions determined totally or even largely by the police themselves. The police always operate in a political arena under public scrutiny (though a good many try to minimize such scrutiny). The police chief heads the police department but is responsible to a city manager, mayor, police commissioner, and city council. In many instances in which city government regards the separate public service agencies as consumer-oriented, chief executive officers are viewed as part of a cooperative team with responsibilities to one another as well. Thus, the chief of police may request new equipment moneys one year, but defer to the fire chief the next. Further, in the vast majority of police agencies, hiring, disciplining (beyond a limited amount), termination, award of benefits, and so on are governed not by the police chief, but by fire and police commissions or civil service boards.

As is the case with all organizations, police departments exist in environments from which they draw resources and in which they provide services. The extent to which these resources are allocated and the manner and type of services provided are largely controlled by external sources. Finally, police departments are only one component of the justice network that sets parameters within which the police must operate. The courts, for example, have indicated clearly that they are willing to intervene in police practices ranging from search and seizure to interrogation to hiring and promotion.

Change in Police Organizations

The way in which an organization deals with change tells a great deal about its effectiveness and efficiency. As we indicated earlier, change is a given in all organizations. Personnel retire or resign or are injured, recruited, or promoted. Resources fluctuate with the state of the economy and the political power of the organization. Change in police agencies has been a major theme throughout this text. Realistically, police personnel must be willing to accept change as a normal part of their occupational world, and police supervisors must be prepared to administer change. Change, whether in personnel, legal requirements, technology, distribution and types of crime, or requests for service, represents a constant challenge; like many of the rest of us, police resist change because they have become comfortable with the status quo. When sudden or drastic change imposed from above occurs, reactions are likely to be negative. As Bobinsky (1994: 17) notes, the change from traditional to community-oriented policing is not always smooth. "While I expected a degree of community skepticism regarding the ambitious program, the negative sentiments expressed by some of my fellow officers represented a more formidable obstacle. These comments, whether directed to one another or to local residents, were difficult to deal with, both on a personal and professional level."

Still, when change is introduced in organized fashion, employees are encouraged to participate in planning and implementing change, and the benefits of change are emphasized, it can be exciting and positive, as well as challenging (Halloran and Frunzi, 1986: 396). Similarly, when change occurs in organizations that are flexible, encourage initiative, and allow for the exercise of discretion in implementing change, the results can be favorable. The tendency among police personnel to resist change results from the fact that they operate in a reactive, paramilitary setting for the most part. As Gaines, Southerland, and Angell (1991: 106) note: "Innovation is stifled in the traditional organization; members of traditional organizations tend to resist changes which challenge the old ways of operating . . . . Members of traditional organizations are also exposed to a conflicting set of expectations—one moment they must make on-the-spot life-and-death decisions, and the next they are treated like children who are not permitted to decide which uniform to wear when the weather changes."

As police administrators adopt less rigid, less hierarchical structures and encourage more participation on the part of personnel at all levels, the police will come to act and think in terms of change rather than to react to change as a crisis.

Police Leadership

The quality of leadership in police organizations varies greatly. Some organizations carefully select entry-level personnel, evaluate their potential for promotion, promote based on merit, and prepare those who are to be promoted by sending them to appropriate training and/or educational programs. Others do none of these things. Many, perhaps most, departments have a difficult time deciding what types of leaders/supervisors they want. Should leadership positions be filled by those with skills in communicating with and supervising personnel and other resources? Should they be filled by personnel with extensive street experience? Are policing skills or management skills more important? Answers to these questions are crucial in determining the criteria for promotion to leadership positions. The issue is further complicated by the fact that, at the level of the chief at least, political savvy and the ability to cooperate as an agency representative with respect to other public service agencies sometimes conflict with expectations of agency personnel.

Field supervisors, typically holding the rank of sergeant, are selected based on years of experience (a minimum of two to three may be required in order to test for the position), performance evaluations based on patrol and/or investigative work, written examinations, and oral interviews. Unfortunately, neither years of service nor performance in investigative or patrol functions necessarily indicate ability to succeed as a supervisor.

Assessment centers may help considerably in this regard, but they are far from perfect. Mistakes made in promotions at this level are likely to be perpetuated because those promoted to the rank of shift supervisor (typically lieutenants) are generally selected from sergeants with a specified minimum level of experience. Similarly, division commanders (captains) are selected from the ranks of shift commanders based on the criteria mentioned above.

Lateral entry at any of these levels is rare, although exempt rank positions, particularly at the upper ranks, are becoming more popular. Exempt rank personnel serve at the pleasure of the chief although they may have continued employment rights (civil service rank) if demoted from their exempt positions. Individuals occupying exempt rank positions are not always well received by other police personnel because they have "jumped" rank and because they sometimes come from outside the ranks of the police.

Police Chiefs

Those occupying the position of police chief run the gamut from "good old boys" who have worked their way through the ranks of the department to become chief to those who are highly skilled, trained/educated professional managers. While the prevalent path to chief is the "insider" path, "outsiders" with police experience and advanced education are increasingly in demand in progressive agencies. "Complete outsiders," those who come from outside the realm of policing, are rare (Bouza, 1990: 40–42).

Goldstein (1977: 228, 230) indicates that the record of providing qualified police chiefs is poor. He notes that as early as 1920, Fosdick found police leadership to be mediocre, and that in 1931 the Wickersham Commission pointed to incompetent leadership as a major problem in policing. In conclusion, Goldstein points out:

> *The costs of having made inadequate provision for police leadership are plainly apparent as one views the overall status of policing in the United States. Many police agencies tend to drift from day to day. They respond excessively to outside pressures; they resort to temporary expedients; they take comfort in technical achievements over substantive accomplishments; their internal procedures become stagnant, cumbersome, and inefficient; and they seem incapable of responding innovatively to new demands and new requirements.*

That the problems identified by Goldstein remain is apparent in Garner's (1993) article, "Leadership in the Nineties," which appears in Highlight 5.1. In the years since Goldstein made his observations, there have been changes in police leadership, though many of his conclusions clearly remain accurate with respect to many police chiefs. Lee Brown (1985), former chief of the Houston and New York City Police Departments, has called for a new type of police leadership that recognizes that the police are basically problem solvers and multiservice providers dependent upon the community for understanding, support, and cooperation. Brown believes that police executives have not been in the forefront of government and business efforts to encourage joint efforts, nor have police executives accepted the fact that one of their primary responsibilities is educating the public with respect to their law enforcement and crime control obligations. Police executives, according to Brown, need to view themselves as "major municipal policymakers" involved in actions that determine the quality of life of community residents. Finally, these executives need to regard themselves as members of public service teams and give up the

---

HIGHLIGHT 5.1   Leadership in the Nineties

By Ronnie Garner, MPA

On a hot, lazy afternoon, a small boy sits barefoot under a shade tree, idly watching a small stream of water from a sprinkler trickle down the street toward him. As tiny rivulets inch their way along the asphalt gutter, they seem to pause at each pebble to build momentum and then push forward again.

Eagerly, the boy grabs handfuls of dirt and builds a small dike that momentarily halts the flow. However, the water slowly wells up in a puddle and edges its way around the barrier. The boy adds more dirt, vainly attempting to outflank and contain the water.

As the battle progresses, it becomes apparent that despite the boy's best efforts, he will never prevail. There are larger forces of nature at work.

How often do organizations struggle in a like manner against the forces of human nature? An organization is, after all, a large pool of human resources. Not unlike the stream of water, this pool seeks movement—*progress*. It cannot stand still; that is not the natural order. It must either move forward or stagnate.

What organizations require is guidance of that movement. This guidance comes in the form of direction and leadership.

Visionary leadership is not for everyone. A gnarled police veteran once counseled me to "never try to teach a pig to sing. It sounds like hell and it annoys the pig."

There is some wisdom in that advice. Many police administrators become so pre-occupied with current problems that they fail to plan for the future. Some do not believe that strategic planning is worth the effort. Others lack the imagination and creativity required to project a detailed guide of behaviors that management accepts and supports within the organization.

A Positive Framework

The organizational vision, mission statement, and values statement form a framework to support management decisions by attaching reasons to actions. The philosophy, goals, and work standards embodied within these documents provide a basis for decision making within the organization. They are the lodestars by which the organization navigates its course through the uncharted waters of both the present and the future.

Creating this framework for leadership is vital to maintain consistency and direction in the management of the organization. However, this framework alone is not sufficient to attract and motivate employees to achieve the organization's mission. Organizations need to incorporate a final leadership principle—empowerment.

Much like the stream discussed earlier, it is the nature of an organization to change and progress. Individual members of the organization continually develop plans and expectations about their roles. Each creates a personal agenda. It is the confluence of these personal agendas that creates a dynamic undercurrent within organizations. Leaders must channel this undercurrent in order to accomplish the organization's objectives.

The cumbersome, monolithic organizational structures in which many agencies currently labor do not allow leaders sufficient latitude to channel individual talents. A more open, flexible participative model must be used so that leaders can successfully empower subordinates.

Empowerment

Empowerment is enabling others to participate in the process of change within the organization. It often involves sharing power

Continued

Reprinted with permission from the *FBI Law Enforcement Bulletin*, 62(12), 1–2.

with subordinates and allowing them sufficient leeway to accomplish tasks in their
own way.

---

*"The organizational vision, mission
statement, and values statement form a
framework to support management decisions by attaching reasons to actions."*

Empowerment is the most effective way
to gain the active participation of others.
When employees are truly empowered to
make meaningful decisions and effect appropriate change within the organization, they
develop a stake in the system—a franchise.
Enfranchised and empowered employees
have a vested interest in the success of the
group. They become important members of
a team with a meaningful purpose.

Most individuals want to believe they
are contributing to a common purpose and
that they are not consumed with pointless
exercises. Leaders who promote such an
atmosphere secure the commitment and
trust of employees.[5] True leadership involves
providing a collaborative atmosphere, where
all workers focus on the critical work of the
organization.[6]

However, some leaders resist sharing
power. They fear that subordinates, if not
sufficiently controlled, may take over the
organization. Although there may be some

rationality to this fear, establishing a positive leadership framework ensures that
employees are both motivated and unified
in achieving the organizational mission. By
focusing on vision, mission, and values, an
enlightened leader empowers and energizes
subordinates toward the attainment of organizational objectives.

Conclusion

The issue of leadership in law enforcement is
neither broad nor obscure. It involves the
concrete process of articulating the vision,
mission, and values of the organization
within the context of a long-range strategic
plan and giving impetus to that plan by
empowering subordinates. Without this base,
police managers serve only as custodians of a
bureaucracy that preoccupies itself with the
present at the expense of the future.

Endnotes

[1]Ted Gaebler and David Osborne, *Reinventing
Government* (Reading, Massachusetts: Addison-
Wesley Publishing Company, 1992), 35.
[2]Ibid.
[3]Ibid.
[4]Ibid.
[5]Burt Nanus, *The Leader's Edge: Seven Keys to
Leadership in a Turbulent World* (Chicago,
Illinois: Contemporary Books, Inc., 1989).
[6]Ibid. Garner, 1993, 1–2.

---

idea of building empires of their own. Fortunately, more and more police executives have come to agree with Brown's assessment.

> *It is widely recognized that the most critical ingredient in the success of an
> organization is the quality of its leadership. Although police leaders cannot
> singlehandedly upgrade law enforcement, there is no other single group as
> important to the process (Witham, 1987: 6).*

Couper and Lobitz (1993) list what they consider to be the seven essential
factors that police leaders must consider in improving and changing police
operations:

1. Leaders must create and nurture a vision (about what the department will
   look like after change has occurred).
2. Leaders must live their values and share them with others.

3. Leaders must listen to their employees and communities.
4. Leaders must hire for tomorrow and to reflect the communities in which they serve.
5. Leaders need to be more concerned about coordinating neighborhoods than filling shifts.
6. Leaders must realize that perceptions are as important as reality.
7. Leaders must practice quality improvement.

Couper and Lobitz view all of these concerns as compatible with community policing.

Dobbs and Field (1993) point out that commitment to organizational success requires shedding traditions that inhibit or are counterproductive to change. They note that many police administrators cling to tradition because they perceive this approach as low risk. Traditional administrators are often unable to admit that there is more than one way to run the organization or that subordinates may have worthwhile suggestions.

Simonsen and Arnold (1993) note that among the alternative strategies for running police organizations is Total Quality Management (TQM). TQM involves four basic elements that might be incorporated in a new model of policing: client identification and feedback; tracking of performance by simple, valid methods; continuous improvement; and employee participation in all change processes. This approach requires police leaders to identify their many clients or customers, to determine the needs of each, and to work, along with other police personnel, toward meeting these needs. Simonsen and Arnold (1993) conclude that if police leaders fail to meet this challenge in a time in which public service agencies are required to do more with what they have, they will soon find themselves trying to do more with less as a result of client dissatisfaction.

Police Unions, Professionalism, and Accreditation

Police Unions

Unionization and collective bargaining in police agencies have received a good deal of attention over the past three decades, although the history of police labor disputes dates back to the 1800s (Gaines, Sutherland, and Angell, 1991). Generally speaking, public sector unionization has lagged behind that of the private sector by at least twenty-five to thirty years. Thus, unionization of police personnel did not become an issue of major importance until the 1960s and 1970s, at which time the increasing complexity of policing was recognized and police officers began to demand compensation commensurate with the task and more comparable to that of the private sector (Sapp, 1985). Today, with the exception of teachers and fire fighters, police are the most organized of public sector employees, with perhaps 75 percent belonging to one union or another. The unions/bargaining agents of choice include the American Federation of State, County, and Municipal Employees (AFSCME), the International Brotherhood of Police Officers (IBPO), the Fraternal Order of Police (FOP), the International Union of Police Associations (IUPA), and the International Brotherhood of Teamsters, Chauffeurs, Warehousemen, and Helpers of America (IBT or Teamsters) among others (Swanson, Territo, and Taylor, 1993: 357–359).

The unionization of police employees proceeded slowly for several reasons. Among the more important causes were public and legislative reactions to the Boston Police Strike in 1919 following which looting, robberies, and general disorder occurred until the state guard was called in to reestablish order. Some 1,100 police officers were fired by Governor Calvin Coolidge and never regained their jobs. Some observers now feel that the effect of the Boston disaster was sufficient to force unionization of police personnel into dormancy for the next forty to fifty years (Thibault, Lynch, and McBride, 1990). The perceived vulnerability of communities to criminal activities during work stoppages has resulted in a generalized rejection of police strikes by the public. Many police officers share this public rejection of any police work stoppage. When strikes have occasionally occurred, there is little evidence to support the belief that crime rates rise rapidly (Gaines, Southerland, and Angell, 1991: 328; Stone and DeLuca, 1994: 458). Nonetheless, some police employees continue to view collective action as self-defeating, because it may result in hostility on the part of the public, the police chief, or others in positions of power.

By 1987, some thirty states had enacted legislation authorizing collective bargaining in public sector agencies, including police departments (Sandver, 1987: 397). In response, in many departments police employees petitioned state labor boards for recognition of exclusive bargaining agents. This petition is typically followed by an election in which it is determined whether the majority of employees want a union to represent them and, if so, which union. Those eligible to vote in police organizations differ from jurisdiction to jurisdiction, but generally include those with a "mutuality of job interests." Thus, rank-and-file employees are likely to be members of one union, but supervisors at different levels may belong to another union or may have separate unions of their own. Regardless of the specific union involved, it appears that police officers have joined unions in increasing numbers in order to gain a stronger voice in the governance of the agency, protect their constitutional rights, establish communications with management, and, perhaps, improve their public image (Bouza, 1990; Alpert and Dunham, 1993; Gaines, Kappeler, and Vaughn, 1994; Langworthy and Travis, 1994).

Among the major concerns of police unions in negotiating with management are salary, insurance, vacation and sick days, pensions, longevity pay, compensatory time/pay, hiring standards, assignment policies, discipline and grievance procedures, promotions, layoffs, productivity, and procedural rights of officers. In short, initial concerns cover the entire range of working conditions, not simply economic factors. When negotiations fail to lead to improvement in any or all of these areas, the possibility of a work stoppage exists in unionized police departments. While police strikes are for the most part prohibited by law, work slowdowns or speedups do occasionally occur.

The former may be accomplished as a result of the "blue flu," which sometimes "surprisingly" affects large numbers of police officers working for the same department at the same time, creating difficulties in providing police coverage. Speedups involve writing considerably more citations than are normally written so that the public complains to the chief or city council members, who will presumably pay more attention to the desires of the officers as a result. The public has traditionally been strongly opposed to the use of work stoppages by the police, and the courts have generally been willing to issue injunctions to bring them to a halt in a relatively short time. Further, many police managers, recognizing the possibility of work stoppages, have prepared contingency plans to guarantee the continuation of police services. When implemented, these plans have generally shown that a community can survive without its regular police force and such plans have cut short police strikes without meeting union demands.

Collective bargaining involves an adversarial relationship between union and management. Typically, the union presents management with a list of its members' demands. Management responds by stating either that it will or will not meet these demands. The demands of the union and the response of management are supported with evidence gathered for their respective purposes. Bargaining sessions are then scheduled to attempt to convince the opposing side of the validity of the arguments presented and/or to reach a compromise acceptable to both parties.

Such bargaining (negotiating) is to be done in good faith by representatives of both sides in an attempt to reach a reasonable solution in a reasonable amount of time. The powers of the two parties are typically spelled out in a labor relations or public employment relations act, as are the rights of the two parties, the procedures to be followed, and the scope of the negotiations. When negotiations, properly conducted in terms of the applicable regulations, fail to lead to an acceptable compromise, an impasse results. Procedures for resolving the impasse are also spelled out in labor relations law. Such procedures typically involve fact finding, mediation, and, if these approaches fail, some form of arbitration (voluntary, binding, final offer). The final product of collective bargaining negotiations is a contract that covers specific areas of employer-employee relations and that binds both parties legally and morally to abide by its provisions during a specified time period.

What factors have been responsible for the growing interest in police unions? First, and in many ways most important, has been the problem of unenlightened managers. Because many police leaders came up through the ranks of paramilitary organizations themselves, they learned how to issue orders and to expect that such orders would be followed. Some also learned the importance of listening to subordinates and explaining the reasons for orders issued, but many did not. Some felt they should be followed because they were in leadership positions, rather than because their arguments made sense. Some felt that policing was a unique enterprise and that principals and procedures that worked in other types of organizations did not apply in their organizations. Others were less concerned about the well-being of their officers than about the trappings of professionalism in the form of new technologies and hardware. Some simply became so far removed from the streets and those who police them that their perceptions of the requirements of the occupation/profession were no longer realistic. Still others apparently felt that fraternizing with subordinates diminished their authority or importance. To some extent, these problems continue to plague police managers and those they supervise. To the extent that such problems continue, they create environments in which union organizers are likely to be successful.

A number of other reasons exist for increasing unionization of police personnel. In the 1960s and 1970s union representatives began to recognize that further organizing in the private sector was likely to become increasingly difficult because of saturation and increasingly enlightened management. They realized the tremendous potential for growth in the expanding public sector and began to explore the new market. At the same time, many of the legal restrictions on collective bargaining among public sector employees were relaxed (Swanson, Territo, and Taylor, 1993: 347–348). Together with police dissatisfaction with wages, working conditions, and level of public support, these changes resulted in a wave of union activities in police agencies. Further, the police had seen the results of well-organized, concerted action among other groups. The protests of the 1960s and early 1970s often resulted in grievances being redressed or at least explored. If such actions could succeed elsewhere, why not among police officers?

Bouza (1990: 266–268) and Murphy and Caplan (1993: 309–310) observe that many police unions and associations are not content to deal with wages and working conditions; they also make their views known on minority hiring, department reorganization/reform, and other issues. Many police unions have become powerful forces in the operation of their departments. Police executives must note this development and be prepared to deal with unions, or they are likely to find themselves involved in controversy.

The bottom line in assessing the effect of police unions is whether they have improved the quality of police services. Some (Bouza, 1990: 267; Murphy and Caplan, 1993: 309) have concluded that unions have often been great obstacles to reform of corrupt departments. They may also fragment the chain of command, contribute to racial tensions, emphasize seniority over merit, and produce inefficiency (Swanson, Territo, and Taylor, 1993: 351; Stone and DeLuca, 1994: 457). However, police unions have improved morale by achieving better salaries, fairer procedures, and better lines of communication (Swanson, Territo, and Taylor, 1993: 350–355; Gaines, Southerland, and Angell, 1991: 312–313; More and Wegener, 1992: 507–511).

Police Professionalism

Police professionalism has been a focal point for police reformers over the past century. However, ambiguity concerning the police role has seriously hampered efforts to professionalize the police: deciding on the proper role of the police is a necessary precursor to outlining and assessing steps towards professionalism. In addition, police professionalism means different things in different places and at different times, making consensus about the requirements for a professional police unlikely.

Finally, it is important to note that professionalism may refer to police organizations, police officers, or both. Some police administrators refer to tangible improvements such as computers, the latest weaponry or communications, or advances in equipment in the crime lab as signs of professionalism. In fact, a department may have all of these tangible indicators but still be unprofessional if officers fail to meet some of the professional requirements spelled out in the following sections. That is, the assumption that changes of this sort will automatically increase professionalism among officers is not necessarily valid. *Professionalization* has been described as the process of legitimation an occupation goes through as it endeavors to improve its social status. *Professionalism* involves the adoption of a set of values and attitudes by members of an occupation that are consistent with a professional ideology (Vollmer and Mills, 1966).

While we generally use the terms interchangeably, it must be recognized that the former does not always lead to the latter. For example, as police agencies become more bureaucratic, rely more on civil service rules and regulations, and become more unionized, officer discretion tends to become more and more restricted; that is, officer autonomy is increasingly curtailed, yet autonomy is highly valued by most professionals. The distinguishing feature of professional work is the freedom to make decisions according to professional norms of conduct, without having to temper every decision by bureaucratic constraint (Caplow, 1983). Thus, it is possible that as organizations become more "professional" in terms of standardized rules and regulations, "professionalization" of employees may become more difficult. To some extent this has no doubt been the case with the police, as we shall see.

Characteristics of professions include:

1. Body of professional literature
2. Research
3. Code of ethics
4. Membership in professional associations
5. Dedication to self-improvement
6. Existence of a unique, identifiable academic field of knowledge attainable through higher education (Swanson, Territo, and Taylor, 1993: 4; Roberg and Kuykendall, 1993: 472; Barker, Hunter, and Rush, 1994: 205–207).

To what extent do the police currently meet these requirements of a profession? With respect to the first two criteria, there clearly is a growing body of professional literature on the police. Journals such as *Police Studies, American Journal of the Police,* and the *Journal of Police Science and Administration* contain reports of police research (the second criterion). Periodicals such as *Police Chief,* the *FBI Law Enforcement Bulletin,* and a rapidly expanding number of government reports and texts on the police contribute additional information on police operations, organizations, and programs. In addition, there are literally hundreds of master's theses and doctoral dissertations concerning the police. Much of the information contained in these publications has been collected using legitimate research techniques, and the body of literature based on police research has expanded dramatically in recent years as grant moneys from a variety of sources have become available.

A code of ethics for the police has been developed and modified by the International Association of Chiefs of Police. The "Police Code of Conduct," discussed in Chapter 4 under Police Ethics (p. 56), is worth repeating here, as it indicates an attempt at further professionalization. It is difficult to determine the extent to which police officers are familiar with these documents (see Highlights 5.2 and 5.3); our observations indicate, however, that many officers know a code exists but are unfamiliar with its contents.

There are a number of professional police associations, mostly for chief executive officers. Organizations such as the Fraternal Order of the Police are oriented toward rank-and-file officers as well, but they have typically served as either social organizations or, more recently, as collective bargaining agents. Associations for staff personnel and field supervisors are far less common, which makes creating and sharing a professional body of knowledge among those occupying such positions difficult. In recent years there has been some expansion of professional organizations among police planners, investigators, and those assigned to the accreditation process.

The evidence is mixed when it comes to dedication to self-improvement. There are currently no national minimum standards for either departments or

---

HIGHLIGHT 5.2   Original Law Enforcement Code of Ethics

AS A LAW ENFORCEMENT OFFICER my fundamental duty is to serve mankind; to safeguard lives and property; to protect the innocent against deception, the weak against oppression or intimidation, and the peaceful against violence or disorder; and to respect the Constitutional rights of all men to liberty, equality and justice.

I WILL keep my private life unsullied as an example to all; maintain courageous calm in the face of danger, scorn, or ridicule; develop self-restraint; and be constantly mindful of the welfare of others. Honest in thought and deed in both my personal and official life, I will be exemplary in obeying the laws of the land and the regulations of my department. Whatever I see or hear of a confidential nature or that is confided to me in my official capacity will be kept secret unless revelation is necessary in the performance of my duty.

I WILL never act officiously or permit personal feelings, prejudices, animosities or friendships to influence my decisions. With no compromise for crime and with relentless prosecution of criminals, I will enforce the law courteously and appropriately without fear or favor, malice or ill will, never employing unnecessary force or violence and never accepting gratuities.

I RECOGNIZE the badge of my office as a symbol of public faith, and I accept it as a public trust to be held so long as I am true to the ethics of the police service. I will constantly strive to achieve these objectives and ideals, dedicating myself before God to my chosen profession . . . law enforcement.

(International Association of Chiefs of Police, 1992)

HIGHLIGHT 5.3   Police Code of Conduct

All law enforcement officers must be fully aware of the ethical responsibilities of their position and must strive constantly to live up to the highest possible standards of professional policing.

The International Association of Chiefs of Police believes it important that police officers have clear advice and counsel available to assist them in performing their duties consistent with these standards, and has adopted the following ethical mandates as guidelines to meet these ends.

Primary Responsibilities of a Police Officer

A police officer acts as an official representative of government who is required and trusted to work within the law. The officer's powers and duties are conferred by statute. The fundamental duties of a police officer include serving the community, safeguarding lives and property, protecting the innocent, keeping the peace and ensuring the rights of all to liberty, equality and justice.

Performance of the Duties of a Police Officer

A police officer shall perform all duties impartially, without favor or affection or ill will and without regard to status, sex, race, religion, political belief or aspiration. All citizens will be treated equally with courtesy, consideration and dignity.

Officers will never allow personal feelings, animosities or friendships to influence official conduct. Laws will be enforced appropriately and courteously and, in carrying out their responsibilities, officers will strive to obtain maximum cooperation from the public. They will conduct themselves in appearance and deportment in such a manner as to inspire confidence and respect for the position of public trust they hold.

Discretion

A police officer will use responsibly the discretion vested in his position and exercise it within the law. The principle of reasonableness will guide the officer's determinations, and the officer will consider all surrounding circumstances in determining whether any legal action shall be taken.

Consistent and wise use of discretion, based on professional policing competence, will do much to preserve good relationships and retain the confidence of the public. There can be difficulty in choosing between conflicting courses of action. It is important to remember that a timely word of advice rather than arrest—which may be correct in appropriate circumstances—can be a more effective means of achieving a desired end.

Use of Force

A police officer will never employ unnecessary force or violence and will use only such force in the discharge of duty as is reasonable in all circumstances.

The use of force should be used only with the greatest restraint and only after discussion, negotiation and persuasion have been found to be inappropriate or ineffective. While the use of force is occasionally unavoidable, every police officer will refrain from unnecessary infliction of pain or suffering and will never engage in cruel, degrading or inhuman treatment of any person.

Confidentiality

Whatever a police officer sees, hears or learns of that is of a confidential nature will be kept secret unless the performance of duty or legal provision requires otherwise.

Members of the public have a right to security and privacy, and information obtained about them must not be improperly divulged.

Continued

Integrity

A police officer will not engage in acts of corruption or bribery, nor will an officer condone such acts by other police officers.

The public demands that the integrity of police officers be above reproach. Police officers must, therefore, avoid any conduct that might compromise integrity and thus undercut the public confidence in a law enforcement agency. Officers will refuse to accept any gifts, presents, subscriptions, favors, gratuities or promises that could be interpreted as seeking to cause the officer to refrain from performing official responsibilities honestly and within the law. Police officers must not receive private or special advantages from their official status. Respect from the public cannot be bought; it can only be earned and cultivated.

Cooperation with Other Police Officers and Agencies

Police officers will cooperate with all legally authorized agencies and their representatives in the pursuit of justice.

An officer or agency may be one among many organizations that may provide law enforcement services to a jurisdiction. It is imperative that a police officer assist colleagues fully and completely with respect and consideration at all times.

Personal-Professional Capabilities

Police officers will be responsible for their own standard of professional performance and will take every reasonable opportunity to enhance and improve their level of knowledge and competence.

Through study and experience, a police officer can acquire the high level of knowledge and competence that is essential for the efficient and effective performance of duty. The acquisition of knowledge is a never-ending process of personal and professional development that should be pursued constantly.

Private Life

Police officers will behave in a manner that does not bring discredit to their agencies or themselves.

A police officer's character and conduct while off duty must always be exemplary, thus maintaining a position of respect in the community in which he or she lives and serves. The officer's personal behavior must be beyond reproach.

(International Association of Chiefs of Police, 1990)

---

police personnel. Many states do not even mandate training on a recurring basis after completion of the basic training program. Concurrently, among more progressive police personnel, there is an increasing interest in establishing police officer standards and in accreditation.

A unique, identifiable field of study in police science has emerged. As we have seen, there are hundreds of college-level academic programs in policing and criminal justice in existence. The quality of these programs varies tremendously, but generally speaking seems to have improved over the past decade. While there is no consensus on precisely what topics should be included in these programs, there is enough agreement to argue that the field is unique and identifiable in general terms at least. Further, an increasing number of officers are earning both undergraduate and graduate degrees in police science, law enforcement, and criminal justice programs.

These achievements notwithstanding, police professionalism remains an elusive goal for a variety of reasons. Dedication to the attainment of professional standards exists among some police executives, is given lip service by some others, and is nonexistent among some. A key determinant of such dedication appears to be the background and particularly the educational level of the police chief executive. "The most salient background characteristic of chiefs is their level of formal education. Education has been described as the centerpiece of professionalization. Professionalized police agencies place proportionally more emphasis on formal education" (Crank et al., 1987: 5).

Another factor involved in the pursuit of professionalism is resistance on behalf of both rank-and-file and midmanagement personnel. When these personnel view their jobs as blue-collar shift work involving little need for advanced education, dedication to self-improvement may be minimized. To some extent, of course, this view is encouraged by both the paramilitary nature of police organizations and the police subculture, which often regards police work as piece work—a certain number of moving citations, nonmoving citations, responses to service requests, and arrests equals a good day's work. To be sure, some police administrations encourage this view as well. Finally, unionization of police officers may inhibit progress toward professionalism. This relationship is complex and deserves a closer look.

Police Unions and Professionalism

Some authors have concluded that unions frequently frustrate attempts at professionalization by taking negative positions on issues such as advanced education, lateral transfer, and changes in recruiting standards (Broderick, 1987; Bouza, 1990). In addition, collective bargaining typically results in highly formalized rules indicating the rights and obligations of both parties. The more formalized these rules become, the less autonomy exists and the more difficult it becomes to bend the rules, even though both parties may be willing. In clarifying the relationships between police administrators and line officers in a union contract, we may go overboard and tie the hands of one or both sides when it comes to the exercise of discretion. For example, a contract that limits the amount of overtime an officer may be required to work may prevent an officer who is willing to work and needed on a particular shift from working. Contracts specifying that every contribution officers make to the organization should be reimbursed in some way (pay, compensatory time, etc.) may limit contributions that officers would willingly make, but for which there is no money to pay them.

There is little doubt that the protection offered by unions in terms of salaries, working conditions, and governance is required in some police organizations. In such organizations, administrative personnel appear to be more concerned about productivity than people, and the rights of employees need to be protected. Unfortunately, some employees are unwilling or unable to contribute their fair share to the organization and they, too, are protected by unions. Finally, the principle of rewards based on merit is most often compromised in the process of unionization, so that those who perform best can be rewarded no more than those who perform worst (or not at all).

It has been argued that unions promote mediocrity by requiring only minimal performance levels and by failing to allow rewards for those who exceed these levels. Those who are self-motivated, dedicated, and interested in advancing themselves and the organization are not encouraged to do so and those who contribute little to the organization are protected. Additionally, unions tend to take on lives of their own, and union leaders sometimes represent their own interests or those of the larger union rather than those of the officers immediately involved. Union representatives may come to see this position as more important than their positions as police officers, and police administrators may come to view them as adversaries rather than employees.

Unions and management need not be adversaries. Both can work toward the betterment of the organization and its employees; this sometimes happens in the case of the police. More frequently, however, unions and managers see each other as adversaries and, even though compromises may be worked out, come to distrust one another. Thus, in some departments we find different unions representing different groups based on rank, race, or some other factor. This divisiveness within the department causes middle management personnel, field supervisors, whites, and blacks to turn to their respective unions to promote each group's welfare. Professional standards are very likely to get caught in the shuffle.

While it is our observation that unions and professionalization as we have discussed them here are basically incompatible, unions in policing appear to be here to stay. Consequently, it behooves police administrators to become or to hire good negotiators and to negotiate, to the extent possible, contracts that are compatible with professional growth. Contracts that provide reimbursement for improving one's education are good examples, as are those that require open, honest evaluations and disciplinary proceedings. Contracts that are viewed in terms of victories or losses are seldom of this type. Contracts that are viewed as representing legitimate efforts on behalf of both parties to improve the organization and the welfare of those employed may achieve this goal. An alternative is enlightened management that seeks to promote the interests of both employees and the organization without the need for third-party intervention.

Accreditation

Through the combined efforts of the International Association of Chiefs of Police, the National Organization for Black Law Enforcement Executives, the National Sheriff's Association, and the Police Executive Research Forum, the Commission for Accreditation of Law Enforcement Agencies was established in 1979. The Commission is a "private, nonprofit corporation working to promote, recognize and maintain professional excellence in law enforcement through accreditation" (Commission on Accreditation for Law Enforcement Agencies, 1984: 1). The commission has developed a voluntary accreditation process through which law enforcement agencies at the state, county, and municipal levels are evaluated in terms of more than nine hundred standards. These standards cover the following areas:

1. Role and responsibilities of law enforcement agencies and relationships with other agencies
2. Organization, management, and administration
3. Personnel administration
4. Law enforcement, traffic operations, and operational support
5. Prisoner- and court-related services
6. Auxiliary and technical services (Commission on Accreditation for Law Enforcement Agencies, 1990)

The standards are intended to assist police agencies in the following areas:

1. Preventing and controlling crime
2. Improving the quality and delivery of services
3. Improving interagency coordination
4. Increasing citizen confidence in police agencies

In order to become accredited, the agency first files an application and receives an agency questionnaire designed to allow agency personnel to conduct a self-evaluation of the agency's current status with respect to applicable standards. Once the self-evaluation is completed, the agency may either determine that it is not yet ready for accreditation and work toward that goal or may request an on-site assessment. In the latter case, a team of assessors is appointed by the commission and an on-site assessment is conducted by impartial assessors. These assessors write a report on their findings and a decision is made by the commission on accreditation. Costs vary depending on the size of the agency involved. Internal preparation costs are relatively high, because it often takes a year to eighteen months for the designated coordinator to prepare for the assessment. Nonetheless, more than two hundred agencies have been accredited and several hundred more are in the process of preparing for accreditation. In order to remain accredited, agencies must apply for reaccreditation after five years; a number of agencies are currently involved in that process.

Several unanticipated consequences of the accreditation process have emerged. A number of states have formed coalitions to assist police agencies in the process of accreditation, thereby improving interagency cooperation. Some departments report decreased insurance costs as a result of accreditation. Also, individuals who serve as assessors are currently updated with respect to the latest developments in policing and can share their experiences with others in the field, thereby promoting both dedication to and attainment of professionalism.

In summary, while professionalism has proved an elusive goal for the police, and while there are still pockets of resistance to meeting the requirements of a profession, a growing number of police personnel appear to be committed to that goal. The role of unions in this process remains unclear, but it is likely that enlightened police administrators will negotiate with unions to convince them to participate as partners in the search for professionalism.

Discussion Questions

1. What are the basic functions of the police?

2. What are the relationships among police discretion, police organization, and police functions?

3. Describe the traditional police organizational structure. Discuss its strengths and weaknesses.

4. What are the three styles of policing described by Wilson and how are they related to organizational structure?

5. Compare and contrast the advantages of small (less than ten personnel) and large police agencies from the perspective of the public, the officers involved, and the chief executive officer.

6. Discuss the context in which police organizations operate and the importance of the environment to the police.

7. Assess the current state of police leadership in your community using whatever sources are available to you (interviews with police supervisors, the media, etc.).

8. Discuss some of the factors that have made the police search for professionalism so difficult.

9. What are the characteristics of a profession? To what extent are these characteristics currently found among police personnel?

10. Why were police unions so slow to emerge? What are some of the reasons for the rapid increase in the number of police unions in the last two decades?

11. Are police unions and police professionalism compatible? Why or why not?

12. What are the relationships between police professionalism and accreditation? What is the rationale behind police accreditation?

13. Are the police currently professionals? If not, will they become professionals in this decade?

References

Alpert, G.P. and Dunham, R.C. 1993. *Policing Urban America* 2 ed. Prospect Heights, IL: Waveland.

American Bar Association, 1973. *The Urban Police Functions*. New York: American Bar Association.

Barker, T., Hunter, R.D., and Rush, J.P. 1994. *Police Systems and Practices: An Introduction*. Englewood Cliffs, NJ: Prentice-Hall.

Berg, B.L. 1992. *Law Enforcement: An Introduction to Police in Society*. Boston: Allyn & Bacon.

Bittner, E. 1967. "The Police on Skidrow: A Study of Peace-Keeping." *American Sociological Review* 32, 699–715.

Bobinsky, R. 1994. "Reflections on Community-Oriented Policing." *FBI Law Enforcement Bulletin* 63(3), 15–19.

Bouza, A.V. 1990. *The Police Mystique*. New York: Plenum.

Bowker, A.L. 1994. "Handle with Care: Dealing with Offenders Who Are Mentally Retarded." *FBI Law Enforcement Bulletin* 63(7), 12–16.

Broderick, J.J. 1987. *Police in a Time of Change* 2 ed. Prospect Heights, IL: Waveland Press.

Brown, L. 1985. "Police-Community Power Sharing." In Geller, W. (ed.), *Police Leadership in America: Crisis and Opportunity*. New York: Praeger.

Caplow, T. 1983. *Managing an Organization*. New York: Holt, Rinehart & Winston.

Commission on Accreditation for Law Enforcement Agencies. 1990. *Standards for Law Enforcement Agencies*. (February). Fairfax, VA.

Couper, D. and Lobitz, S. 1993. "Leadership for Change: A National Agenda." *Police Chief* 60(12), 15–19.

Cox, S.M. and Fitzgerald, J.D. 1991. *Police in Community Relations: Critical Issues* 2 ed. Dubuque, IA: Wm. C. Brown.

Crank, J.P., Regoli, R.M., Culbertson, R.G., and Poole, E.D. 1987. "Linkages Between Professionalization and Professionalism Among Police Chiefs." Paper presented at the Academy of Criminal Justice Sciences Annual Meeting St. Louis, MO.

Dobbs, C. and Field, M.W. 1993. "Rational Risk: Leadership Success or failure?" *Police Chief* 60(12), 64–66.

Franz, V. and Jones, D. 1987. "Perceptions of Organizational Performance in Suburban Police Departments: A Critique of the Military Model." *Journal of Police Science and Administration* 15(2), 153–161.

Gaines, L.K., Kappeler, V.E., and Vaughn, J.B. 1994. *Policing in America*. Cincinnati: Anderson.

Gaines, L.K., Southerland, M.D., and Angell, J.E. 1991. Police Administration. New York: McGraw-Hill.

Goldstein, H. 1977. *Policing a Free Society*. Cambridge, MA: Ballinger.

Greenwood, P.W., Chaiken, J., and Petersilia, J.R. 1977. *The Criminal Investigation Process*. Lexington, MA: D.C. Heath, Ch. 14 and 15.

Halloran, J. and Frunzi, G.L. 1986. *Supervision: The Art of Management*. Englewood Cliffs, NJ: Prentice-Hall.

Hernandez, J., Jr. 1989. *The Custer Syndrome*. Salem, WI: Sheffield.

Illinois Compiled Statutes, 1993, ch. 24, 125.

International Association of Chiefs of Police. 1990. *Police Chief* (January), 18.

International Association of Chiefs of Police. 1992. *Police Chief* (January), 16.

Kelling, G.L., Pate, T., Dieckman, D., and Brown, C.E. 1974. *The Kansas City Preventive Patrol Experiment: A Summary Report*. Washington, D.C.: Police Foundation.

Langworthy, R.H. and Travis, L.F. 1994. *Policing in America: A Balance of Forces*. New York: Macmillan.

Moore, D.T. and Morrow, J.G. 1987. "Evaluation of the Four/Ten Schedule in Three Illinois Department of State Police Districts." *Journal of Police Science and Administration* (15), 105–109.

More, H.W. and Wegener, W.F. 1992. *Behavioral Police Management*. New York: Macmillan.

Murphy, P.V. and Caplan, D.G. 1993. "Fostering Integrity." In Dunham, R.G. and Alpert, G.P. (eds.), *Critical Issues in Policing: Contemporary Issues*. Prospect Heights, IL: Waveland Press, 304–324.

National Institute of Justice, 1988. "Police Response to Special Populations." (May/June) Washington, D.C.: U.S. Government Printing Office.

Perrow, C. 1967. "A Framework for Comparative Organizational Analysis." *American Sociological Review* 32(2), 194–208.

Roberg, R.R. and Kuykendall, J. 1993. *Police and Society*. Belmont, CA: Wadsworth.

Sandver, M. 1987. *Labor Relations: Process and Outcomes*. Boston: Little, Brown.

Sapp, A.D. 1985. "Police Unionism as a Developmental Process." In Blumberg, A.S. and Niederhoffer, E. (eds.), *The Ambivalent Force: Perspectives on the Police* 3 ed. New York: Holt, Rinehart & Winston, 412–419.

Simonsen, C.E. and Arnold, D. 1993. "TQM: Is It Right for Law Enforcement?" *Police Chief* 60(12), 20–22.

Skolnick, J.H. and Bayley, D.H. 1986. *The New Blue Line: Police Innovation in Six American Cities*. New York: Free Press.

Sparrow, M.K., Moore, M.H., and Kennedy, D.M. 1990. *Beyond 911: A New Era for Policing*. New York: Basic Books.

Stone, A.R. and DeLuca, S.M. 1994. *Police Administration: An Introduction* 2 ed. Englewood Cliffs, NJ: Prentice-Hall.

Swanson, C.R., Territo, L., and Taylor, R.W. 1993. *Police Administration* 3 ed. New York: Macmillan.

Thibault, E.A., Lynch, L.M., and McBride, R.B. 1985. *Proactive Police Management*. Englewood Cliffs, NJ: Prentice-Hall.

Thibault, E.A., Lynch, L.M., and McBride, R.B. 1990. *Proactive Police Management* 2 ed. Englewood Cliffs, NJ: Prentice-Hall.

Toch, H. and Grant, J.D. 1991. *Police as Problem Solvers*. New York: Plenum.

Vollmer, H.M. and Mills, D.L. 1966. *Professionalization*. Englewood Cliffs, NJ: Prentice-Hall.

Wilson, J. 1968. *Varieties of Police Behavior: The Management of Law and Order in Eight Communities*. Cambridge, MA: Harvard University Press.

Witham, D.C. 1987. "Transformational Police Leadership." *FBI Law Enforcement Bulletin* (December), 2–6.

Wrobleski, H.M. and Hess, K.M. 1990. *Introduction to Law Enforcement and Criminal Justice* 3 ed. St. Paul, MN: West.

6

POLICE RECRUITMENT AND SELECTION

Every police department is faced with the necessity of recruiting and selecting personnel to fill the complex role discussed in the preceding chapters. Personnel must be recruited and selected to fill positions at three different levels: the entry level, the supervisory level, and the chief's level. We will discuss the recruiting and selecting processes involved at each of these levels in this chapter.

The Importance of Recruitment and Selection

The importance of productive recruitment and selection procedures cannot be overemphasized, regardless of the level involved. Poor recruiting and selection procedures result in hiring or promoting personnel who cannot or will not communicate effectively with diverse populations, exercise discretion properly, or perform the multitude of functions required of the police (see Highlight 6.1). Recognizing this, most, though certainly not all, departments and their representatives (fire and police commissions or civil service commissions) expend considerable time and money in the process. The extent to which they are successful largely determines the effectiveness and efficiency of the department.

We must point out that the process of recruiting and selecting officers and chiefs and promoting supervisors is in many cases done in large part by those outside policing. That is, police and fire commissioners, personnel departments, or civil service board members often determine who will be eligible for hiring and promotion, and assessment teams, city manager, mayor, and council members typically determine who will fill the position of chief. To be sure, in the former case, police officials may select the officers they choose from among those on the eligibility list and in the case of promotions have a good deal of input as we shall see later. Still, much of the recruiting and selecting of police personnel is done by civilians with varying degrees of input from police administrators.

HIGHLIGHT 6.1   Personnel Selection

The personnel selection process is one of the most important administrative functions in a police department. It is the process through which the agency is rejuvenated by importing vital new human resources. Since officers often have complete careers with one agency, if the initial selection decision is poorly made, the department is faced with retaining an inferior officer for twenty years or more. Thus, selection decisions have long-term, momentous implications for a department. No matter how well a department is organized or administered, if the police officers who must perform daily police responsibilities are not of the highest caliber, the department will not reach its full potential in terms of maintaining order, reducing crime, and providing important services to the community (Gaines and Kappeler, 1992: 107–123).

It is important to note that recruitment and selection are ongoing processes that recur throughout the career of an officer. Once selected for an entry-level position by a specific department, the officer is likely to be involved in selection procedures involving appointment to different assignments (detective, juvenile officer, crime technician, patrol officer, and so forth), to different ranks (promotional examinations), to different schools/training programs, and so on. For some, the process ends with their selection as chief, for others the process continues as they seek the position of chief in other agencies, and for some the process begins and ends at the rank of patrol officer.

Nonetheless, even for the latter, the process is repeated over and over throughout their careers, even though they may choose not to participate directly. That is, some officers make a conscious choice to remain patrol officers and not to seek opportunities for training. These officers, too, are important in understanding the recruitment and selection process involved in promotions, because they may become perceived as outside the pool of candidates to be recruited for such advancement or training. In addition, those who are selected for such assignments must be prepared to deal with them, just as they must be prepared to deal with those promoted around them. An examination of the various requirements and strategies employed in the recruitment process will reveal some of the difficulties involved in selecting personnel who will both fill the official vacancy and meet the situation-specific needs of various departments. However, before we turn our attention to recruitment and selection at the various levels, we need to understand the legal context in which such processes currently occur.

Equal Employment Opportunity and Affirmative Action

For most of our history, U.S. employers, both public and private, have felt relatively free to hire and promote employees according to whatever criteria they established and, similarly, to exclude from employment and promotion those they deemed, for whatever reasons, to be unfit. This was true even though the U.S. Constitution, in the First, Fifth, and Fourteenth Amendments prohibited deprivation of employment rights without due process of law. Further, the Civil Rights Acts of 1866, 1870, and 1871 (based on the Thirteenth and Fourteenth Amendments) prohibited racial discrimination in hiring and placement as well as deprivation of equal employment rights under the cover of state law (Bell, 1992).

Still, it wasn't until 1964 and the passage of the Civil Rights Act of that year—and specifically Title VII of the act—that many employers began to take equal employment rights seriously. The Act prohibited discrimination in employment based on race, color, and national origin and applied to all employers receiving federal financial assistance. Title VII of the 1964 Civil

Rights Act, as amended in 1972, extended the prohibition of discrimination in hiring to religion, sex, and national origin and applied to federal, state, and local governments, among others. This act, the Equal Employment Opportunity Act (EEOA), established a commission (EEOC) to investigate complaints of discrimination. Following these changes in federal law, states also began passing such laws in the form of fair employment statutes (Bell, 1992).

In general terms, these laws hold that discrimination occurs when requirements for hiring and promotion are not *bona fide* (that is, they do not actually relate to the job) and when they adversely affect members of a minority group. The burden of demonstrating that requirements are job related falls on the employer, while the burden of showing an adverse affect falls on the complainant. For an employer to be successfully sued in this regard, both conditions must be met; that is, it is possible to have job requirements that have an adverse effect, but are nonetheless valid. For example, if it could be demonstrated that police officers routinely have to remove accident victims from vehicles, and if this job requirement also eliminated from policing categories of applicants unable to physically do so, the requirement would not be discriminatory under the law. If, however, these actions are seldom if ever required of police officers, the requirement would be discriminatory. We will have more to say about such requirements later in this chapter, but it is important to understand here the context within which charges of discrimination are filed and decided.

The combined effect of equal employment opportunity laws and executive orders eventually came to be realized by government agencies, among them the police. Prior to the early 1970s, most police departments had employed predominantly white males, a practice that became the focus of numerous legal challenges. These challenges came in the form of both court actions and complaints to the Equal Employment Opportunity Commission alleging discrimination on the part of employers.

During the same period, the concept of affirmative action gained prominence. Affirmative action programs have two goals. First, they are intended to prevent discrimination in current hiring and promotional practices. Second, they may be used to help remedy past discrimination in hiring and promotion.

Equal employment opportunity and affirmative action programs may be implemented in a number of different ways. First, some employers voluntarily establish affirmative action programs because they recognize the importance of hiring without regard to race, creed, or gender. Second, some employers implement such programs when threatened with legal action based on alleged discrimination. Third, some employers fight charges of discrimination in the courts and are found to be in violation. When this occurs, such employers are in danger of losing federal financial support, and in order to prevent this from occurring, agree to develop and implement affirmative action programs. An employer is able to retain financial aid through the use of a consent decree in which the employer agrees to strive to achieve some sort of balance in terms of race, ethnicity, and/or gender in the work force. In other cases the courts impose plans and time tables on employers and can impose severe sanctions in the form of fines if the goals of the plan are not met within the specified period.

The use of consent decrees has led to much confusion and widespread ill feelings on behalf of employers and white, male employees. On the one hand, the Equal Employment Opportunity Act prohibits discrimination based on race, creed, religion, gender, or national origin and states that employers will not be forced to hire less qualified employees over more qualified employees. On the other hand, the courts have reached agreements with employers that would seem to discriminate against white, male employees and have, although the EEOA prohibits the use of quotas to achieve racial balance, imposed quota systems on some employers (Berg, 1992).

For example, in 1987, the U.S. Supreme Court upheld promotional quotas that required that the Alabama State Police promote one black officer for each white officer until blacks hold at least 25 percent of the top ranks in the department (Gest, 1987). More importantly, perhaps, this decision protected over a hundred affirmative action cases that included quotas (Sullivan, 1989: 337).

A number of police administrators have complained that they have been forced to hire minority employees who do not meet the standards they have established to improve police services and thousands of white, male applicants for police positions complain that, although they are better qualified than minority candidates in terms of test results, the latter have been hired or promoted. Both of these complaints are, in individual instances, justified, but they must be viewed in light of the goals of affirmative action—especially the goal of remedying past discrimination.

In essence, white males applying for police positions or promotions in some areas are suffering the same fate their black and Hispanic counterparts have suffered over the past three centuries in U.S. society. Now that the opportunities have shifted, white males are facing the same difficulties minorities and women have faced for years. In some cases, white, male applicants have filed suits claiming discrimination and have prevailed. The shift from discriminatory employment practices in policing, as well as in many other areas, has been slow and sometimes painful. Yet, it is necessary in order to maximize the number of qualified applicants and to make police agencies representative of the communities they serve. As Cox and Fitzgerald (1991) note, the police will not be seen as understanding community problems unless they have members who can view them from the community's perspective.

Unfortunately, in spite of the fact that the International Association of Chiefs of Police unanimously adopted a resolution in 1975 supporting minority recruitment (Broderick, 1987: 214), in many cases police agencies and the municipalities in which they operate have chosen to continue discriminatory hiring and/or promotional practices until and unless someone files legal action to force change. Others, though perhaps a minority, made and are making deliberate attempts to hire and promote minority group members for the obvious advantages that result. In either case, it is clear that certain requirements must be met in order to avoid charges of discrimination in employment:

1. Requirements must be job related
2. Requirements must be validated
3. Requirements must be free from "inherent bias"
4. Requirements must be properly administered
5. Candidates must be properly graded (Sullivan, 1989: 337)

As a result of numerous claims of reverse discrimination by white males, the Supreme Court considered the issue in 1989 (it had previously done so to some extent in 1987 in the case of *Baake v. California*). The Court's decision indicates that statistical comparisons of populations alone are insufficient to show discrimination and that cases of overt discrimination are the only cases covered by Title VII (Gaines, Kappeler, and Vaughn, 1994: 73). The Court recognized in a number of cases the concept of reverse discrimination and in a case involving firefighters in the city of Birmingham, Alabama, found that qualified whites who are passed over for promotion in order to promote less qualified blacks have a cause of action against the city (presumably, this decision applies across the country). Thus, municipalities operating under consent decrees in which agreement has been reached to preferentially hire minorities may, by adhering to the conditions of the decree, be opening themselves up to suit in the name of reverse discrimination.

In 1992, President Bush signed legislation intended to clarify issues arising from what appear to be conflicting Supreme Court decisions. As a result of that legislation, "statistical and other adjustments that would give minorities an advantage over majority candidates in the selection process" were prohibited. "Such things as adding points, using dual lists, or using quotas" became prohibited. In addition "the act reintroduced disparate impact as a method of determining whether discrimination existed" (Gaines, Kappeler, and Vaughn, 1994: 73).

The Americans with Disabilities Act

In 1990, the Americans with Disabilities Act (ADA) was enacted. While the impact of the act on policing is not yet entirely clear, at least a brief description of the ADA is in order: There is little doubt that many police agencies will be involved in litigation as a result of the act. The ADA makes it illegal to discriminate against persons with certain categories of disabilities, limits blanket exclusions, and requires that the selection process deal with individuals on a case-by-case basis. To be protected under the ADA, the individual must have a disability or impairment (physical or mental), a record of such disability, or be regarded as having such a disability and must be otherwise qualified for the position in question. *Otherwise qualified* means that the applicant must be able to perform the essential elements of the job with or without reasonable accommodation. Reasonable accommodation refers to new construction or the modification of existing facilities, work schedules, or equipment, so long as such modification does not cause the agency undue hardship (significant expense or difficulty). Examples of disabilities covered by the ADA include vision, hearing, breathing, and learning problems, as well as AIDS and HIV infection (Rubin, 1993). Examples of accommodation include building ramps to provide access to buildings or work sites, designating parking spaces for those with disabilities, installing elevators, and redesigning workstations and restrooms.

The ADA places considerable emphasis on job-task analysis to determine the essential functions of positions and, of course, requires that job requirements be *bona fide* (Schneid and Gaines, 1991). Further, it appears that the ADA will change police hiring practices with respect to psychological testing, which may be viewed as part of a medical examination; the ADA protects those with mental impairments who are otherwise job-qualified. It may be, then, that the psychological test, like the medical examination, will have to be delayed until after an employment offer is made. Additionally, the ADA may require changes in application forms that previously inquired as to "potentially disabling impairments" and in oral board interviews in which inquiries as to the extent and nature of existing disabilities are prohibited (Higginbotham, 1991: 28).

Let us now turn our attention to the entry-level requirements that have been established for police officers, as well as the recruitment and selection process at this level.

Entry-Level Recruitment and Selection

> *It must be remembered that police work is a labor-intensive service industry, in which roughly eighty-five percent of the agencies' budgets are devoted to various personnel costs. The most significant investment police departments make is in the recruiting, selection and training of their personnel, or, in other words, on the police officer (Alpert and Dunham, 1988: 35).*

One important personnel cost for any organization is that associated with attracting qualified applicants to fill vacancies; this is certainly true in policing, which is, as indicated above, labor intensive. The costs of recruitment begin with the advertising process and, hopefully, end with the successful completion of the probationary period. In other words, the objective of the recruitment process is to select potential police officers who can not only meet entry-level requirements, but who can successfully complete training academy requirements and the probationary period. While recruit qualifications vary tremendously among different departments, some general requirements and concerns can be discussed.

The objective in advertising is to attract from the total pool of potential applicants for police work those, and only those, who are both qualified and seriously interested in becoming police officers. The more applicants attracted who do not meet both of these requirements, the more expensive the recruiting process becomes. Let us assume, hypothetically, that the cost of processing one police recruit from application to placement on the eligibility list is five hundred dollars. Suppose that the agency attracts fifty applicants for the one vacancy available, and suppose that forty of the fifty applicants pass all the tests given in the early stages of the selection process. When the agency conducts background investigations of those who have successfully completed the tests, however, it is discovered that ten of the applicants have prior felony convictions. In essence, the municipality has wasted the money spent on testing these individuals since, in most jurisdictions, they could not be hired as police officers regardless of performance on the tests. Again, suppose that ten more of the applicants really have no interest in police work once they discover something about its nature and would not accept a police position if it were offered. The time and money spent on these individuals is also wasted. Now there are thirty applicants remaining, but the agency has only one vacancy. As you can see, the cost of recruiting the one individual who is selected is quite high.

To some extent these difficulties are inherent in the recruiting/selecting process, but they may be offset by the establishment of an eligibility list (if there are other vacancies within a relatively short period of time). That is, those involved in the hiring process probably cannot determine at the outset who will and will not decide to accept the position, if it is offered. If several of the people who qualify are hired, the costs may be reduced. Costs may also be reduced, however, by developing an advertising campaign that clearly states the requirements of the position and that, to the extent possible, accurately describes the duties to be performed. Thus, a statement that those with prior felony convictions need not apply might be part of the advertisement. While this statement does not guarantee that such persons will not apply, it at least indicates to them that they have no chance of being hired if discovered and probably prevents many with prior convictions from applying. The point is that the more accurately the qualities sought are described, the less likely it is that large numbers of unqualified people will apply, thus helping to keep recruiting costs as low as possible.

At the same time, however, advertisements must be designed so as to attract as many qualified applicants as possible. This includes not only describing the benefits associated with the position available, but also indicating that the police department is an equal opportunity employer and that women and minorities are invited to apply. This is especially necessary in police recruitment because police departments, for reasons detailed above, have traditionally been viewed by both minorities and women as basically white, male domains. Advertising campaigns must take this fact into account, and advertisements should be placed in magazines likely to be read by women and minorities, as well as in the more traditional professional journals and newspapers.

Further recruiting efforts may be directed at college campuses, high schools, and minority neighborhoods. Conducting orientation sessions that provide a realistic picture of police work in the department in question is another valuable tool in eliminating those who find they have no interest in such work. While those responsible for recruiting police personnel have made strides in these areas in recent years, there is still much to be done. The bottom line is that if those charged with hiring police officers want to have representative police departments in order to provide the best services available to the communities served, they must attract the most qualified candidates.

When the application deadline indicated in the advertisements has been reached, the applications that have been filed must be analyzed. The better the application form, the easier it is to analyze the applications. The form might request information on prior experience in policing, any criminal convictions, educational background, reasons for the interest in police work, current drug and alcohol use, and other information considered pertinent by specific departments. It should also provide some indication of the applicant's ability to express him or herself in writing. Some departments have found that charging a nominal fee for the application eliminates some applicants who might be simply "testing the waters"; detailed application forms requesting specific information probably also eliminate some who are using narcotics, have prior felony convictions, and so on. The more of these potential applicants eliminated at this stage, the less costly the recruiting process will be. Once the applications have been reviewed, the actual testing of qualified applicants can begin.

As we have seen, standards of selection for police officers were virtually nonexistent in the early days of U.S. policing. When standards began to emerge, they often required little more than allegiance to a particular politician or political party. The last two decades have seen an increase in the concern with establishing minimum entry-level requirements for police officers, and only in the past ten to fifteen years has what has been called the "Multiple-Hurdle Procedure" become common (Stone and DeLuca, 1985). The term refers to a battery of tests or hurdles that must be successfully completed before the recruit can become a police officer. In the following sections, we will critically analyze each of these tests, which may be generally divided into the following categories:

1. Status tests
2. Physical tests
3. Mental tests
4. Tests of morality
5. Tests of ability to communicate

It's important to remember that the different types of tests sometimes overlap, but we will discuss each independently.

Status Tests

Status tests have to do with things such as citizenship, possession or ability to obtain a driver's license, residency, service in the military, educational level, and age. Police officers are virtually always required to be citizens, though some court challenges to this requirement are being made. Is citizenship a *bona fide* job requirement? Can one who is a citizen perform police functions better than one who is, for example, a permanent resident who has passed a test covering the U.S. and state constitutions? This is an issue that will eventually be decided by the courts, but for now it is safe to say that citizen status is typically required. The requirement that the applicant have or be able to obtain a driver's license seems likely to be upheld for obvious reasons. Some municipalities and states require that newly hired personnel be residents (or be willing to become residents) of the jurisdiction involved. This requirement, too, has been and continues to be subject to court battles, and a majority of jurisdictions have modified the requirement (Gaines, Kappeler, and Vaughn, 1994: 78). Many suburban police departments, for example, simply require that officers live no more than twenty or thirty minutes from their place of duty.

Questions concerning prior military service arise because bonus points (veterans' preference points) may be added to the test scores of applicants if they have such prior service, thus affecting the final eligibility list. Most departments have minimal educational standards—typically, possession of a high school diploma or its equivalent—which must be met by applicants, and these have been upheld by the courts.

Finally, the vast majority of departments require that applicants be adults (the age of majority) at the time of employment and not be more than thirty-six to forty years of age at the time of initial employment in policing. The minimum age requirement makes sense in terms of maturity and meeting statutory requirements for entering certain types of establishments. The upper age limit, however, has been called into question as a result of the Age Discrimination Act of 1990, which prohibits age discrimination with respect to those over forty. Whether the applicant meets the status requirements can be largely determined from the application form.

Physical Tests

Physical tests include physical agility tests, height/weight proportionate tests, vision tests, and medical examinations.

Physical Agility Tests

Physical agility tests are used by about 80 percent of police agencies to determine whether applicants are agile enough, in good enough condition, strong enough, and have enough endurance to perform police work (Ash, Slora, and Britton, 1990). These tests must be job related; many have fallen by the wayside as the result of court challenges. Tests of coordination and actual agility can typically be shown to be job related, whereas tests based on sheer strength are more difficult to validate. Many departments at one time required that applicants be able to complete a specified number of pull-ups or push-ups in a certain time period. It is difficult to justify such tests on the basis of job relatedness, however. How often does a police officer have to do pull-ups in the performance of his or her duty? A more realistic test is the wall test in which the applicant must clear a wall of a certain height. One can at least envision the possibility of this type of activity occurring in the performance of police duties.

It may be that the basis for such strength tests was a desire to eliminate female applicants from police employment, or police administrators may have sincerely believed that strength was an important requirement for police officers. Whatever the case, the requirement that such tests be validated has led to a number of changes in the types of physical tests now administered and a wide variety of testing strategies characterizes different police departments. One study by Booth and Hornick (1984: 40) concluded that the ability to react quickly is the most critical and frequently required physical attribute of police officers, while brute force and long-term endurance are the least frequently performed and least critical of the physical activities performed by police personnel.

Height/Weight Tests
Height/weight proportionate tests have replaced traditional height requirements, which eliminated most women and many minority group members from policing. Such tests make sense in the context of police work and the agility requirements discussed previously. As originally used, these tests seemed largely superfluous because few departments required that proportionate height and weight be maintained after initial employment, but many if not most departments now test for proportionate height and weight on a regular basis. This requirement makes the initial employment requirement more meaningful; it seems apparent that if the requirement is important for young officers, it is doubly important for current employees whose age may make them more vulnerable to problems related to disproportionate height and weight (McCormack, 1994).

Vision Requirements
Vision requirements vary greatly among departments and are the subject of controversy. When such requirements are for uncorrected vision they are especially controversial. Most departments have established corrected vision requirements, which may be justified on the basis of driving ability, ability to identify license plates or persons, or weapons qualification (Holden and Gammeltoft, 1991). While it is certainly possible that an officer may have his or her glasses broken or lose a contact lens in an altercation, we know of no strong evidence that indicates these happenings occur frequently enough to be problematic or to justify stringent uncorrected vision requirements.

Medical Examinations
The medical examination is a critical part of the testing process from the point of view of the department because an officer who becomes disabled as a result of injury or illness is often eligible for life-long disability payments. In order to detect conditions that may lead to such illnesses or injuries, virtually all police agencies require a medical examination, which is intended to detect problems of the heart, back, legs, and feet, among others. These conditions may be aggravated by police work and the department would prefer to eliminate from consideration applicants with such problems. Due consideration must be given to the requirements of the Americans with Disabilities Act, of course.

Mental Tests

Mental tests may be divided into two categories: those designed to measure intelligence, knowledge, or aptitude, and those designed to evaluate psychological fitness.

Tests of Intelligence, Knowledge, or Aptitude

Written tests are used as an early screening device by the vast majority of police agencies (Ash, Slora, and Britton, 1990). These paper-and-pencil tests come in a variety of forms intended to measure a variety of things. To be of value, the tests must deal with job-related issues and must have predictive value; that is, they should be able to predict whether or not an applicant has the ability to perform police work well. Such prediction is attempted despite the fact that there is no accepted definition of a competent police officer or of what qualities are required for or likely to increase competence (Burbeck and Furnham, 1985: 64–65).

In addition, these written tests have historically eliminated most minority group members. Millions of dollars have been spent in attempts to develop "culture-fair" tests to avoid this bias with, at best, only moderate success (Winters, 1992). Perhaps for lack of a better screening device, the vast majority of departments continue to use written tests in spite of their obvious inadequacies. In most departments in which such tests are used, they are scored on a point system and the score obtained becomes a part of the overall point total used to determine the eligibility list. Differences of one or two points might, therefore, make the difference between hiring one applicant and another, even though differences of up to five to ten points probably indicate little difference between candidates. While a score of seventy is often established as the cutoff point for passing, this score may be raised or lowered depending on the candidate pool, indicating that there is nothing magical about the score itself. The very fact that there are many different tests and forms of tests available implies that there is no consensus about a best test or form.

While there are some difficulties involved in conducting the research necessary to evaluate written entry-level tests, such research is essential if we are to develop a test with predictive power. Such research would require that a department hire applicants regardless of their scores on the test (including those who failed), keep the test results secret from those who evaluate the officers' performance over a period of time (preferably at least eighteen months to two years), and then compare performance evaluations over the time period with initial test scores. If those who scored high on the written test were also the best performers on the job, the validity of the test would be demonstrated, all other factors being equal—which they seldom are. While the research required is relatively simple, questions of liability exist for a department choosing to participate in such research. What happens, for instance, if an applicant who failed the test is hired and performs so badly that someone is injured or killed as a result? In addition, the time period involved is quite long and many agencies and test constructors are unwilling to wait the required time to obtain meaningful results.

Some research has been done that suggests that situational tests, which place the potential officer in situations designed to test whether he or she possesses the necessary skills to perform police work, recognizes when such skills are required, and demonstrates the motivation or willingness to apply these skills, appear to be indicative of job performance over the first two years of employment (Pugh, 1985; Pynes and Bernardin, 1992). It may be that tests of this type—actually a form of the assessment center discussed below as it relates to promotions—prove to be more valuable than paper-and-pencil tests.

Still, most police agencies continue to use written entry-level tests as screening devices in spite of their obvious shortcomings. Despite the intensive effort to improve written tests, there is little convincing evidence that test scores can predict officer performance over any extensive period of time.

Psychological Tests

Psychological tests present even more difficulties than written tests of intelligence, knowledge, or aptitude. They have been used increasingly over the last thirty years and the President's Commission in 1967 recommended that they be used by all police departments to determine emotional stability (Meier, Farmer, and Maxwell, 1987). In spite of the many weaknesses discussed here, psychological tests continue to be administered both because of the liability that may result from hiring police officers without the use of such tests and because many police administrators believe that they at least screen out those applicants who are clearly suffering from emotional disorders. "Over one hundred books and articles have been published on the subject of psychological assessment in police selection in the past twenty years. Some of this activity has no doubt been stimulated by court decisions in which police departments have been held liable for dangerous behavior of employees, both on and off duty, when no adequate screening for psychological stability was performed" (Pendergrass, 1987: 8).

Meier et al. (1987: 215) note in their review of psychological screening as it relates to police officers that there may be other reasons for the continuation of the practice. They list the defense against negligent hiring and retention as one motivating factor and note that equally relevant are the social responsibilities of protecting the public and assisting officers who face serious problems.

The task of predicting psychological stability for short time periods—let alone the career of a police officer—is a formidable one. It is an especially difficult task since the psychological characteristics of the ideal police officer have not been and perhaps cannot be identified. The very diversity in U.S. policing discussed in the first two chapters, combined with the complexity of the police role make obtaining a consensus about the characteristics of the ideal officer highly unlikely. Pugh (1985: 176), for example, suggests that policing makes varying demands on police officers and that the personality qualities required early in an officer's career may differ from those required later.

Benner (1989: 83) discusses the extent to which psychological tests can eliminate police applicants who are either unstable or unsuitable (or both) and concludes: "It matters little that the field of psychology is only marginally capable of predicting 'bad' officer candidates. Psychologists and psychiatrists are expected not only to screen out the 'bad' but to be able to screen in the 'good.' Unfortunately, consensus definitions of 'good' or 'suitable' have not been developed either among the professionals or members of the lay public."

Tests commonly used to help determine suitability and stability of prospective police officers include the Minnesota Multiphasic Personality Inventory (MMPI), the California Personality Inventory (CPI), the Fundamental Interpersonal Relations Orientation-B (FIRO-B), the Inwald Personality Inventory (IPI), and others. These tests are sometimes used in combination with others to form "test batteries," which are thought to be more comprehensive than individual tests (Pendergrass, 1987; Ash, Slora, and Britton, 1990). In addition, personal interviews with psychologists or psychiatrists frequently supplement the paper-and-pencil tests.

According to Pendergrass (1987: 25–29) and Hiatt and Hargrave (1988: 125), there are several studies indicating that the use of psychological tests for screening entry-level police officers has led to the recognition of certain characteristics—including level of cognitive functioning, personal history, and possibly work interests—that may help predict success. Burbeck and Furnham (1985: 68) conclude that psychological testing may eliminate applicants suffering from some mental abnormality. The tests, however, are not infallible because subjects can successfully fake results, and they are "expensive to administer for a very small return of aberrant scores" (Burbeck and Furnham, 1985: 68).

Pendergrass (1987: 29) indicates that psychological tests can make a contribution to the selection process but should not "replace other methods nor are the results of psychological assessment without error in prediction of success of candidates. . . . Selection based entirely upon psychological testing is likely to eliminate a number of good candidates and retain some poor candidates in error."

While the literature on psychological testing of police recruits is confusing at best, it appears certain that such testing, unless used to supplement the other procedures discussed here, is of limited value. Meier et al. (1987: 213) conclude that there is no convincing evidence for the use of psychological instruments to predict long-term successful employment in policing, although they believe research in this area should continue because there is some consensus that the techniques can identify applicants who may represent a real risk to the public.

Dwyer, Prien, and Bernardi (1990) and Wright, Doerner, and Speir (1990) conclude that psychological tests are of unknown validity and the available research does not support their use. Still, about two thirds of all police departments continue to use them in the selection process (Ash, Slora, and Britton, 1990), perhaps more because they believe in the value of the tests as a defense against litigation than in their value as a tool in predicting success as a police officer.

Tests of Morality

Tests of morality include background investigations, drug tests, and polygraph examinations. We refer to these requirements as tests of morality because they are used to evaluate the moral character of police applicants. Certainly drug testing also constitutes a physical test, but it is typically the use of drugs itself rather than the effect of the drugs on the physical well-being of the applicant that is of primary concern.

Background Investigations

The importance of background investigations is clearly demonstrated in an example cited by Ferguson (1987: 6). In a community in the Southwest, a new police chief was appointed based on the favorable impression he made during his visit and the references listed on his application. He then hired his own officers. The city failed to check the references listed by the chief or those of the new officers. Eventually, reporters checked these references and found that the chief's were phony and that one of the officers he had hired and promoted to the rank of sergeant was a wanted felon in another state. Even the most precursory background investigation could have saved the city the embarrassment that obviously ensued.

Background investigations are used by almost all police departments, but the extent and intensiveness of these investigations vary considerably. In some cases, listed references are simply checked by phone, while in others a good deal of time and money are expended to ensure the character of the applicant. In cases of the latter type, the investigation normally includes:

1. A check of education and training accomplishments listed on the application
2. A check of former employers
3. A neighborhood investigation
4. An investigation of the circumstances surrounding separation from the military in appropriate cases
5. An investigation of financial history
6. A check on the place of residence
7. A check with state and national crime information centers to determine prior criminal history (Swanson, Territo, and Taylor, 1988; Roberg and Kuykendall, 1990).

In short, a major purpose of the background investigation is to determine the honesty of the applicant as reflected by the information he or she provided on the application form and in subsequent communications with those in charge of recruiting and selecting. Background investigations may exclude, or highlight for further inquiry, applicants with prior felony convictions or who are currently wanted, those with a history of serious employment, family, or financial problems, those who have been dishonorably discharged from the military, and those who have failed to tell the truth during the application process. In addition, prior and current use of alcohol or other drugs is typically explored in the context of making reference contacts.

The rationale for excluding or further investigating applicants with problems in these areas is relatively clear. It makes little sense to hire as a police officer an individual who has serious drug-related problems, and in virtually all jurisdictions those with prior felony convictions are excluded from policing by statute. Those with histories of domestic violence or bankruptcy also present problems since they may be corruptible or prone to the use of force in their positions as police officers. In short, the background investigation represents an attempt to admit into policing only those with what is defined as good moral character.

Drug Tests

Possession, manufacture, distribution, and sale of illegal drugs are all serious problems in our society and applicants for police work are not immune to these problems. One recent study of police applicants found that one out of every three police candidates was rejected because of drug use (Van, 1986). One survey of thirty-three major police departments found that twenty-four had drug-testing programs, that virtually all had written policies and procedures relating to drug testing, and that twenty-four indicated that treatment as opposed to dismissal would be appropriate for some officers using drugs (McEwen et al., 1986). About a quarter of all municipal police departments require drug testing of all applicants and the percentage requiring such testing increases with the size of the department (U.S. Department of Justice, 1992). Increasingly, police departments are finding many applicants reporting drug use, which would make them unacceptable for police employment (Gaines, Kappeler, and Vaughn, 1994: 83).

The International Association of Chiefs of Police has developed a model drug-testing policy that calls for all recruits to be tested prior to employment, testing of current employees under certain circumstances, and requiring that officers assigned to narcotics units submit to periodic testing (McEwen et al., 1986). While the issue of drug testing, usually accomplished through urinalysis, has led to a great deal of litigation, it appears that when such testing is done according to a schedule (as opposed to random testing), and when it is done in reasonable fashion and on reasonable grounds, the courts will allow the testing as it relates to policing. It appears legitimate because of police departments' interests in protecting the safety of the public and of other employees. The possibility of a drug-impaired police officer injuring a colleague or another citizen as the result of a vehicle accident, firearm discharge, or use of excessive force clearly exists. Thus, drug testing is likely to become even more prevalent among police agencies as the legal requirements for such testing are more clearly elaborated by court decisions and revision of statutes.

Polygraph Examinations

Polygraph examinations are used by close to half of the municipal police agencies in the United States (Ash, Slora, and Britton, 1990), although recent changes in federal legislation have already greatly restricted their use in the private sector and may eventually have the same effect on the public sector. The rationale behind the use of the polygraph for recruiting and selection purposes appears to be twofold. First, the results of the examination are used as one indicator of the honesty of the job applicant. Second, the results are used to eliminate applicants whose responses are not acceptable to the police agency in question, regardless of the honesty of the applicant. Either or both of these purposes may be justifiable, but there remains considerable controversy over the accuracy of polygraph tests, raising the issue of rejecting some qualified applicants while accepting others who are deceitful. While supporters of the polygraph test claim accuracy in the 85 to 90 percent category, opponents claim results are little more reliable than guessing and argue that a margin of error of 10 to 15 percent is unacceptably large.

The problem with polygraph tests does not lie with the machine, which simply measures blood pressure, rate of breathing, and Galvanic Skin Response (changes in electrical resistance in the skin) over time. The interpretation of the results and the way in which the test is administered depend on the polygrapher. Training, skills, and competence of polygraphers vary widely and the conditions (anxiety and nervousness on behalf of applicants) under which employment and promotional polygraph interviews are conducted are less than ideal for accurate results. "[Another] use of polygraph testing is in pre-employment screening of applicants for police work. The use of the polygraph for this purpose is very controversial and is, in fact, illegal in some jurisdictions" (Horvath, 1989: 509). If the tests have any value in recruiting and selecting it would appear to be as one small part of the overall process.

Tests of Ability to Communicate

As we indicated earlier, many of the recruiting and selecting procedures used with respect to the police are overlapping. This interdependence of procedures is perhaps best illustrated by tests of ability to communicate. Properly conceived, these tests include the application form, the written tests taken by applicants, and the oral interview typically required of potential police officers. Since we have already discussed the application and written tests, we will concentrate here on the oral interview or oral "board" as it is often called. Let us simply note that it is both possible and desirable to evaluate the written communication skills of applicants by requiring them to write a job history or autobiographical statement as a part of the application form because a large measure of police work involves writing reports that require accuracy and comprehensiveness. While a misspelled word or two is probably no cause for concern, serious defects in the ability to communicate in writing at the very minimum indicate the need for some remedial work in this area.

The Oral Board

Oral interviews of police applicants are used by most agencies. These interviews or boards are typically conducted by members of the fire and police or civil service commission or the personnel department in larger police agencies, often in conjunction with representatives of the police agency. In some cases the latter actually participate in the interview, in others they simply observe. The number of interviewers varies, but three to five seems typical.

The express purpose of the oral board is to select a suitable applicant to fill the existing police vacancy. There is, however, often a second goal in these interviews: that of selecting a certain kind of person to fill the vacancy. In addition to demonstrating the skills necessary to fill the formal organizational position, the applicant's loyalty to the department, trustworthiness with respect to other police officers, and, while legally and formally forbidden, race, gender, and general presentation of self may be considered (Gray, 1975; Cox and Fitzgerald, 1991). While it is undoubtedly true that efforts to reduce the amount of subjectivity in oral interviews have been made in the form of standardized questions and independent evaluation by the raters, it is equally true that the way we look (dress, skin color, gender, etc.) and act (eye contact, handshake, degree of self-confidence expressed) affect our daily interactions. While attempts may be made to minimize the effect of these variables on the scoring of the interview, the issues also affect the interviewers (Falkenberg, Gaines, and Cox, 1990). The general impression from conversations with other board members is that factors that are expressly forbidden from consideration, in terms of equal employment opportunity guidelines for example, *do* affect the judgment of interviewers in subtle, if not in obvious, ways.

The interview format varies greatly. In most cases general questions about the applicant's background, experiences, education, prior training, interest in police work in general, and police work in the specific department in question are asked. These questions may be followed by a series of questions to test the applicant's knowledge of some legal, moral, and ethical issues relating to police work. For example, the applicant may be asked how he or she would respond to the apparent corruption of another officer, what response would be appropriate if the traffic violator stopped turned out to be the mayor, or how much force is justified in a certain type of incident.

These questions may be asked slowly with follow-up questions or may be asked and followed up in such a fashion that they create stress for the interviewee. The responses to the questions are evaluated by each of the raters independently and, should major differences in evaluation occur, may be discussed among the raters in an attempt to reach some consensus about the applicant's worthiness. The final scores for the oral board are then added to the scores from the other portions of the testing procedure to establish an eligibility list from which the chief of police or personnel department may select candidates to fill existing and future vacancies.

There is a definite irony here that needs to be emphasized. Although the selection process today is conducted under the guise of objectivity, including having the written tests sent elsewhere for scoring, scoring by identification numbers as opposed to names, rating interviewees independently, and calculating scores to the nearest point (or, in some cases, tenth of a point), when the process is completed, the final rank order based on the complex scoring system may be ignored by the chief or personnel department. That is, the applicant who scored third highest overall may be selected to fill the vacancy instead of the applicant who scored highest. While there is perhaps nothing wrong with giving the chief some input at this stage of the selection process, it tends to call into question the value of the apparent objectivity surrounding the process, particularly during the promotion process to which we shall soon turn our attention.

We need to keep in mind that the recruitment and selection process does not end with the establishment of the eligibility list. Rather, it continues as those selected for hiring go to the training academy, as they return to the department to serve their probationary period, and as they proceed through their careers in policing.

Supervisory Recruitment and Selection

As we indicated earlier, the recruiting and selection process does not end with initial employment, but continues as some individuals are promoted to supervisory positions and special assignments. If it is important to select prospective police officers carefully, it is equally important to promote carefully to ensure that those who supervise new recruits are well prepared to do so.

The same equal employment opportunity and affirmative action rules discussed previously apply in selecting and recruiting police supervisors, including chiefs. The vast majority of police supervisors are promoted from within the ranks of the department (with the exception of police chiefs about whom we shall have more to say in the following section), since lateral entry is the exception rather than the rule in U.S. policing. As Bouza (1990: 40–41) notes, there are two ways of shaping supervisory talent: formal education and on-the-job training. For the latter to produce a highly skilled supervisor, a wide variety of experiences (assignments) should be included. Because the police culture largely downplays the importance of theories of management and liberal arts education, on-the-job training becomes critical. However, on-the-job training often fails to provide the breadth of training necessary because the skills of the up-and-coming officer may be so valuable to the chief that he or she comes to rely almost totally on that officer for certain kinds of information or input. Thus, the about-to-be promoted may remain in the same positions for most of their prepromotional careers. This narrow focus makes it difficult for those promoted to understand the broader police picture and leads to scorn on behalf of line officers. Further, the testing procedure itself is almost always suspect from the perspective of both those applying for advancement and those who will be affected by having new supervisors. In short, observers tend to believe that it is who you know, rather than what you know, that leads to promotion.

Advertisements typically consist of position vacancy announcements posted within the police agency. Outside advertisement, while it may sometimes occur, is greatly limited (for example, to other agencies that employ city workers).

Since most police departments retain paramilitary structures, promotional opportunities exist at the level of the field supervisor (typically at the rank of sergeant), shift or watch commander (typically lieutenant or commander rank), division commander (typically with the rank of captain or above), and for a host of specializations in larger departments (juvenile, burglary, fraud, vice, and so on). As is the case at the entry level, the vacancy announcements should clearly state the qualifications for the position in question and indicate how interested parties may go about applying. Individuals applying for these positions are required to pass status tests similar to those discussed for entry-level employees, with the additional stipulation that they have served a specified number of years in policing or at the level immediately below the one for which they are applying. In other words, to become a lieutenant, an officer would have to meet the basic status requirements of the department and, in addition, might be required to have served three years at the rank of sergeant.

Typically, physical tests are not employed in selecting supervisors. The assumption may be that they have already passed tests that the department requires or that the position to which they aspire does not require the same degree of physical agility required of line officers. Neither of these assumptions is entirely justified, however, and some measures of physical fitness appear to be appropriate. At a minimum, a thorough medical examination should be required and proportionate height and weight requirements would appear to be reasonable.

Paper-and-pencil tests are often part of the supervisory selection process, although they have not been demonstrated to be any more successful in predicting success as a supervisor than as an entry-level officer. As a result, another technique known as the assessment center has been used increasingly in recent years.

Assessment Centers

The assessment center had its origins in the military in World War II and the concept was furthered in the 1950s in private industry (Bray et al., 1974). As O'Leary (1989: 28) indicates, prior to the 1970s many police departments promoted people because they had "influential contacts, or did well in objective paper-and-pencil tests, or impressed a civil-service board made up of a variety of people from law-enforcement in neighboring departments, state highway patrol, private-sector managers, and perhaps representatives of the local department of human resources." Such promotions often resulted in ineffective supervisors because the interviewers had an inaccurate picture of the duties and responsibilities accompanying the position. The interview, as a predictive tool, proved to be only marginally effective. Paper-and-pencil tests also turned out to be poor at predicting supervisory performance.

Pynes and Bernardin (1992) found that assessment centers for entry-level police officers predicted both training academy and on-the-job performance, the latter better than paper-and-pencil tests (see Highlight 6.2). They also found that assessment centers had a less adverse impact on blacks and Hispanics than did cognitive paper-and-pencil tests. The assessment center may prove to have these same benefits at the supervisory level.

In order to use the assesment center, there must first be a comprehensive, accurate job description of the position advertised. Second, a group of trained observers (usually three to five) must observe the candidates for the position

---

HIGHLIGHT 6.2   Assessment Centers

The newest selection procedure . . . is called the *assessment center method*. . . . Applicants are required to complete several *performance tests* in which they are expected to demonstrate their ability to perform tasks similar to those actually performed by police officers. The performance tests often take the form of simulated police activities. Other simulations involve situational testing.

An important aspect of the assessment center method is that each applicant is rated not by one evaluator, but by several, and the applicant's final score on performance tests is a composite of the several evaluators' ratings. . . . The idea behind the assessment center method is to treat the applicant as a whole person and to evaluate a number of possible areas of strengths and weaknesses,

rather than merely to set arbitrary pass-or-fail criteria.

The advantage of the assessment center method is that it allows applicants to be rated on their overall performance on both objective tests and situational tests. The use of several evaluators whose ratings are combined in some manner helps to overcome the possibility that a single evaluator might be biased for or against an applicant.

However, the assessment center method is . . . a very costly procedure. The testing process is more time-consuming . . . and requires teams of well-trained evaluators. There are no well-established standards against which to measure the applicant's performance on simulations and situational tests (Stone and DeLuca, 1994: 268–287).

---

as they go through a number of job-related activities. Such activities might include giving an oral presentation; dealing with incoming memos, mail, and phone calls; handling a grievance; fielding questions at a press conference; and so forth. The assessors rate the applicants individually on each of the tasks assigned over a one- or two-day period.

In some cases the applicants' performances are videotaped so they may be reviewed by the assessors at their convenience. Then the candidates are interviewed by the assessors using a standardized format, which, however, provides latitude for assessors to raise questions concerning issues brought to light by the various exercises in which the candidates have engaged.

Finally, the assessors, usually under the direction of a team leader, meet to discuss their scores and impressions of the applicants. Each assessor must be prepared to defend his or her scores, and discrepant scores often become topics of heated debate. In the ideal case, differences can be resolved through discussion, and the applicants are listed in order of the assessors' preferences. Final selection is then made by the personnel department, police chief, city manager, mayor/council, or some combination of these. While the costs of the assessment center are high, success in predicting good performance may be equally high, and, when measured against the costs of making a bad appointment, are less imposing than they might seem.

Polygraph, drug, and psychological tests, as well as updated background investigations, may also be required for promotion. Tests of ability to communicate are incorporated into the assessment center or may be evaluated by an oral board in a fashion similar to that discussed for entry-level personnel.

Evaluations based on past performance are also frequently used when considering applicants for promotion. The usefulness of these measures remains to be established, because they are typically based on behaviors relevant to the current position of the applicant, which may or may not be related to the position for which he or she is applying. That is, excellent performance as a street officer may be totally unrelated to performance as a supervisor. Nonetheless, in many departments, these evaluations account for 20 to 30 percent of the total score considered for promotion.

Recruiting and Selecting Police Chiefs

The skills required of a police chief are, in many instances, significantly different from those required of new recruits or lower-ranking supervisors. The chief not only maintains general control over the department, but is its representative in dealing with other municipal agencies, other police agencies, and elected officials. In some very small departments, the police chief must perform patrol and investigative functions and has few supervisory responsibilities. In police agencies with more than four or five employees, however, administrative and supervisory responsibilities become more important than street work.

Advertising for police chiefs is generally done through professional police publications as well as through the use of area newspapers and bulletins. Recruitment for the position of chief may involve going outside the department, staying within the department, or a combination of the two. Thus, lateral entry, while seldom a possibility at other police ranks, is possible at the level of the chief. Chiefs recruited from outside appear to be better educated, more likely to have held a variety of administrative positions, and have shorter careers than those recruited from inside (Enter, 1986).

The status requirements discussed with respect to other supervisory personnel typically apply, with the number of years of service and the level of police experience required varying greatly across communities. Hiring is done primarily by the mayor or city manager in conjunction with the city council or a committee (police and/or personnel) of the council. Similar to hiring practices for other supervisory personnel, written tests related to administrative and supervisory tasks are often employed and, in addition, attempts may be made to assess the extent to which the candidates view themselves as part of a management team. Educational and training requirements also vary considerably, ranging from high school graduation and basic police training to possession of a master's degree and attendance at one of the more prestigious police management schools (such as the F.B.I. Academy or the Southern Police Institute).

While many chiefs are hired based on interviews with officials of city government, performance on written tests, and background investigations, more and more are being processed through assessment centers designed to test their administrative skills.

The vast majority of police chiefs come from the police ranks and hiring those without prior police experience, though it does occasionally occur, is the exception. Unlike other police personnel, chiefs are seldom required to attend training schools after being hired, although the political and public relations skills required to be successful indicate the need for further training in many, if not most, cases.

Couper and Lobitz (1993: 19) indicate that leadership styles in police agencies must change if the needs of community residents are to be met. "Unfortunately, the dominant model of leadership and management in America—from commando units to retail stores—has been the use of coercion to get the job done. No employee liked to be on the receiving end of that coercion, but most people thought it was the only way to run an organization." Many police chiefs have clearly operated according to this philosophy. (Couper and Lobitz, 1993: 19) Garner (1993: 1) notes some other deficiencies: "Many police administrators become so preoccupied with current problems that they fail to plan for the future. Some do not believe that strategic planning is worth the effort. Others lack the imagination and creativity required to project in the abstract." Such imagination and creativity are clearly required for the transition from traditional policing to community policing, empowerment of police officers and the public, and meeting budgetary and other challenges.

Bouza (1990: 41) perhaps sums up the difficulties in selecting a police chief best: "A chief's selection by the mayor probably accommodates some narrow and probably temporary political objective, which undoubtedly did not include considerations of competence. It is no small wonder that two former chiefs dubbed these chief executives 'fifty-year-old cops' and 'pet rocks.'" While some improvement has occurred in this area, promotion to rank of chief from within undoubtedly contributes to continuing resistance to change in a good many police agencies.

Some chiefs are basically contract chiefs, serving for a specified period of time with periodic reviews at the end of this period. Others are essentially given tenure when hired, though almost all serve at the pleasure of the head of city government and the council, and job security is often a major concern (Frankel, 1992). When the chief reports directly to the mayor/council, political considerations are often extremely important. The city-manager form of government provides some insulation from direct political ties and, from the perspective of promoting a professional, somewhat apolitical department, the latter arrangement is probably superior.

Discussion Questions

1. Why are the costs of recruitment of police personnel so high? How can such costs reasonably be reduced?

2. Why is recruitment of qualified personnel so important to police agencies?

3. Discuss some of the changes in the selection of police officers that have occurred as a result of equal employment opportunity laws and affirmative action pro-

grams. What are some of the positive and negative consequences of EEOC and affirmative action programs?

4. List and discuss the five basic types of police officer selection requirements. How do such requirements apply to promotions?

5. What is an assessment center, why are such centers being used increasingly, and what, if any, disadvantages do they have?

6. What are the backgrounds of most police chiefs and what implications do these backgrounds have for policing as a profession?

7. How do the provisions of the Americans with Disabilities Act affect the police? How do you feel about ADA requirements?

References

Alpert, G.P. and Dunham, R.G. 1988. *Policing Urban America*. Prospect Heights, IL: Waveland.

Ash, P., Slora, K.B., and Britton, C.F. 1990. "Police Agency Officer Selection Practices." *Journal of Police Science and Administration* 17(4), 258–269.

Bell, D. 1992. *Race, Racism and American Law* 3 ed. Boston: Little, Brown.

Benner, A.W. 1989. "Psychological Screening of Police Applicants." In Dunham, R.G. and Alpert, G.P. (eds.), *Critical Issues in Policing: Contemporary Readings*. Prospect Heights, IL: Waveland Press: 72–86.

Berg, B.L. 1992. *Law Enforcement: An Introduction to Police in Society*. Boston: Allyn & Bacon.

Booth, W.S. and Hornick, C.W. 1984. "Physical Ability Testing for Police Officers." *The Police Chief* (January), 39–41.

Bouza, A.V. 1990. *The Police Mystique: An Insider's Look at Cops, Crime, and the Criminal Justice System*. New York: Plenum.

Bray, D.W. et al. 1974. *Formative Years in Business: A Long Term AT & T Study of Managerial Lives*. New York: Wiley Interscience.

Broderick, J.J. 1987. *Police in a Time of Change* 2 ed. Prospect Heights, IL: Waveland Press.

Burbeck, E. and Furnham, A. 1985. "Police Officer Selection: A Critical Review of the Literature." *Journal of Police Science and Administration* 13, 58–69.

Couper, D. and Lobitz, S. 1993. "Leadership for Change: A National Agenda." *The Police Chief* 60(12), 15–19.

Cox, S.M. and Fitzgerald, J.D. 1991. *Police in Community Relations: Critical Issues* 2 ed. Dubuque, IA: Wm. C. Brown.

Dwyer, W.O., Prien, E.P., and Bernard, J.L. 1990. "Psychological Screening of Law Enforcement Officers: A Case for Job Relatedness." *Journal of Police Science and Administration* 17(3), 176–182.

Enter, J.E. 1986. "The Rise to the Top: An Analysis of Police Chief Career Patterns." *Journal of Police Science and Administration* (14)4, 334–346.

Falkenberg, S., Gaines, L.K., and Cox, T.C. 1990. "The Oral Interview Board: What Does It Measure?" *Journal of Police Science and Administration* 17(1), 32–39.

Ferguson, R. 1987. "Pre-screening of Police Applicants." *The Chief of Police* 2(1), 6.

Frankel, B. 1992. "Police Chiefs Worry About Job Security." *USA TODAY* (19 November), p. 10A.

Gaines, L.K. and Kappeler, V.E. 1992. "Selection and Testing." In Cordner, G.W. and Hale, D.C. eds. *What Works in Policing? Operations and Administration Examined*. Cincinnati: ACJS/Anderson.

Gaines, L.K., Kappeler, V.E., and Vaughn, J.B. 1994. *Policing in America*. Cincinnati: Anderson.

Garner, R. 1993. "Leadership in the Nineties." *FBI Law Enforcement Bulletin* 62(12), 1–4.

Gest, T. 1987. "A One-White, One-Black Quota for Promotions." *U.S. News and World Report* (March), 8.

Goldstein, H. 1977. *Policing a Free Society.* Cambridge, MA: Ballinger.

Gray, T.C. 1975. "Selecting for a Police Subculture." In Skolnick, J. and Gray, T.C. (eds.), *Police in America.* Boston: Little, Brown, 46–54.

Hiatt, D. and Hargrave, G.E. 1988. "Predicting Job Performance Problems with Psychological Screening." *Journal of Police Science and Administration* 16(1), 122–125.

Higginbotham, J. 1991. "The Americans with Disabilities Act." *FBI Law Enforcement Bulletin* (August), 25–32.

Holden, R.N. and Gammeltoft, L.L. 1991. "*Toonen v. Brown County:* The Legality of Police Vision Standards." *American Journal of Police* 10(1), 59–66.

Horvath, F. 1989. "Polygraph." In Bailey, W.G. (ed.), *The Encyclopedia of Police Science.* New York: Garland, 507–511.

McCormack, W.U. 1994. "Grooming and Weight Standards for Law Enforcement: The Legal Issues." *FBI Law Enforcement Bulletin* 63(7), 27–31.

McEwen, J.T., Manili, B., and Connors, J. 1986. "Employee Drug Testing Policies in Police Departments." *Research in Brief.* (October) National Institute of Justice. Washington, DC: U.S. Government Printing Office.

Meier, R.D., Farmer, R.E., and Maxwell, D. 1987. "Psychological Screening of Police Candidates: Current Perspectives." *Journal of Police Science and Administration* 15(3), 210–215.

O'Leary, L. R. 1989. "Assessment Centers." In Bailey, W. G. (ed.), *The Encyclopedia of Police Science.* New York: Garland Press.

Pendergrass, V.E. 1987. "Psychological Assessment of Police for Entry-Level Selection." *The Chief of Police* 11(1), 8–14.

Pugh, G. 1985. "Situation Tests and Police Selection." *Journal of Police Science and Administration* 13(1), 30–35.

Pynes, J. and Bernardin, H.J. 1992. "Entry-level Police Selection: The Assessment Center is an Alternative." *Journal of Criminal Justice.* 20(1), 41–52.

Rubin, P.N. 1993. "The Americans with Disabilities Act and Criminal Justice: An Overview." *Research in Action.* (September) National Institute of Justice. Washington, DC: U.S. Government Printing Office.

Roberg, R.R. and Kuykendall, L. 1990. *Police Organization and Management.* Pacific Grove, CA: Brooks/Cole.

Schneid, T.D. and Gaines, L.K. 1991. "The Americans with Disabilities Act: Implications for Police Administrators." *American Journal of Police* 10(1), 47–58.

Stone, A. and DeLuca, S. 1985. *Police Administration.* New York: Wiley.

Stone, A.R. and DeLuca, S.M. 1994. *Police Administration: An Introduction* 2 ed. Englewood Cliffs, NJ: Prentice-Hall, 268–287.

Sullivan, P.S. 1989. "Minority Officers: Current Issues." In Dunham, R. G. and Alpert, G. P. (eds.), *Critical Issues in Policing: Contemporary Readings.* Prospect Heights, IL: Waveland Press: 331–345.

Swanson, C.R., Territo, L., and Taylor, R.W. 1988. *Police Administration* 2 ed. New York: Macmillan.

U.S. Department of Justice. 1992. "Drug Enforcement by Police and Sheriff's Departments, 1990." *Bureau of Justice Statistics Bulletin* (May). Washington, DC: U.S. Government Printing Office.

Van, J. 1986. "1 in 3 Police Candidates Found to Use Drugs." *Chicago Tribune* (17 February), pp. 1, 5.

Willman, M.T. and Snortum, J.R. 1984. "Detective Work: The Criminal Investigation Process in a Medium-Size Police Department." *Criminal Justice Review* 9(1), 33–39.

Winters, C.A. 1992. "Socio-Economic Status, Test Bias, and the Selection of Police." *Police Journal* 65(2), 125–135.

Wright, B.S., Doerner, W.G., and Speir, J.C. 1990. "Pre-employment Psychological Testing as a Predictor of Police Performance During an FTO Program." *American Journal of Police* 9(4), 65–84.

7

POLICE TRAINING AND EDUCATION

The extent and nature of police training and education have been controversial issues since at least 1908 when August Vollmer began formal training for police officers. Although the two issues are closely interrelated, they are distinct and we will address them separately in this chapter.

One of the most frequently debated issues concerning the police revolves around the distinction between training and education. While there is clearly a good deal of overlap, training may be regarded as the provision of basic skills necessary to do the job, and education may be viewed as providing familiarity with the concepts and principles underlying the training. From this perspective, training is more concrete and practical, education more abstract and theoretical. The discussion that follows is based on these distinctions, although the reader should note that there is no absolute agreement concerning the distinctions made.

Police Training

Policing is a difficult and complex career. The police officer is called on to play psychiatrist, doctor, lawyer, judge, juror, priest, counselor, fighter, and dog catcher. The training requirements to become a police officer have long been neglected, however. "Police officers must be experts in interpersonal communications, possess intimate knowledge of counseling and crisis intervention strategies, and be able to defuse potentially volatile domestic disturbances. Yet the time allotted to these topics in my police academy is a paltry seven hours total. . . . Police officers . . . can and do make decisions to arrest and restrict a person's freedom, and the power of life and death is literally at their fingertips, but on the average they receive less than one-quarter of the training required to give someone a haircut" (Nowicki, 1990b: 4).

Police administrators and the governmental bodies they represent spend millions of dollars on training personnel. There is no longer any debate whether training for police officers should be mandatory, both to improve their performance and as protection against liability that may result from failure to train (Phillips, 1988). Inadequate or inappropriate training can lead to poor decision making, too much or too little self-confidence, and inaccurate assessments of situations (Graves, 1991: 62). How much training should be done, though? Who should do it? What should the content of the training be? The form? How can training best be used to benefit officers and the citizens they serve? How effective is the training received? Answers to these questions are not always easily found, but they are essential if our goal is to develop highly trained, competent police officers.

How Much Training Is Enough?

Simply put, police officers can never have enough training and training is, therefore, a career-long commitment. This observation is based on the assumption that the world is constantly changing and that police officers must respond to that changing world. Consider the recent concern among police personnel with communicable diseases resulting largely from the recognition of AIDS. How many officers annually contract AIDS in the performance of their duties? How does infection occur? How can it best be prevented? These questions are all extremely pertinent when you consider that just over 10 years ago we were training police officers in mouth-to-mouth resuscitation techniques without the aid of plastic airways and unprotected pressure point strategies to control bleeding. Similarly, there was little concern about contamination by bodily fluids found at crime scenes or in the handling of drug paraphernalia. Today our thinking about these issues and events has changed dramatically, and practically every patrol car is equipped with plastic airways and latex gloves. Further, with the passage of the Americans with Disabilities Act in 1990, those with AIDS or HIV cannot be excluded from police work if they are otherwise qualified, raising the possibility of contagion from within (Blumberg, 1993). The concern over protecting themselves from contamination is apparent in the vast majority of police officers. Both as a cause and result of these concerns, communicable disease policies are now part of most policy manuals and most departments have offered training in proper techniques to avoid infection.

So much is happening so rapidly that no one can possibly keep up with the changes in technology and theory. Only proper training and education (as we shall see later in this chapter) can keep police officers current. This is indicated by the increase in the use of computers for communications, forensics, crime analysis, and so on. The need for training pervades all levels of police agencies. Unfortunately, many police administrators fail to take advantage of training opportunities because of busy schedules, lack of interest, or the mistaken belief that they already know all there is to know. A frequently heard comment in training sessions is, "I wish the chief could hear this." A police administrator who wants a well-trained department must send the message that training is important in a variety of ways, including at least his or her own occasional attendance at training sessions.

It is important to note that a number of states now mandate training both at the entry level and on a continuing basis. Peace Officer Standards and Training Commissions now operate in all states prescribing and supervising training for police officers; the National Association of State Directors of Law Enforcement Training (NASDLET) was established in 1970 to provide a mechanism for sharing information and innovation in the field of police training.

Types of Training

Basic Recruit Training

Most new police recruits attend police training institutes or academies. Such training is referred to as basic or recruit training and consists of (roughly in order of the amount of time spent on each): patrol techniques and criminal investigation, force and weaponry, legal issues, administration, communications, criminal justice systems, and human relations (see Table 7.1). A 1986 survey of state

TABLE 7.1   Requirements for Police Entry-Level Training Programs by Type of Competency Area and State, as of December 1985 (in Hours)

State	Total number of hours required	Human relations	Force and weaponry	Communi-cations	Legal	Patrol and criminal investi-gations	Criminal justice systems	Adminis-tration
Hawaii	954	17	153	65	133	444	29	113
Rhode Island	661	42	65	0	48	480	0	26
Vermont	553	4	80	30	74	330	3	32
Maine	504	27	62	17	73	277	21	27
West Virginia	495	14	98	20	120	195	36	12
Pennsylvania	480	76	88	10	94	196	16	0
Maryland	471	0	0	0	73	366	0	32
Massachusetts	460	35	132	28	90	167	8	0
Utah	450	19	73	27	49	247	15	20
Connecticut	443	23	48	8	64	284	11	5
Indiana	440	21	73	4	83	192	32	35
Michigan	440	9	105	8	48	244	0	26
Washington	440	34	152	24	85	145	0	0
New Hampshire	426	20	75	8	60	205	8	50
New Mexico	421	30	69.5	18	56	238.5	9	0
Arizona	400	24	110	16	78	135	12	25
California	400	15	80	15	60	185	10	35
Iowa	400	33	75	12	44	175	13	48
Kentucky	400	6.5	84.5	3.5	75.5	182.5	6	41.5
South Carolina	382	18	77	12	72	178	2	23
Texas	381	14	48	18	68	233	0	0
North Carolina	369	28	64	20	72	170	0	15
Delaware	362	12	64	17	87	174	6	2
Montana	346	22	77.5	14	19.5	183.5	15	14.5
Nebraska	341	36	58	10	62	158	2	15
Colorado	334	19	55	22	79	141	18	0
Florida	320	24	39	18	54	158	9	18
Kansas	320	34	42	20	45	170	1	8
Mississippi	320	8	70	20	50	153	7	12
Wyoming	320	10	71	14	53	119	33	20
North Dakota	313	10	23	20	84	139	16	21
Idaho	310	0	47	9	51	169	16	18
New Jersey	310	26	40	13	49	116	17	49
Arkansas	304	14	60	6	19	190	0	15
New York	285	9	38	7	44	169	10	8
Alabama	280	14	49	8	48	138	3	20
Ohio	280	16	42	10	76	111	20	5
Oregon	280	14	64	12	62	104	8	16

TABLE 7.1 *Continued*

State	Total number of hours required	Human relations	Force and weaponry	Communi-cations	Legal	Patrol and criminal investi-gations	Criminal justice systems	Adminis-tration
Alaska	276	1	20	7	74	139	13	22
Georgia	240	18	45	5	47	110	2	13
Louisiana	240	16	57	8	36	78	5	40
Tennessee	240	2	50	7	31	136	8	6
Wisconsin	240	18	30	9	16	121	10	36
Nevada	200	8	28	11	46	96	2	9
South Dakota	200	17	32	8	22	109	6	6
Missouri	120	3	23	10	28	55	1	0

The header spans: Competency area covers Human relations, Force and weaponry, Communications, Legal, Patrol and criminal investigations, Criminal justice systems, Administration.

Source: Robert J. Meadows, "An Assessment of Police Entry Level Training in the United States: Conformity or Conflict with the Police Role?" Boone, NC: Appalachian State University, 1985. (Mimeographed.) Table 11. Table adapted by SOURCEBOOK staff. *Sourcebook for Criminal Justice Statistics,* 1986. Used with permission.

Note: These data were obtained through a mail survey of law enforcement training directors. Oklahoma, Illinois, Virginia, and Minnesota were omitted from the study due to incomplete data regarding their curriculum content. Each State mandates the minimum hourly requirements reported above, but police agencies within each State may establish entry-level training in addition to State requirements.

"Human relations" training stresses the development of the whole person in dealing with the problems of society. Training involves subjects such as human relations, crisis intervention, and stress awareness. "Force and weaponry" involves the development of skills in the use of firearms, chemical agents, hand to hand combat, and other measures of physical force. "Communications" is the development of interpersonal skills for conducting interviews and interrogations: included in this category are report writing, basic training in grammar, spelling, and body language. "Legal" training encompasses criminal law, rules of evidence, basic Constitutional law, laws of arrest, search and seizure, civil rights, and liability. "Patrol and criminal investigation" training focuses on patrol techniques and procedures, defensive driving, basic criminal investigation, emergency medical aid, traffic control, physical fitness, accident investigation, jail/custody procedures, and other technical competencies. "Criminal justice systems" training stresses the knowledge needed for understanding the criminal justice system; included in this area are corrections and courts, and professional conduct and ethics. "Administration" covers training matters related to the use of equipment, basic orientation to the training program, and diagnostic testing and/or examination time (pp. 8–10).

and municipal police agencies (in cities with at least 50,000 population) indicated that the mean (average) length of basic training was 13.5 weeks or 541.5 hours (Sapp, 1986: 62). In none of these academies does the amount of time spent on human/community relations exceed 10 percent, although the vast majority of a police officer's time is spent in encounters/duties requiring skills in these areas.

Field Training
Although the information provided in basic training academies is crucial, there is often a considerable gap between what is taught and what actually occurs on the streets. In a very real sense, academy training is simply a preparatory step to on-the-job or field training. The first opportunity to practice what

the recruit has been taught comes during the first year to eighteen months of service, often referred to as the "probationary period." During this period, new officers are or should be involved in field training under the supervision of field training officers (FTOs) who have been selected and trained to direct, evaluate, and correct the performance of recruits. Such programs have become widespread since their inception in San Jose, California, in 1972. They provide for the daily evaluation of recruits' performance by two or more FTOs as well as for weekly or monthly evaluations by other supervisory personnel. The programs are typically divided into introductory, training, and evaluation phases. If the recruit successfully completes these phases, he or she becomes a full-fledged police officer at the end of the probationary period. Remedial training is provided if required. If remedial training fails to produce the desired results, FTO evaluations may serve as a basis for terminating undesirable or ineffective personnel. Formalized field training programs make it easier for both the FTOs and the recruit to assess progress. Since each recruit has two or more FTOs during the course of the training, the possibility of personality conflicts or bias leading to unfair judgments is reduced (McCambell, 1986). As Nowicki (1990a: 34) indicates, FTOs are no longer "macho" types, although certain physical and survival skills remain important. Good FTOs teach their trainees how to recognize and effectively deal with problems in ways other than the use of physical force. Trained FTOs know that an officer's verbalizations should be used to avoid problems rather than create them.

In-Service Training

Most police personnel receive periodic in-service training provided either by department personnel, training consultants hired by the department, or regional or local training boards. While most departments offer occasional in-service training, many conduct it on a hit-and-miss basis with no real plan or program in mind. Further, it is sometimes viewed as a necessary evil both by those conducting it and those being trained, rather than as a valuable means of keeping current in the field. It appears that supervisory personnel are unlikely to participate in such training unless specifically required to do so. As a result, many are not as up-to-date as they could be; this is frequently noticed and commented on by patrol personnel.

In order to help remedy some of the problems associated with in-service training, some states have developed mobile training units responsible for planning and providing training within specified geographic areas on a regular basis. These training units frequently arrange training at different locales within their territories in order to make it easier for police personnel from rural areas and small towns to attend. Unfortunately, budgetary cutbacks (and in some instances union contracts) have made it increasingly difficult for departments to release personnel to attend such training.

Other Types of Training

Selected police personnel have the opportunity to participate in longer, more intensive training offered by a variety of training institutes around the country.

Among the more popular of these training groups are the Northwestern Traffic Institute, the Southern Police Institute, and the F.B.I. National Academy, all of which offer courses ranging in length from a week to several months. Courses offered by these institutions cover topics ranging from traffic investigation to executive management. At California's Command College, future concerns of police officers and agencies are addressed. The college opened in 1984 and covers topics such as "Defining the Future," "Human Resource Management," and "Handling Conflict." Controversial topics and ideas are discussed and alternatives to traditional policing are outlined (Lieberman, 1990).

"Operation Bootstrap," which began in 1985, arranges tuition-free corporate management training programs for police administrators and officers. With support from private foundations and the National Institute for Justice, the program now extends into forty states, offering state-of-the-art management training programs ranging in length from one day to one week and covering subjects ranging from effective supervision techniques to conflict resolution to stress management. While formal evaluation of the program has yet to be conducted, strong support has been expressed by those who have attended the programs (Bruns, 1989).

In many instances, these longer training courses are offered to senior-level personnel as a reward for longevity rather than to personnel in positions in which they could make active use of the information provided. In addition, much of the information provided during these courses remains locked in the minds of those who attend rather than being disseminated to others in the department through in-service training sessions designed to make the information accessible to others.

All training should be interrelated. Those with specialty skills need to update these skills on a continuing basis and can share these skills with others through in-service training. This sharing will be effective, however, only when it includes supervisory personnel who may otherwise find the disseminated concepts difficult to understand and continue to operate using outdated information. Again, the commitment to training must come from the top, along with the recognition that training is one of the few forms of recognition available to police personnel. Selection on the basis of merit for a specialized training course conducted at the department's expense is a rewarding experience, as is recognition of an officer's ability to train others. Without such recognition, training may be viewed in an unfavorable light.

Training and Police Leaders

None of the subjects dealt with in training seminars is static; each one is constantly changing, and what we knew to be true yesterday may turn out to be myth tomorrow (Bracey, 1990b). One way of determining the value police supervisors attach to training is to examine the extent to which they subject themselves to it. Currently, many supervisors (including chiefs) avoid training and rationalize their absences by pointing out the demands on their time in terms of meetings, planning, administrative chores, and bureaucratic requirements. In reality, the absence of police supervisors from training sessions may have more to do with other factors. Why should those at the top sacrifice their time and energy to attend training when those still striving for such positions may benefit more? Bracey (1990b) believes it is unhealthy for the functioning or morale of an organization if the people at the top cannot communicate in an informed and sophisticated manner about concepts and ideas suggested by those who work for them due to their education and training. It is clearly very frustrating, then, to return from a period of training and education with an idea that seems ideal for implementation in one's own organization, only to be misunderstood or ignored by supervisors.

Last, but not least, police executives often like to operate as if they were omniscient, with no need for additional information. Related to this may be doubts about how well he or she will perform in the classroom. What if he or she appears ill-informed before classmates, including subordinates? What if the police executives' contributions to the training session are not appreciated or well received? What if his or her performance is exceeded by that of other, lower-ranking trainees? While these concerns are real, they should be worth risking in order to demonstrate that training is not a frill, or a superficial symbol of the progressive nature of the organization but a valued, ongoing part of that organization.

Training Effectiveness

The effects of training are relatively easy to determine but are infrequently properly assessed by police agencies. Does training provide useful information? Did those attending understand the material presented? The answers to these questions lie in a simple evaluation process that is too often neglected because of the assumption that the information provided is understandable and absorbed. The only way to assess the value of training is to conduct routine evaluations. Ideally, such evaluations would include a pretest of attendees' knowledge of the material to be presented and a posttest of such knowledge.

If the training is presented in understandable fashion and is relevant to the needs of the attendees, the posttest should show some increase in knowledge and understanding. If no such increase is observed, the training may be too basic, the material presented irrelevant to the officers attending, the method of presentation inappropriate, or the trainees either unable or unwilling to benefit from the training. No difference between pre- and posttest scores should lead to further investigation to determine and correct the problems. Failure to evaluate training leads to a waste of training resources. Too often, a simple after-the-fact evaluation of the trainer, training, and/or training facilities by participants is conducted instead of attempting to evaluate the actual effect of the training.

Content of Training

The content of police training, of course, varies with time, place, type of personnel involved, subject matter, and training goals established. As Alpert and

Dunham (1992: 52) point out, training thought to be important for the police during the 1960s may be irrelevant or unnecessary in the 1990s. In general, however, it may be said that content should be relevant to the needs of trainees, timely, well organized, and clearly presented. When these requirements are met, trainees can best appreciate the value of the training. It is imperative that the information conveyed in training sessions be current and accurately conveyed. The range of subjects that may be covered in training sessions is limited only by the imaginations of planners and presenters.

Purposes of Training

A basic purpose of training is to keep police personnel up-to-date with respect to important changes in the profession. In a larger sense, however, the purposes of training depend on the way in which the role of the police is defined. In the 1960s and 1970s, crime fighting and law enforcement were emphasized and, to some extent, many officers still view these aspects of the police role as the most important part of police work. As a result, training courses dealing with survival techniques, patrol techniques, criminal investigation, use of force, and the law are among the most popular courses; it is typically easy to recruit officers for courses dealing with these issues.

However, in the 1990s we have come to recognize that while law enforcement and crime fighting are critical parts of the police role, they are not the most important in terms of time spent or citizen satisfaction. As we have seen (Chapter 2), police personnel spend the majority of their time negotiating settlements between spouses, lovers, or neighbors and providing other services that have little or nothing to do with law enforcement. As buffers between aggrieved parties, police personnel need to develop skills in this area. Successful intervention into the daily lives of citizens requires such skills, as well as cooperation on the part of the nonpolice citizens involved. Increasingly then, communication skills (both verbal and nonverbal) and human/community/minority relations skills are emerging as among the most important assets of a competent, effective police officer.

Where are these skills to be learned, though? Many police training programs pay little attention to the importance of developing effective communication skills, and many police administrators assume that officers' communication skills will develop as they gain experience. Without formal training, however, officers can learn only from the examples set by others, which may or may not be appropriate (Pritchett, 1993: 25).

A look at basic training curricula indicates that little emphasis is placed on these skills in that setting. Yet, communicating with others in the process of negotiating is what police officers do most often. Some police officers have excellent skills in these areas, others practically none. The importance of these skills is most clearly illustrated by focusing on those officers who lack them. Such officers are unlikely to get cooperation from diverse segments of the public, either because they alienate other citizens by assuming an authoritative stance as a defense for their poor communications skills, or because they cannot express clearly and convincingly what they want or need the public to do. They receive little input from the public about crime or their own performances. They routinely enforce the law in an attempt to maintain order when their more skilled colleagues could have maintained order without resorting to arrest. They become unnecessarily involved in physical encounters (Reiss, 1971; Pritchett, 1993). They create numerous and constant headaches for their superiors, or, if they are supervisors, for those who work for them.

Training in communications, human relations, minority relations, analysis of encounters, and negotiating is available, but, while more popular than a decade or two ago, such training is often not well attended unless officers are required to be present. Typically, officers who are forced to attend such training fail to see the benefits that may accrue. Such benefits are present, of course, whether a crime is being investigated (interviewing and interrogation skills), a police action is being questioned by the public (public relations), orders or directives are involved (departmental policies cannot be successfully implemented unless they are understood), or evaluations or promotions are involved (both require clear communication between those being evaluated/promoted and those doing the evaluating/promoting).

Such skills are also at a premium when the police are trying to educate the public, whether about crime prevention programs, new police policies, proper complaint procedures, or other issues. Such training is increasingly being recognized as a major aspect of the police role. Finally, not least important, communication skills are critical when the police are training their own (Pritchett, 1993; Overton and Black, 1994).

One of the major purposes of police training, then, is to make better communicators of the public servants responsible for maintaining order. Courses dealing with both verbal and nonverbal communication should be required of all police personnel. It is also possible, however, to improve communication skills regardless of the specific content of the training. Any topic can be presented in an organized fashion that requires feedback from the participants. Dealing with that feedback can help participants learn to express themselves more clearly as well as to be better listeners. Police officers who are trained to express themselves clearly and to be good listeners are likely to be better at both order maintenance and law enforcement.

Who Should Do Police Training?

Based on the information contained in the preceding discussion, it is clear that police trainers come from diverse backgrounds. Certainly police officers themselves may be trainers when they have both information to share and the skills to present the information. Let us be clear that these are two separate, equally important requirements. It does little good to use an expert in any area as a trainer unless he or she has good communication skills. Similarly, it does little good to have an expert communicator present useless (out-of-date or irrelevant) information. Both extremes are found in the arena of police training. When an in-service or retired officer meets both requirements of a trainer, he or she often has a significant advantage over other trainers, provided the material presented requires an understanding of the police world. While others may have such understanding, the fact that the trainer is or has been a police officer often heightens his or her credibility among police personnel.

It is essential, however, that police training also be conducted by those outside the profession for two important reasons. First, many of the skills required of police officers are not frequently found among police officers. Skills needed to set up and run a computer software package, analyze interaction patterns, and prevent infection resulting from communicable diseases are only a few examples. Second, relying only on those within the profession for training typically leads to a myopic world view that serves to isolate members from the rest of society and the police can ill afford further isolation. Who should train the police? Those meeting the requirements outlined above, regardless of the area of their expertise, are the most qualified. Trainers may include police officers, physicians, computer experts, self-defense experts, college professors, members of minority groups, and business leaders, to name just a few. In general, the broader the spectrum of qualified trainers and the greater the exposure to different skills the more useful the training will be (Marsh and Grosskopf, 1991).

It has been suggested that police training must be viewed positively within the police community; this is difficult to accomplish because police training has few easily measurable results. The effect of training is often measured in terms of the numbers of hours or programs attended annually, but what happens when the number of hours or programs is cut? There is typically no measurable effect since training often does not result in clearly measurable end products. Thus, training is relatively easy to eliminate in times of budgetary cuts. In order for training to gain and maintain a degree of importance, it must be shown that resources expended for training lead to positive results for both the police and the community they serve.

According to The Nationwide Law Enforcement Training Needs Assessment Project, areas in which such results might be attained include, among others, the following:

1. Handling personal stress
2. Maintaining physical fitness
3. Conducting interviews and interrogations
4. Procedures related to evidence collecting and preserving
5. Emergency and pursuit driving
6. Promoting a positive police image
7. Testifying in court
8. Report writing
9. Effective supervisory procedures
10. Handling domestic violence situations (Phillips, 1988: 12)

Further, alternate means of delivering training need to be developed in order to make more training available to more officers on a cost-effective basis. Along these lines, training videos and satellite broadcasting have emerged during the past decade. Both media have the potential to reach large, widely scattered groups of police personnel and, in some formats at least, still allow for interaction between trainers and trainees through the use of direct telephone communication between the two.

Yet another innovation in police training involves the use of job analysis and assessment centers. The former enables trainers to determine the nature of the skills required for performance of specified jobs, while the latter enables trainers or administrators to measure what trainees learn through the use of situational and written tests and oral presentations covering one or more areas in which training has been provided (Mullins, 1985).

Mentoring is another means of assisting police training. Experienced officers with proven skills in specific areas are assigned (or volunteer for) the task of sharing their expertise with other officers. Mentors demonstrate the skills involved, answer questions, provide instruction, and regularly assess the progress of their students (Marsh and Grosskopf, 1991: 65).

In the next decade, two major aspects of police training clearly require further assessment. First, further study of the relationship between training and job performance is necessary. Second, more comprehensive and timely training for those wishing to fill supervisory roles must be made available. Over the past two decades, the value of traditional police training techniques—verbal harassment, harsh criticism, physical activity as punishment—have been called into question. Techniques that build self-esteem and motivate recruits are more appropriate to applicants seeking challenge, participation in decision making, and career development (Post, 1992). While advances in training techniques have been made in the past decade, many questions remain to be answered, and the impact of training on the job has yet to be clarified.

Police Education

One of the most popular proposals for improving the quality of policing in the United States has focused on better educated officers. The idea that a college-educated police officer would be a better police officer spawned a federal program (LEAA) that provided millions of dollars annually in support of such education, a dramatic increase in the numbers of college programs related to policing, and an increase in the number of police officers with at least some college education (Carter and Sapp, 1992). The debate over the importance of police education continues, federal funding for such education has diminished considerably, new federal programs are being proposed, and there are continuing concerns over the content and quality of police education (see Highlights 7.1 and 7.2).

Many of the current concerns surrounding police education result from our inability or unwillingness to decide exactly what we want the police to be and

---

HIGHLIGHT 7.1　Is a College Degree Needed for Police Work?

Douglas Hinkle, an auxiliary member of the Essex County, Virginia, Sheriff's Department, argues that a college degree is an impractical prerequisite for police work. "We are speaking here of the growth in belief that police officers of the future should have a college degree. . . . The real question is: is the additional training, and attendant expense, commensurate with the demands of the street? Or with the benefits derived? . . . Requiring a college degree as a prerequisite to police work is impractical in the extreme. It fails to answer the basic question. Would a degree help in the preponderance of situations a street officer has to face? . . . A college degree would certainly not be a detriment to a cop. But would it justify the time and expense needed to obtain it? . . . Many officers hold college degrees and even Ph.D.'s. I respect and admire them, and I insist that formal education no doubt helps. Yet it is my belief that these officers would be good cops with or without advanced education. . . . A good cop must have certain attributes—compassion, courage, self-confidence, intelligence, a sense of humor, and a feeling for right and wrong. A college degree is not among them" (Hinkle, 1991: 105).

Reprinted with permission of *Law and Order*.

HIGHLIGHT 7.2　The Future of Police Education and Training

Dorothy Bracey of John Jay College, in discussing the preparation of future police leaders, emphasizes a number of important points. "To work successfully in an environment in constant flux calls for the command of a large body of information; the learning skills that make it possible to add to that body continuously and relevantly; the ability to analyze and synthesize, induce and deduce; a copious amount of self-knowledge; and the self-confidence that permits a novel situation to be faced with determination and zest, rather than with the hope that if it is ignored, it will go away." Bracey goes on to indicate that training and education in areas such as language, culture, and technology are critical for effective administration of justice. "(But) most important, all members of the system must be constantly reminded that none of these subjects, once learned, stays learned forever. Each one is constantly changing and yesterday's knowledge is tomorrow's myth. . . . Certainly institutions of tertiary education must be heavily involved, in providing lecturers and researchers for in-house training, for the development of diploma and degree programs, and for admitting members of the justice system into lectures, programs, and events that would be valuable even if not obviously related to justice administration. . . . If career-long education and training are to contribute all they can to the process of doing justice, they cannot be treated as a frill or as a symbol to demonstrate the enlightened and progressive nature of the organization. They must be systematically planned . . . they must have proper financial support. . . . Effective participation must be a prerequisite to recognition and advancement . . . " (Bracey, 1990b).

Reprinted with permission.

do in our society. It is extremely difficult to develop courses and curricula for the police under these circumstances. Some believe that liberal arts courses provide the best background for police officers in a multi-ethnic/cultural society, others are convinced that specialized courses in criminal justice are preferable, while still others question the value of college education for police officers. In spite of these continuing concerns, the number of programs in criminal justice and related areas increased dramatically in the 1970s.

Broderick (1987: 217) notes, for example, that criminal justice education grew rapidly in the early 1970s so that by 1976 there were 699 colleges and universities offering over 1,200 degree programs, ranging from the associate to the doctorate. Many of these programs, however, were of poor quality, consisting of "war stories" and technical and vocational training. Data collected in 1985 indicated that many in academia still perceived criminal justice education as being basically technical or vocational training, often taught by faculty without proper credentials. Carter and Sapp (1992: 14) conclude that this remains a problem in the 1990s.

Types of Police Education

Assuming that higher education for police officers is desirable, what type of education provides the best background? One survey of police departments serving cities with populations of 50,000 or more found that about half of all police executives who responded prefer to hire officers who have majored in criminal justice (Carter and Sapp, 1992). A similar number indicated no preference in college degrees/majors. Those who preferred criminal justice majors did so because of the graduates' knowledge of policing and criminal justice, while those stating no preference indicated they preferred a broader education to prepare officers to deal with a wide variety of situations, including those not dealing with law enforcement.

The same study indicated a general perception among police executives that colleges and universities do not have curricula that meet the contemporary needs of law enforcement agencies. While the respondents found that criminal justice graduates are knowledgeable about the criminal justice system and policing in general, they are often "narrow in ideology" and lack the broader understanding of divergent cultures and social issues confronting the police. These executives do not want colleges and universities to teach police skills but are seeking graduates who can integrate the duties of a police officer with an understanding of democratic values (Carter and Sapp, 1992). The consensus is that liberal arts curricula should be part of college/university criminal justice programs. Many respondents noted that a quality education is needed, particularly in the area of communications skills. Other areas perceived as requiring greater attention include critical thinking, decision making, research, ability to integrate, and understanding of diverse cultures. Finally, the police executives saw a lack of communication between colleges and universities and police agencies, with less than 25 percent indicating they were regularly consulted by these institutions and more than a fourth indicating they were never consulted about issues of common interest. The authors conclude:

> *The results of this national study suggest that colleges and universities should be developing policies, changing and modifying curricula, and focusing on providing the educational background needed by students and society. Criminal justice educators must introspectively give detailed attention to curricula to ensure that today's curricula fit today's needs in law enforcement and other areas of the criminal justice system (Sapp, Carter and Stephens, 1989: 5).*

Police Educational Requirements

In the survey conducted by Sapp, Carter, and Stephens (1989) for the Police Executive Research Forum, only about 14 percent of the responding agencies reported requiring any college at all and less than 1 percent required a bachelor's degree. Yet, almost two thirds of these agencies had some form of educational incentive program. This apparent discrepancy appears to be due in part to a belief among agency officials that higher education requirements could be effectively challenged in the courts or in contract negotiations. This belief is based on concerns about possible discrimination against minorities and the difficulty in demonstrating that higher education is a *bona fide* job requirement for police personnel (Sapp, Carter, and Stephens, 1988: 1; Carter and Sapp, 1992: 11).

As a result, it appears that while many departments do in fact give preference to recruits with college educations, few are willing to make college education a formal requirement. This conclusion is supported by the fact that the mean educational level of police officers, as determined by this survey of over 250,000 officers, is 13.6 years as compared to 12.4 years in 1967. The authors conclude that in light of the fact that some departments require college education as a condition of initial employment and the willingness of the courts to uphold college education as a requirement in at least some cases, it is possible to establish a "defensible college education entrance requirement for employment" (and, for that matter, for promotion) in law enforcement (Sapp, Carter, and Stephens, 1988: 23; Carter and Sapp, 1992: 11). The college requirement would mean developing a policy outlining the rationale for the requirement by individual police agencies desiring to implement educational requirements.

Facts in support of such a rationale are available, although they may be more qualitative than quantitative. In the case of *Davis v. Dallas*, the U. S. Supreme Court allowed the Dallas Police Department's 45-semester-hour college requirement for entry-level officers to stand *(Davis v. City of Dallas, 1986)*. Other police departments, such as San Jose, California, and Lakewood, Colorado, have had long-standing entry-level educational requirements as well; numerous other court decisions support educational requirements for the police (Scott, 1986).

College Education and Police Performance

It has been argued by some that police work, especially at the local level, does not require a formal education beyond high school because such tasks as directing traffic, writing parking tickets, conducting permit inspections, and performing clerical tasks do not require higher education. In addition, it has been suggested that a highly intelligent and well-educated person would soon become bored with these mundane and repetitive tasks and either resign or remain and become either an ineffective member of the force or a malcontent (Swanson, Territo, and Taylor, 1988: 211–212).

Others have argued that the complex role of policing a multiethnic, culturally diverse society requires nothing less than a college degree as a condition of initial employment for police officers (National Advisory Commission on Criminal Justice Standards and Goals, 1973; Carter and Sapp, 1992).

In a review of the evidence on the relationship between higher education and police performance, Hayeslip (1989: 49) highlights the assumed benefits of college education for police officers: greater motivation, more ability to utilize innovative techniques, clearer thinking, better understanding of the occupation/profession, and so on. Based on the studies reviewed, Hayeslip concludes that education and police performance are consistently related, though the relationship is moderate.

Sherman and Blumberg (1981) found no consistent relationship between educational level and police use of deadly force. Daniels (1982), examining the relationship between educational level and absenteeism among police personnel, found that employees without college degrees missed more than three times as many work days through unscheduled absences as those with a four-year degree.

Griffin (1980) found an inverse relationship between educational levels of patrol officers and performance ratings, but a significant relationship between educational levels and what he refers to as job achievement. Meagher (1983) examined police officer educational levels and differences in delivery of services and concluded that college graduates are more likely to explain the nature of complaints to offenders, talk with people to establish rapport, analyze and compare incidents for similarity of *modus operandi*, recruit confidential informants, and verify reliability and credibility of witnesses than officers with some college or high school education. However, Meagher was unwilling to attribute these performance differences solely to educational differences.

Other studies of the relationship between higher education and police performance have found that those officers with the best performance evaluations also have significantly higher education (Baehr, Furcon, and Froemel, 1968), college-educated police officers are less authoritarian than those without college educations (Smith, Locke, and Walker, 1968), that those with at least some college education had fewer civilian complaints and less sick time than those without such education (Cohen and Chaiken, 1972).

Worden (1990: 587) concludes that college education is weakly related to some police officer attitudes and unrelated to others. He found that officers' performance in police-citizen encounters, as measured by citizen evaluations, is "largely unrelated to officers' educational backgrounds" (Worden, 1990: 587).

Kappeler, Sapp, and Carter (1992) conclude that while officers with four-year degrees generate at least as many violations of departmental policy as those with two-year degrees, the former perform better than the latter in the areas of courtesy and citizen complaints.

Higher Education and the Police: A Continuing Controversy

The controversy surrounding the need for higher education for police personnel continues in spite of the fact that virtually every national commission on the police over the last half century has recommended such education. One basic argument against college education for the police is that there is insufficient empirical evidence to indicate that such education is necessary for performing the police function. This argument is countered by recognizing that there is scant evidence to indicate that college education is necessary for performing any occupation, but considerable evidence that such education may improve the performance of those in the occupation (Scott, 1986). Additionally, there is a good deal of evidence that indicates that the college experience increases critical thinking, the amount of factual information available, self-confidence, open-mindedness, and adaptability (Feldman and Newcomb, 1969; Bowen, 1977). While these abilities and skills may not have been deemed critical to police personnel in previous decades, they are of paramount importance to the police as order maintainers and negotiators. As we have pointed out throughout this book, the police role has changed and is changing.

> *Police must have the ability to understand human problems in their community and they must be trained to identify and understand a variety of social, economic, and developmental ills for which they must be able to refer, recommend, or involve themselves in an effort to seek the best available solution. College education does appear to develop and enhance these abilities and skills, if the education is administered outside the narrow parameters of a vocational training program or the classic criminal justice or law enforcement programs found in most two-year and four-year programs (Scott, 1986: 26).*

Scott concludes that entry-level requirements for police officers include a four-year degree requirement and that police officers already in the field should take any opportunities to pursue bachelor's degrees. This is the same conclusion reached by the National Advisory Commission on Higher Education for the Police some years ago.

Commitment to education, like commitment to training, should be career-long for police personnel. For officers who already have college degrees, as well as for those without such degrees, continuing education courses can be challenging, motivating, and worthwhile. Such courses are also beneficial for officers who do not wish to pursue a college degree.

The benefits of continuing education for police officers are not limited to course content. It has been observed over the past twenty years that a good deal of benefit accrues from having police officers and other students share the same classroom, coming to know each other as individuals, and hearing one another's perspectives on a variety of issues. This is perhaps particularly true when the class is diverse with respect to age, race ethnicity, gender, size of hometown, and cultural background.

Departmental incentives for becoming involved in continuing education indicate to officers that their efforts are appreciated. Such incentives may include tuition reimbursement, time off to attend classes (or allowing officers to attend class while on duty in an "on-call" status), reimbursement for the cost of books, and so on. In many departments that provide these incentives, enhanced chances for promotion also exist. As is the case with training, commitment to education and continuing education must come from the top (Carter and Sapp, 1992).

The debate over the proper extent and nature of police training and education continue. An increasing body of legal evidence is accumulating to indicate that failure to train may lead to serious financial consequences for police agencies, agents, and municipalities alike. Further, there appears to be increasing legal support for higher education of police officers. Coupled with the fact that the perceived role of the police has changed dramatically in recent years, these facts would appear to support increasingly higher standards for police training and education.

The transition to police officers with higher education has not, however, been smooth or easy. Conflict and uneasiness between college-educated officers and those without such education is typical in many agencies. This conflict is particularly present when college-educated officers are supervised by those lacking such education. The former often consider themselves superior to the latter based on educational background while the latter often consider such education a waste of time and believe that street experience and common sense are far more important than a college degree. Given these conditions, developing common ground and mutual respect is not easy.

Although only a small proportion of police agencies now require a college education for initial employment or promotion, discussions with police executives informally indicate that such education is of considerable importance. Similarly, the increasingly complex nature of crime, requests for police services, and the laws regulating activities in these areas would appear to support the need for better educated and trained police. In order to reach these ends, colleges and universities, as well as police training institutes and academies, must continually revise and update curricula while maintaining high standards. Vocational training for police officers is necessary but should not be confused with education. The two types of programs can and must coexist; improved cooperation between proponents of each can only lead to more prepared police officers. As Carter and Sapp (1992: 14) note, law enforcement agencies can no longer can fail to recognize the changes that are taking place in policing. These changes include an increase in the educational level of citizens and an increase in the number of police programs based on increased police-citizen interactions. These two developments alone require review of law enforcement educational policies. Carter and Sapp (1992: 14) are convinced that "the question is not whether college education is necessary for police officers, but how much and how soon."

Discussion Questions

1. Why is recurrent training so important to police personnel? What are some of the possible consequences of failure to train?

2. What kinds of topics should be included in police training? Who should conduct the training?

3. How would you go about evaluating the effectiveness of a police training program? Why is evaluation so important?

4. What is the relationship between education and training? Can one replace the other? Why or why not?

5. Discuss the arguments for and against college education for police officers.

6. What are some of the weaknesses of existing college programs in criminal justice/law enforcement noted by police executives in recent surveys? How might these weaknesses be corrected?

7. Is there legal justification for requiring some college for entry-level police officers? What are the legal issues involved with this requirement?

8. Has the relationship between college education and improved police performance been thoroughly documented? What needs to be done in order to further examine this relationship?

References

Alpert, G.P. and Dunham, R.G. 1992. *Policing Urban America* 2 ed. Prospect Heights, Il: Waveland Press.

Baeher, E.M., Furcon, J.E., and Froemel, E. 1968. *Psychological Assessment of Patrolman Qualifications in Relation to Field Performance*. Washington, DC: U.S. Government Printing Office.

Blumberg, M. 1993. "The AIDS Epidemic and the Police: An Examination of the Issues." In Dunham, R. G. and Alpert, G. P. (eds.) *Critical Issues in Policing: Contemporary Readings*. Prospect Heights, IL: Waveland Press, 208–219.

Bowen, H.R. 1977. *Investment in Learning: The Individual and the Social Value of Higher Education*. San Francisco: Jossey-Bass.

Bracey, D.H. 1990a. "Future Trends in Police Training." Paper presented at the Third Annual Sino-American Criminal Justice Institute, Taipei, Taiwan.

Bracey, D.H. 1990b. "Preparing Police Leaders for the Future." *Police Studies* 13(4), 178–182.

Broderick, J.J. 1987. *Police in a Time of Change*. Prospect Heights, IL: Waveland Press.

Bruns, B. 1989. "Operation Bootstrap: Opening Corporate Classrooms to Police Managers." *NIJ Reports*. National Institute of Justice 217, 2–6.

Carter, D.L. and Sapp, A.D. 1992. "College Education and Policing: Coming of Age." *FBI Law Enforcement Bulletin* (January), 8–14.

Cohen, B. and Chaiken, J.M. 1972. *Police Background Characteristics: Summary Report*.

Washington, DC: U.S. Government Printing Office.

Daniels, E. 1982. "The Effect of a College Degree on Police Absenteeism." *The Police Chief* (September), 70–71.

Davis v. City of Dallas 777 F. 2d 205 (5th Cir. 1985, Certiorari Denied to Supreme Court May 19, 1986).

Feldman, K.A. and Newcomb, T.M. 1969. *The Impact of College on Students. Vol. 1: An Analysis of Four Decades of Research.* San Francisco: Jossey-Bass.

Graves, F.R. 1991. "Trainers Technique Syndrome." *Police Chief* 58 (11), 62–63.

Griffin, G.R. 1980. *A Study of Relationships Between Level of College Education and Police Patrolman's Performance.* Saratoga, NY: Twenty-One Publishing.

Hayeslip, D., Jr. 1989. "Higher Education and Police Performance Revisited: The Evidence Examined Through Meta-Analysis." *American Journal of Police* 8 (2), 49–59.

Hinkle, D.P. 1991. "Cop's Commentary: College Degree and Impractical Prerequisite for Police Work." *Law and Order* 39 (7), 105.

Kappeler, V.E., Sapp, A.D., and Carter, D.L. 1992. "Police Officer Higher Education, Citizen Complaints and Departmental Rule Violations." *American Journal of the Police* 11 (2), 37–54.

Lieberman, P. 1990. "Facing the Future." *Police* 14 (1), 44–71.

Marsh, H.L. and Grosskopf, E. 1991. "The Key Factors in Law Enforcement Training: Requirements, Assessments and Methods." *Police Chief* 58 (11), 64–66.

McCambell, M.S. 1986. "Field Training for Police Officers: State of the Art." *Research in Brief.* National Institute of Justice. (November)

Meagher, M.S. 1983. "Perceptions of the Police Patrol Function: Does Officer Education Make a Difference?" Paper presented at ACJS Meeting San Antonio, Tx.

Mullins, W.C. 1985. "Improving Police Officer Training: The Use of Job Analysis Procedures and Assessment Center Technology." *The Journal of Police and Criminal Psychology* 1 (March), 2–9.

National Advisory Commission on Criminal Justice Standards and Goals. 1973. *Report on the Police.* Washington, DC: U.S. Government Printing Office.

———— 1990a. "New Dogs, New Tricks." *Police* 14 (1), 31–51.

Nowicki, E. 1990b. "Police Training: A Sense of Priority." *Police* 14 (1), 4.

Overton, W.C. and Black, J.J. 1994. "Language as a Weapon." *Police Chief* 65 (8), 46.

Phillips, R.G. 1988. "Training Priorities in State and Local Law Enforcement." *FBI Law Enforcement Bulletin* (August), 10–16.

"Police Chiefs: CJ Curricula Inconsistent with Contemporary Police Needs." *ACJS Today* 7 (4), 1,5.

Post, G.M. 1992. "Police Recruits: Training Tomorrow's Workforce." *FBI Law Enforcement Bulletin* 61 (3), 19–24.

Pritchett, G.L. 1993. "Interpersonal Communication: Improving Law Enforcement's Image." *FBI Law Enforcement Bulletin* 62 (7), 22–26.

Reiss, A.J., Jr. 1971. *The Police and the Public.* New Haven: Yale University Press.

Sapp, A.D. 1986. "Education and Training Requirements in Law Enforcement: A National Comparison." *The Police Chief* (November), 48–62.

Sapp, A. D., Carter, D., and Stephens, D. 1988. "Higher Education as a Bona Fide Occupational Qualification (BFOQ) for Police: A Blueprint." *American Journal of Police* 7 (2), 15–59.

Scott, W.R. 1986. "College Educational Requirements for Entry Level and Promotion: A Study." *Journal of Police and Criminal Psychology* 2 (1), 10–28.

Sherman, L.W. and Blumberg, M. 1981. "Higher Education and Police Use of Force." *Journal of Criminal Justice* 9(4), 317–331.

Smith, A.B., Locke, B., and Walker, W.F. 1968. "Authoritarianism in Police College Students and Non-Police College Students." *Journal of Criminal Law, Criminology, and Police Science* 59 (3), 440–443.

Swanson, C.R., Territo, L., and Taylor, R.W. 1988. *Police Administration: Structures, Processes, and Behavior* 2 ed. New York: Macmillan.

Worden, R.E. 1990. "A Badge and a Baccalaureate: Policies, Hypotheses, and Further Evidence." *Justice Quarterly* 7 (3), 580–592.

8

WOMEN AND MINORITIES
IN POLICING

As we indicated in Chapter 6, in recent years there have been attempts to recruit more women and minorities into policing. These attempts have come largely in response to affirmative action and equal employment opportunity requirements, rather than as a direct result of the belief that such recruits can in fact perform the police roles as well as white males. In 1990, 80 percent of local police personnel were white, 10.5 percent black, and 5.2 percent Hispanic. Women comprised 8.1 percent of local police officers (Maguire, Pastore, and Flanagan, 1993). We will now examine the impact of efforts to recruit women and minority group members into policing.

Women in Policing

On September 3, 1910, in the city of Los Angeles, Alice Stebbin Wells became the first official policewoman in the United States (Horne, 1980: 28). Her duties included supervising and enforcing laws pertaining to dance halls, skating rinks, theaters, and other public recreation areas. She lectured to various groups around the nation in the next few years about the place of women in police service and her efforts resulted in the Chicago City Council passing an ordinance that provided for the hiring of policewomen. By 1915, Chicago had employed 30 policewomen (Swan, 1988: 11). Wells became the first president of the International Association of Policewomen in 1915. At that time, policewomen worked mainly with troubled youth and women victims and offenders. During World War I, policewomen were utilized to keep prostitutes away from military camps and to assist in the return of runaway women and girls (Bell, 1982: 113; House, 1993: 139). The "women's bureau" was a separate division, policewomen did not wear uniforms, and they were not armed. They typically received less pay than their male counterparts, although their educational qualifications were considerably better (Horne, 1980: 30). Still, at the Chief's Association convention in 1922, a resolution was passed stating that policewomen were indispensable to the modern police department (Swan, 1988: 11).

Very few policewomen were hired during the Depression, and while women were used as auxiliary police officers during World War II, this ended with the war. Not until the 1960s did opportunities for policewomen begin to improve. The President's Commission on Law Enforcement and Administration of Justice (1967) found that policewomen could be an "invaluable asset" to modern law enforcement and recommended their present role be broadened to include patrol and investigative duties, as well as administrative responsibilities. The first woman assigned to full-time field patrol was hired in Indianapolis in 1968 (McDowell, 1992).

In 1972, Congress amended Title VII of the 1964 Civil Rights Act to prohibit discrimination by both private and public employers based on the gender of the applicant. At about the same time, *Women in Policing* was published by the Police Foundation and the report was generally favorable toward policewomen. In the same period, the Federal Bureau of Investigation and the Secret Service appointed their first female field agents. Finally, a number of cities (St. Louis, Washington, DC, New York) placed uniformed female officers in patrol positions and conducted studies to evaluate their performances. These studies in the 1970s led to the conclusion that policewomen perform as well as policemen, although sometimes in different fashion. There was also an early study that indicated that the attitudes of policewomen and policemen are fairly similar (Koenig, 1978). Bartol, Bergen, and Volckens (1992) more recently studied thirty full-time female police officers and found that overall, in small towns at least, they experienced stressors similar to those of their male counterparts. Other studies found that organizational commitment, job satisfaction, stress levels and job-related anxiety, and attitudes toward law and order do not differ significantly by gender (McGeorge and Wolfe, 1976; Fry and Greenfield, 1980). Felkenes and Lasley (1992) surveyed over one thousand officers and found that regardless of gender or race, levels of job satisfaction were high.

One researcher concluded that policewomen, at least in the southwestern part of the United States, are more authoritarian and cynical than their male counterparts (Davis, 1984). Nonetheless, male officers and administrators continue to doubt their ability to perform, particularly in violent or potentially violent situations. To some extent, these doubts may be based on the development of different entry-level requirements, particularly in the area of physical ability, resulting from attempts to attract and hire female officers. To many male officers, in some cases with justification, different standards imply lower standards, and stories about being passed over for employment or promotion as a result of affirmative action requirements are prevalent among male officers and potential officers.

Once hired, however, Block and Anderson (1974) found that female and male officers responded to calls in generally similar fashion and that citizen respect for the police was similar for the two groups, though male and female officers performed the jobs in somewhat different ways. Female officers, for example, tended to make fewer arrests than their male colleagues. Kerber et al. (1977) found that citizens generally judged male and female officers as equally competent and over three-fourths of the respondents to their survey indicated that both male and female officers should be hired in order to improve the quality of police services. To be sure, Kerber et al.'s study was conducted in a university community and may not be representative of attitudes in other types of communities. Kerber et al., (1977), 346 however, conclude: "respondents from larger cities with higher levels of education and better jobs" have more liberal views on female police officers and that, in the long run, demonstrated competence on the job is the basic criterion policewomen must satisfy to gain acceptance.

The number of policewomen in the United States has gradually increased so that by 1990 they accounted for about 8 percent of sworn police personnel. In that year, more than 114,000 women were employed as sworn officers. The number of female police officers more than tripled between 1980 and 1990 with the increase being greatest in departments serving populations over 250,000 and in suburban departments in which women accounted for nearly 10 percent of sworn personnel. Still, the number of female supervisors remains low (see Highlight 8.1).

In spite of the fact that the Washington, DC, study conducted in the early 1970s led to the conclusion that policewomen performed capably, male patrol officers and supervisory officers continued to express predominantly negative attitudes toward their female counterparts. They continued to indicate that female officers were less capable in violent situations or as backup in such situations. More studies of policewomen soon followed. An evaluation of policewomen patrolling alone in St. Louis County indicated that they performed their duties as well as men, as measured by police supervisors, observers, and citizens (Sherman, 1975). The attitudes of policemen remained largely negative, although somewhat less so after the evaluation.

A study done by the California Highway Patrol in 1976 concluded that, although it cost more to recruit and train women, they performed capably

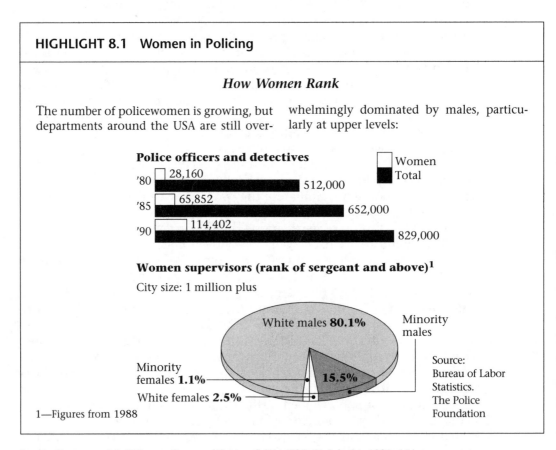

HIGHLIGHT 8.1   Women in Policing

How Women Rank

The number of policewomen is growing, but departments around the USA are still overwhelmingly dominated by males, particularly at upper levels:

Police officers and detectives

☐ Women
■ Total

'80 28,160 / 512,000
'85 65,852 / 652,000
'90 114,402 / 829,000

Women supervisors (rank of sergeant and above)[1]

City size: 1 million plus

White males **80.1%**
Minority males
15.5%
Minority females **1.1%**
White females **2.5%**

Source: Bureau of Labor Statistics. The Police Foundation

1—Figures from 1988

(Balkin, 1988). A study done in Denver at about the same time reached similar conclusions (Bartlett and Rosenblum, 1977), as did a New York City study conducted in 1976 (Sichel et al., 1978). Numerous other studies have led to the same conclusion—women perform patrol functions acceptably. Only one study concluded that women are not as capable on patrol as men. This study, done in the Philadelphia Police Department, found that women do not project the image of power and strength that policemen project and that they do not conduct building searches as well. The report concluded that women fail to handle patrol duties as safely and efficiently as men. Critics have noted that this information is relevant only if the major concerns of the police have to do with appearing powerful and conducting building searches (Horne, 1980).

Policewomen as Viewed by the Public, Their Supervisors, and Male Officers

Although public attitudes toward policewomen have not been extensively investigated, the information that is available indicates these attitudes are mostly positive and, in fact, in the St. Louis and New York studies discussed above, women were regarded more favorably than male officers (Balkin, 1988). In other studies, policewomen have been rated higher by the public when it comes to handling domestic disputes and showing appropriate concern and sensitivity. A study by Bell (1982) found that while citizens generally believed that policemen are preferable in violent situations, they also generally approved of policewomen.

Studies of supervisors' attitudes toward policewomen are also scarce and those that exist are conflicting. The Washington study, for example, indicated predominantly negative attitudes on the part of supervisors, while studies in St. Louis and New York showed supervisors to be more positive (Balkin, 1988).

Policemen's opinions of their female counterparts have been better documented and, as indicated previously, have been found to be generally negative. Policemen tend to view policewomen as incompetent and unfit for police work and working with female police officers does not appear to have a positive effect on such opinions (Balkin, 1988). A good deal of the skepticism among male officers is undoubtedly due to gender-role socialization. Even though significant changes have occurred over the past decade with respect to integration of occupations by gender, some occupational groups have been slow to accept such changes. This inertia is perhaps particularly true in occupations imbued with traditional conceptions of masculinity as a required trait, such as the construction trades, airline and fighter pilots, and, of course, the police. With changes brought about by movements for equal rights for women, by hiring more educated officers, and as a result of competent performance of women in the police role, these gender-role stereotypes are gradually changing. A study by Grown and Carlson (1993), for example, found that there has been a small shift toward more favorable attitudes concerning female officers, but still about 20 percent of male officers do not want to work with female officers on patrol.

Factors Affecting the Performance of Policewomen

Not surprisingly, the greatest source of work-related stress reported by female police officers is male police officers (Wexler and Logan, 1983). Bartol, Bergne, and Volckens (1992) found that police women experienced stress as a result of working in a male-dominated occupation, but that stress did not appear to affect their job performance as supervisors evaluated male and female officers as performing the job equally well.

As Balkin (1988: 34) points out, the negative attitudes of policemen toward policewomen are based on personal belief, not actual experience. "No research has shown that strength is related to an individual's ability to manage successfully a dangerous situation. . . . There are no reports in the literature of bad outcomes because a policewoman did not have enough strength or aggression."

Others have noted that agility, a cool head, and good communication skills may be more important than strength in dangerous situations (Charles, 1982; Rogers, 1987; McDowell, 1992). Some suggest that the presence of a policewoman may actually help to defuse a potentially violent situation (Sherman, 1975; Homant and Kennedy, 1985; Martin, 1993).

In spite of all these defenses of policewomen, most male police officers continue to be highly critical of them. Explanations for this persistent hostility on behalf of male officers are varied. As indicated previously, some suggest that traditional gender roles involving sex-typing of occupations are widely held by male police officers. The presence of women in what has typically been referred to as the police "fraternity" may undermine the sense of masculine identity that accompanies that subculture. Wives of male police officers sometimes object strenuously to their husbands spending eight hours a day with "another woman."

Whatever the reasons, policemen's attitudes toward policewomen have some very real consequences for both. First, policewomen are continually in the spotlight and must repeatedly prove themselves capable before they have a chance of being accepted as "real" police officers. Some perform most capably under this added strain, others do not and those who fail become legend among tradition-oriented male officers. We have heard numerous stories about policewomen who were involved in traffic accidents while on duty, failed to qualify the first time around with their firearms, and are never the first to arrive at a potentially violent call in their zones. These things do, of course, occur. They also occur with a good deal of regularity among male police officers.

Second, because male officers often feel uncomfortable about dealing with potentially violent situations when their partners are female, they sometimes over protect policewomen by instructing them to stay in the car, to stay on the radio, or to stay back away from the altercation. Thus, policewomen are sometimes denied the opportunity to demonstrate their skills. Further, the same officers who require their female partners not to get involved may then criticize these partners to other male officers for failing to provide adequate backup.

Third, negative attitudes toward policewomen have undoubtedly played a role in promotional processes. Taking orders from a policewoman when one has no respect for women in the occupation is difficult. The ability of police-women to perform at supervisory levels thus remains to be tested, but there is little reason to believe that, given adequate preparation, they will prove less worthy than their male counterparts (Koenig, 1978; Martin, 1993).

Nonetheless, when women enter a male-dominated workplace, there is an excellent chance that they will be viewed as "tokens," at least initially. As has been noted (Kanter, 1977; Martin, 1993), this status means they will be sub-ject to enhanced scrutiny, differences between themselves and those who have traditionally filled the work role will be polarized, and they will be stereotyped. The stress implied by token status is over and above that experi-enced by others occupying the same role who are not considered tokens.

Alex (1969), in discussing the stresses experienced by black police officers, used the term "double marginality" to refer to the fact that black officers are not fully accepted by their white co-workers and are also distrusted by other blacks. The same term may be applied to women in police work who are not fully accepted as equals by their male co-workers and who often find other women (especially male officers' wives) somewhat suspect of their motives for entering police work. Based on these considerations, we might expect that policewomen would have relatively high turnover rates; this appears to be the case at least in some departments (Fry, 1983). Martin (1993) found that such turnover is due to discrimination on behalf of male officers, lack of equal promotional opportuni-ties, and the constant pressure on policewomen to prove themselves.

Sexual harassment continues to be a problem for policewomen. According to McDowell (1992), the harassment that persists in many police agencies includes lewd jokes transmitted over police radios and sexist remarks in the halls. Martin (1993: 336) notes: "Frequent sexual jokes and gossip remind the women that they are desired sexual objects, visible outsiders, and feared com-petitors." Kathleen Burke, a former New York City police officer concludes: "On the surface, women seem to have all the opportunities that the men have. They are, for the most part, in every unit in the police department [New York City]. But, have all the discrimination fences been knocked down? Absolutely not, not until the last dinosaur's bones are buried" (House, 1993: 144).

Interestingly, male officers were particularly critical of female officers who performed well and who did not allow themselves to be treated in conde-scending fashion. These women were frequently stereotyped as "bitchy" or "lesbians" by male officers (Martin, 1993).

Further, Poole and Pogrebin (1988: 54) found that "After just three years on the force, only a small proportion of women officers still aspire to rise in the police organization. It is likely that these officers have recognized in a rel-atively short period of time that few women actually get promoted; conse-quently policewomen lack a variety of female role models in higher ranks whom they could realistically strive to emulate."

One national survey of policewomen found that 40 percent felt that their skills were being under-utilized in their departments. Those with higher edu-cational levels were more likely to report that their skills were not being uti-lized properly (Garrison, Grant, and McCormick, 1988).

The advantages of hiring women for police work are perhaps best summarized by Linn and Price (1985): It is illegal to discriminate on the basis of gender in hiring and promoting police officers; women are often better at collecting certain kinds of police information than men; the presence of female officers shows commitment to serving the entire community; diverse views are needed when formulating police policies; policewomen demonstrate that women can successfully occupy positions of authority and respect and thereby serve as role models to the community.

Linn and Price (1985: 75) indicate that the policeman is often resistant to change, in part, "because so little of his world is safe and predictable. His opposition to women on patrol stems in part from his not knowing *how* to treat a woman as a peer. Should he watch his language? Offer to drive? Buy her coffee? Talk about sports? Initiate friendliness? Could he share hours of tension, or even hours of boredom, and not become too involved?"

While these problems may be overcome, dealing with an officer's wife may be more difficult. Policemen's wives have demonstrated in several cities over the assignment of women to patrol duty. The outward concern in such demonstrations has been the safety of the male officer, but questions of fidelity don't appear to be far beneath the surface.

Linn and Price (1985) conclude that the outlook for policewomen is not entirely bleak in spite of the difficulties discussed above. In Miami and in Dayton, Ohio, policewomen have been accepted by male coworkers and the public alike. Further, there is evidence that minorities and more educated officers are more likely accept women—and *their* numbers are increasing. Because women account for about 51 percent of the population, and the evidence is clear that they are capable of performing a wide variety of police functions, they should be viewed as a valuable asset in the struggle to make police departments more representative of the communities they serve and, ultimately, in the battle to reintegrate police and community. As McDowell (1992: 70) indicates, female police officers "are bringing a distinctly different, and valuable, set of skills to the streets and the station house that may change the way the police are perceived in the community." This is clearly one of the goals of community policing and female officers who display negotiation and mediation skills are an important part of this movement (see Highlight 8.2).

Black Police Officers

As noted earlier, some of the most problematic encounters involving the police occur between white police officers and minority citizens. Encounters between the police and blacks, Hispanics, American Indians, and, increasingly, Asians indicate that a good deal of hostility remains as a result of racist attitudes, historical distrust, and past discrimination. A national survey of 1,223 adults found broad agreement that the United States has moved toward racial equality since 1963 and 71 percent of those surveyed felt equality is attainable. Yet, 40 percent felt that racial equality would not occur during their lifetimes, 55 percent said U.S. society is racist overall, and 43 percent felt

---

HIGHLIGHT 8.2   Breaking Ground Wasn't Always Easy

Retired Police Captain Paved the Way for Women on the Force

By Warletta Johnson of the Journal Star

When Detroit police command officer Jeanne Miller was hired as Peoria's assistant police superintendent in January, it was history in the making for the city.

Miller reached a level no other woman had reached in the Peoria Police Department. But it wasn't that no other woman had tried.

Retired Peoria Police Capt. Mary Ann Dunlavey fought the male-dominated system to pave the way for herself and to blaze the path that other women were to follow.

Although she lost her own battle to be named department chief, Dunlavey says she's pleased to see Miller so close to the helm.

"I'm glad Assistant Chief Miller is in there. It will make people realize that women can do the job," Dunlavey said.

Dunlavey, who joined the police force on March 2, 1964, retired last year after 27 years on the job. During her tenure, she was what some would describe as a "mover and shaker."

She fought for everything that she got, Dunlavey said.

She was the first female officer to ride in a city squad car; the first allowed to take the sergeants' promotional exam; the first promoted to sergeant; and the only woman promoted to lieutenant and captain.

In 1985, she filed a complaint with Illinois Human Rights Commission against the city after she lost her bid for the police chief's job to a man with less education and experience.

Dunlavey settled the sex discrimination case out of court a year ago and received a $150,000 settlement. The agreement Dunlavey made with the city was worded in a way to bar other women from citing Dunlavey's case as precedent.

Besides Miller, Dunlavey is the only other female who has held a command position in the department.

When Dunlavey joined the department there were five women police officers. Today there are 12.

Although the female officers interviewed said they had no ambition to climb the administrative ladder, some indicated that their lack of interest stemmed from controversy over the sergeants' exam. The test establishes the order in which officers will be promoted to sergeant.

Before 1988, the last sergeants' exam was given in 1979. When the promotions list expired in 1982, the city hired a consultant to develop a new test which the Police Benevolent Association successfully challenged in court.

The court battled delayed the promotion process until 1988. Of the 78 officers who took the test, 55 names appear on the current eligibility list.

Fourteen officers—none of whom were women—have been promoted from the list thus far, which expires Nov. 1, 1993.

Training officer Martha Schoch and traffic officer Elizabeth Buck remain on the list. However, Buck and nine other officers are appealing their rankings on the list in court.

Meanwhile, other female officers said they are satisfied just being a police officer.

Vice officer Ann Ruggles said she has no desire to be a sergeant and has never taken the test. She said the highest rank positions require more paper work and less dealing with people in the community.

"I came into the job to serve the community and that's what I am doing," Ruggles said.

Dunvaley said Miller's spot near the top leaves hope for other women who aspire to higher positions.

Miller admits advancing to the male-dominated field has not always been easy.

Continued

When some men are open to seeing women in high places, others are not, she said.

Miller, who was among the first group of women officers allowed to patrol the streets of Detroit, recalled an incident in which one male colleague congratulated her on scoring high on a sergeants' exam while the other announced loudly that he was much better suited for the job than she could ever be.

Miller said she became even more determined to excel as a result.

Schoch, among the few women to patrol Peoria streets recalled an incident in which a male officer, who is no longer with the force, complained about the quality of work of female officers. She was called in to discuss her performance.

"He couldn't point out a thing I was doing wrong. He just had a problem with working with female officers," Schoch said.

Today, the men are more open to working with female officers, the women said.

Miller said she realizes there's not a lot she can do to get women promoted, but still she hopes they will assert themselves in a way that can bring promotions.

"I wish there were women command officers I could talk with and become friends with, but there are not," Miller said.

that minorities do not receive equal treatment in the criminal justice system. Interestingly, 61 percent of blacks surveyed felt discrimination occurs in the criminal justice system compared to 40 percent of white respondents (Langer, 1988). Because the police are a reflection of society, it is not surprising that they sometimes have poor working relationships with minority group members. In fact the National Advisory Commission on Civil Disorders found that poor minority relations were an important factor in precipitating the ghetto riots of the 1960s and recommended increased hiring of minority officers as one possible solution to the problem.

Racial tensions remain high in some parts of the country, which is indicated by the now famous Howard Beach incident that occurred in 1987 and the Rodney King incident in Los Angeles in 1991. In the former case, three black males wandered into a predominantly white community and were attacked by a group of white teenagers. One of the black males was hit by a car and killed while trying to flee his pursuers and another was seriously injured. A jury eventually found three white teens guilty of manslaughter and assault charges, but the city was portrayed as an example of the racial division. Protests by hundreds of blacks over various forms of racial discrimination followed (*Newsweek*, 1988).

In 1991, several white police were caught on videotape beating, shooting with a stun gun, and stomping Rodney King, a black motorist who had attempted to outrun the police. When the officers were acquitted by a jury, parts of Los Angeles erupted in violence, including the near fatal beating of a white truck driver, Reginald Denny, by blacks (Church, 1992).

In December of 1989, two black teenagers filed a federal lawsuit against two white police officers who allegedly picked the teens up in a black neighborhood, harassed them, and dropped them off in a largely white neighborhood where they were later beaten. The suit also names the city of Chicago on grounds that there is a pattern of failure to discipline police officers who violate the civil rights of other citizens (*Journal Star*, 1989).

The proportion of black (and other minority) officers remains relatively low and police-minority relations continue to be problematic. In fact, the number of black applicants for police positions remains extremely low in some areas and tension between black and white officers periodically runs high. This may be due to a perception among blacks that they are unwelcome or at least suspect in many police agencies (Fountain, 1991). Given these facts, one wonders why some blacks *do* apply for police positions. Alex (1969) noted some time ago that police work is attractive to blacks for the same reasons it is attractive to whites—reasonable salary, job security, and reasonable pension. In addition, police departments have a good deal to gain by hiring blacks in terms of the benefits of "protective coloration." Black police officers can often gather information that would be extremely difficult for white officers to gather: black police officers may make charges of racial brutality against the police less likely, and federal funding is partly dependent on equal employment opportunity and affirmative action programs.

It is also obvious that white police officers, whether undercover or not, will arouse suspicion in predominantly black groups. With respect to police brutality toward minority groups, it is apparent that when black police officers resort to the use of force in dealing with black citizens the issue of interracial brutality is avoided (although the issue of police brutality remains).

Perhaps the best reason for hiring and promoting qualified black applicants is the fact that a tremendous amount of talent is wasted if we exclude them from police work. Since there is no evidence that white officers perform the policing function better than black officers, it is ethically and morally proper to hire officers of both races. Further, integrated police departments are more representative of the public they serve, and black officers may serve as much needed role models in the community.

Problems for Black Police Officers

Kuykendall and Burns (1980) indicate that blacks first served as police officers in Washington, DC, in 1861. Their numbers remained low until World War II when gradual increases began. These early black officers were largely confined to black neighborhoods, and their powers of arrest did not extend to whites. In some cities, restrictions on the powers of black officers remained in place until the 1960s (Kuykendall and Burns, 1980). Leinen (1984) found that in the mid-1960s, only twenty-two law enforcement agencies employed blacks in positions above the level of patrol officers. A 1971 report of the Commission on Civil Rights affirmed the need to bring minority officers into law enforcement (Margolis, 1971). Litigation involving discrimination in hiring and promotion followed in the 1970s and 1980s and consent decrees of the type discussed earlier frequently resulted, leading to the hiring of more minority (particularly black) officers.

During the same period, the National Black Police Association and the National Organization for Black Law Enforcement Executives were established to promote minority hiring, improved community relations, and fair hiring practices (Sullivan, 1989). When these policies came under fire, the Supreme Court responded by handing down an endorsement of racial quotas in police departments that were recalcitrant in hiring and promoting minority group members. In 1987, the Court upheld promotional quotas requiring that the Alabama State Police promote one black officer for each white officer promoted until blacks hold 25 percent of the top ranks in the department (Gest, 1987).

In 1992, President Bush signed into law a new civil rights act that prohibited the use of adjusting tests scores based on race, gender, religion, or national origin except in specified cases involving, for example, physical differences between the sexes or cases in which preferential treatment is accorded to rectify past discrimination (Sauls, 1992). The effect of this new civil rights legislation was to continue a trend toward recognizing reverse discrimination originating with *Bakke v. California* and carrying over into the late 1980s. The new legislation and an accumulating body of case law has, to some extent at least, led to a movement away from court-imposed quotas and toward new forms of ranking candidates for both entry-level and promotional positions (Gaines, Kappeler, and Vaughn, 1994: 73).

Black police officers confront a number of problems in addition to those confronted by their white counterparts. While many black officers are assigned to police the ghettos in hopes of alleviating racial tensions, not all black citizens prefer black officers to white. Jackson and Wallach (1973) and Alex (1969, 1976) have noted that black officers sometimes have more trouble dealing with black citizens than do white officers. As noted previously, Alex (1969) found that black police officers suffer from double marginality resulting from distrust by their white counterparts and perception as traitors by other members of the black community. Black officers may be perceived as more black than blue (police-oriented) by white officers and more blue than black by those in the black community.

As a result, black officers often report difficulties in dealing with black citizens, particularly young, black males who call on officers to see themselves, and to act first as racial brothers/sisters instead of police officers. Taunts and slogans indicating the role of black officers as "lackeys" for white society are commonplace in encounters between black officers and young, black males. Being the target of such epithets places an additional burden on black officers to retain their composure in confrontations; not all are able to do so. Thus, encounters between black officers and other black citizens are not always civil. In fact, there is some evidence that police brutality is largely an intraracial phenomenon, at least in high-crime areas in urban centers (Reiss, 1968).

Hacker (1992: 189), in discussing the fact that blacks are three times more likely to die from a police officer's bullet than whites, notes: "As it happens, a disproportionately high number of these killings of blacks are by black policemen, which suggests that departments tend to give black officers assignments where they encounter suspects of their own race. . . . For many years, police forces hired few if any blacks; now there is a tendency to use blacks to control blacks."

Jacobs and Cohen (1978: 171) concluded that "Black policemen, like their white colleagues, must still arrest unwilling suspects, intervene in domestic squabbles, and keep order on ghetto streets. In the end, they represent the interests of order, property, and the status quo in an environment where large numbers of unemployed minority youth among others do not share this same commitment."

Encounters between black officers and white citizens do not always proceed smoothly either. As recently as 1988, citizens of a Chicago suburb called police to report that a black man was impersonating a police officer, wearing a police uniform, and driving a patrol car. The officer received, on a daily basis, "racial insults and humiliation not only from the people he has sworn to protect but also from some of his fellow officers upon whom his life may depend" (Gup, 1988: 25). Other black officers also report being subjected to racial slurs, distrust, and outright avoidance. Some whites are concerned about whether black officers will respond first as members of their race or as police officers when dealing with interracial situations. In some parts of the country, blacks in positions of authority are uncommon and whites are apprehensive about being subject to such authority. In a multiracial society, this is perhaps inevitable to some extent as we divide the world into "we" and "they" groups, interact with and tend to support members of the "we" group, and distrust members of the "they" groups. As long as skin color continues to be as important as—or more important than—an individual's actions, encounters between police officers and other citizens of different racial groups are likely to remain uncomfortable, regardless of the qualifications and expertise of the officers involved.

It is important to note that in spite of the many difficulties confronting black police officers, they report that their relationships with white officers, at least while on duty, are satisfactory. They feel confident that white officers will back them up in emergency situations and they indicate that they would do the same for white officers. While there may be little socialization after hours, on-duty encounters are likely to be civil (Alex, 1969, Leinen, 1984). There are exceptions, of course. In some instances, black officers have formed their own associations in police departments with agendas different from and sometimes in sharp contrast with those of white officers (see Highlight 8.3). In 1985, for example, a federal judge awarded almost six hundred thousand dollars to the Afro-American Police League of the Chicago Police Department and seven of its members after finding that discrimination had occurred in assignments, promotions, and other areas.

Promotions of black officers appear to be problematic in many departments. There is a general consensus that officers of all minority groups are greatly underrepresented at levels above the patrol level (Williams, 1988; Sullivan, 1989: 342). In part, this underrepresentation may be due to their

---

HIGHLIGHT 8.3   Black Women in Blue

According to a recent article in *Ebony*, black women in policing continue to experience at least periodic episodes of sexism and racism. Sheriff Jacquelyn Barrett, the first black woman ever to be elected to that office, manages a staff of seven hundred and a budget of thirty million dollars in Fulton County, Georgia. Barrett indicated that some people doubt she can contribute to law enforcement because she is a woman. Others have difficulty accepting the fact that she is black, a woman, and the sheriff. She recognizes that the black, woman sheriff is something new, but says that with the exception of a few incidents, she has been positively received.

Dr. Elsie L. Scott, named deputy commissioner of training for the New York City Police Academy in 1991, has met resistance from white, male co-workers who would prefer not to work for a black woman. Even though Scott has a doctorate in criminal justice and has taught at Howard and Rutgers, she says her white, male colleagues believed she was not capable of managing the 640 employees and $3 million dollar budget (Haynes, 1993: 64–68).

---

relatively recent entry into police in many locales, but it is also due in part to institutional discrimination (biased testing procedures, job assignments, and educational requirements, for example) and to the fact that federal agencies wishing to satisfy affirmative action requirements often recruit minorities from the ranks of municipal departments. The increasing number of black politicians occupying positions as mayors and chiefs of police may, over time, alleviate the promotional dilemma.

Hispanic Police Officers

Police-minority relations are not only problematic for white officers and the black community, as a recent Miami incident illustrates. In this case, a Hispanic police officer shot at two black motorcyclists, resulting in their deaths. The deaths resulted in three days of looting, burning, and rock throwing in the community and heightened racial tensions for almost a year. So serious was the concern about further violence that the jurors' verdict in the case against the police officer was delayed for more than two hours to allow the police time to position themselves to prevent such violence. Further, the return of a guilty verdict against the officer was immediately denounced by some Miami police officers, thus raising the possibility of continued tensions (Parker, 1989).

The Hispanic population in the United States has increased dramatically in the past decade. The Hispanic population was estimated at almost twenty-two million in 1991, up over 50 percent from 1980, making Hispanics one of the fastest growing minorities in the country. It has been estimated that about 150,000 Hispanics illegally enter the country annually and the total illegal Hispanic population is estimated at about three million. Family median income among Hispanics averages about ten thousand dollars per year less than that of non-Hispanics; about 25 percent are below the poverty line (Clancy, 1987: 1a; Schaefer, 1993: 265). All of these facts taken together indicate that police contacts with Hispanics are already frequent and are likely to increase dramatically as the minority group increases in size. These contacts are likely to be somewhat problematic because of language differences, as well as the fact that, in addition to whatever immediate reason the police have for initiating contact with Hispanics, they may also be dealing with illegal immigrants who can be deported if detected and reported. Further, at least one study has found that Hispanics of Mexican origin view the police in a less favorable light than whites and about as favorably as blacks (Carter, 1983).

Hispanics in the United States are not a homogeneous group, but consist of those whose origins are in Mexico, Cuba, Puerto Rico, and other Central and South American countries. Further, some of these groups are concentrated in specific areas (Cubans in Southern Florida, Mexican Americans in the Southwest), although most metropolitan areas include sizable numbers of Hispanics. In these areas, if the police are to be representative of the communities they serve, Hispanic officers must be recruited.

The rationale for recruiting Hispanic officers is much the same as for women and blacks, with the additional consideration of being bilingual, and, ideally perhaps, bicultural. It should be noted here that if being bilingual is an important job-related qualification, it should be specified when advertising the vacancies because there are many individuals with Hispanic surnames who do not speak Spanish. Because many Hispanics are not fluent in English, police officers serving in heavily Hispanic areas need to speak at least basic Spanish in order to render assistance as well as to engage in order maintenance and law enforcement functions. Further, a basic understanding of Hispanic culture is likely to make the officer who polices in Hispanic neighborhoods more comfortable with his or her surroundings and more understanding of the lifestyle encountered.

There is little information about Hispanic police officers, in part because their numbers have been very small until recently. Walker (1989), in a study of some fifty of the largest police departments in the United States, found that 42 percent of those responding reported significant increases in the number of Hispanic officers employed between the years 1983–1988, about 11 percent reported reductions, and 17 percent reported no change. A study by Carter (1986) concluded that Hispanic police officers in a Hispanic-American community perceive that they are discriminated against by the police organization, even though the department in question consisted of 70 percent minority group members.

A study by Winters (1991) of Hispanic police officers in the Chicago area found that fewer dollars for policing and a high drop-out rate among Hispanic high school students accounted for many of the hiring problems that existed. Carter and Sapp (1991) noted that college education is still disproportionately inaccessible to blacks and Hispanics, raising the possibility that a college-degree requirement for entry-level officers may be discriminatory.

The language barrier, physical size requirements, general belief that Hispanics were not highly sought after by police departments, and belief that other occupations/professions were to be more highly prized probably account for the relatively small number of Hispanic officers in the past. With changing physical requirements, greater emphasis on unbiased, job-related tests, and affirmative action programs, opportunities for Hispanics in policing have increased.

What we know suggests that they seek police positions for the same reasons as officers from all other racial or ethnic groups and share basically the same problems, including double marginality and discrimination in promotions and assignments discussed previously with respect to black police officers. In 1988, for example, a U.S. District Court judge found that hundreds of Latino agents had been victims of discrimination by the F.B.I. The judge found that Hispanics were often given unpleasant assignments rarely handed out to their white counterparts. "A frequent complaint supported by the preponderance of the evidence is that an Hispanic agent with five years of Bureau tenure who has ridden the 'Taco Circuit' may not have the experience of an Anglo on duty for two years" (Kennedy, 1988). The obvious result of such discrimination can be seen in terms of promotions, which often depend on a variety of different police experiences and other factors.

Chinese-American Police Officers

As the Asian-American population continues to increase, crime rates in Asian-American communities increase, and Asian-Americans become more organized in pursuit of equality, the need for Asian-American police officers becomes apparent. While there is little information about Asian-American police officers, one study of Chinese-American officers has been completed (Lin, 1987). In this study, all 120 Chinese-American police officers in New York City were sent questionnaires soliciting information about their attitudes and self-conceptions.

Seventy of the questionnaires were returned and the results of the survey indicate that Chinese-American police officers share many of the same problems as other minority officers. For example, over three-fourths of the officers responding indicated that they have good working relationships with other Chinese-American officers as well as with officers of all other ethnic groups. However, only 3 percent preferred Chinese-American partners, while 41 percent indicated a clear preference for partners who are not Chinese-American.

Only 7 percent preferred Chinese-American supervisors, while 46 percent indicated a preference for supervisors who are not Chinese-American. Over two-thirds felt the department should hire more Chinese-American police officers, but only 10 percent indicated they would seek the advice of other Chinese-American officers with respect to their work. While over 60 percent felt that Chinese-Americans would prefer to make complaints to Chinese-American officers, only 20 percent expressed a preference for policing in heavily Chinese-American neighborhoods. Less than half felt that choosing policing as a career had improved their social status, although 86 percent viewed policing as a worthwhile career and more than half would encourage friends or relatives to pursue a career in policing. Unlike members of some other minorities in policing, 86 percent agreed that there are promotional opportunities for them in policing, 78 percent felt they were fairly evaluated, and 68 percent agreed that their duties had been fairly assigned.

Lin concludes that Chinese-American officers are well integrated into policing in New York City and that they tend to distance themselves from other Chinese-Americans in some ways, much as some officers who represent other minority groups tend to distance themselves from their racial or ethnic groups. It appears, as seems to be the case with black officers as well, that Chinese-American officers prefer to be viewed first and foremost as police officers, at least while on duty.

Other Asian minorities also require the attention of the police. Refugees from Vietnam, Cambodia, and Laos have formed enclaves in many urban areas, establishing subcultural pockets as their numbers increase. Numerous officers have reported difficulties in communicating with and understanding the culture of such refugees. Korean and Japanese neighborhoods also exist in cities around the country, and residents of these areas, too, may present difficulties in terms of providing (or requesting) police services. Further, Asian and Oriental neighborhoods are not the crime-free areas we once thought them to be. There is clear evidence of Chinese involvement in organized numbers operations and racketeering, of Vietnamese involvement in drug rings, of Korean involvement in illegal massage parlors, and so on (O'Connor, 1985).

The Dilemma of Recruiting and Promoting Minority Police Officers

The recruitment and promotion of qualified minority group members by police departments are essential for several reasons. When police agencies do not represent the communities they serve in terms of race and ethnicity, and perhaps to some extent gender as well, suspicion and distrust arise among members of both the police organization and the minority groups in question. Research has shown that interaction that occurs among those equally well qualified for the positions they occupy tends to reduce such suspicion and distrust. Further, understanding and communicating with members of different racial and ethnic groups that are characterized by different cultural or subcultural values, attitudes, and beliefs are essential for any public servant in a multicultural, multiethnic society. In addition, minority group members who become police officers may serve as living proof that it is possible to succeed for minority youngsters who need such role models. Finally, equal treatment regardless of race, ethnicity, religion, or gender is the foundation for a truly democratic society.

Yet, there is a down side to minority recruitment as well. In some cases minority group members are recruited or promoted for reasons other than ability and competency. When this occurs, members of the dominant group are adversely affected and a backlash may be expected. Minority group members, whether qualified or not, are in the spotlight in many police organizations. Their behavior is critically scrutinized at every turn and this is especially true if the standards according to which they were hired are different from those that applied to dominant group members. This scrutiny may make the minority group members feel as if they are on trial, or have been singled out for close observation and criticism—increasing the stress under which they operate—which may, in turn, make it more difficult for them to perform well.

In some cases, as a result of our desire to correct past wrongs as quickly as possible, we quite simply hire and promote personnel who should not have been hired or promoted. When the city of Miami responded to demands from minority communities that more minorities be hired by consenting to hire 80 percent minorities, minority citizens were pleased but police administrators and many white police officers were outraged. In what some perceive as a direct result of hiring and promoting large numbers of minority group members in a relatively short (seven-year) period, some twenty-five Miami police officers have been arrested for crimes ranging from burglary to murder, the morale of the police is extremely low, and there is considerable talk about a need for change in city and department administration (Dorschner, 1987).

The solution to this dilemma is obvious, but difficult to achieve. In simple terms, race, ethnicity, and gender should not be considerations when hiring or promoting police personnel. There is no evidence to support the belief that any of these factors determine success or lack of success in policing. Eliminating these factors in the hiring and promotional process means developing tests that are not inherently biased in terms of such factors; herein lies the difficulty. Such tests are likely to be considerably different from those traditionally employed and are likely to be perceived as inferior to those previously taken by officers who were hired in the past. Of course, different does not necessarily imply inferior, either in testing or with respect to race, ethnicity, and gender, and we must find ways to make this point clearly and certainly.

Until the suggested reforms in hiring and promoting become widespread, we must work hard at dealing with biases of those already employed in police work. Occupational discrimination continues to occur on a regular basis in squad rooms, locker rooms, and patrol cars in many police agencies. While most police officers are smart enough to understand that outright racial slurs to other citizens are likely to lead to disciplinary action sooner or later, many continue to use such terms among themselves and with respect to minority officers. Indeed, in order to be more accepted in the fraternity, some minority group members use derogatory terms to describe members of their own racial or ethnic group, allowing white officers to rationalize their behavior by pointing to this fact. In spite of their lack of widespread popularity, human relations and community relations courses need to be offered on a regular basis, if for no other reason than to combat occupational discrimination, which too often becomes institutionalized.

To sum up the current situation with respect to minority police officers, the following observations are made. Minority officers have largely achieved representation commensurate with their population share and now have the same legal rights and responsibilities as other police officers. However, it is clear that minority officers still face discrimination in duty assignments and promotion. While numerous law enforcement agencies have made attempts to eliminate discrimination in hiring and promoting minority officers, this has proven to be a difficult and complex task. Minority officers often lack the skills necessary to gain access to higher education, and many do not compete well using traditional measures such as written tests. As a result of these factors, court decisions, and civil rights legislation, police entry-level and promotional requirements have sometimes been changed. Such changes have caused some to argue that police agencies are lowering their standards and recruiting unqualified minorities.

These fears that hiring minorities for police work will result in a more negative image of the police, based upon lower standards and performance, remain real for many white, male police officers. It is our belief that such changes will lead to better, more representative, police departments and that changing standards so that they are equitable to members of both genders and all racial and ethnic groups need not be equated with lowering standards and poor performance. At least at present, the information we have appears to support this belief.

Discussion Questions

1. Why and how have women and minority group members been excluded from police work over the years?

2. Summarize the research relating to the performance of policewomen on patrol. Are you convinced that policewomen are as capable as policemen? Why or why not?

3. What are the basic advantages police departments gain when hiring members of racial or ethnic minorities?

4. Do affirmative action programs sometimes result in reverse discrimination? What pressures do affirmative action programs place on minority group members who are hired?

5. What stresses do minority officers experience in addition to those experienced by white police officers?

6. What steps can be taken to address occupational discrimination? To improve understanding among police officers of different racial/ethnic groups?

References

Alex, N. 1969. *Black in Blue*. New York: Appleton-Century-Crofts.

Alex, N. 1976. *New York Cops Talk Back*. New York: Wiley.

Balkin, J. 1988. "Why Policemen Don't Like Policewomen." *Journal of Police Science and Administration* 16(1), 29–37.

Bartlett, H.W. and Rosenblum, A. 1977. "Policewomen Effectiveness." Denver, CO: Denver Civil Service Commission.

Bartol, C.R., Bergen, G.T., and Volckens, J.S. 1992. "Women in Small-Town Policing: Job Performance and Stress." *Criminal Justice and Behavior* 19(3), 240–260.

Baumann, M. 1991. "Women Cops and Sexism." *USA TODAY* (24 July), p. 11A.

Bell, D.J. 1982. "Policewomen—Myths and Reality." *Journal of Police Science and Administration* 10, 112–120.

Block, P. and Anderson, D. 1974. *Policewomen on Patrol: Final Report*. Washington, DC: Urban Institute.

Carter, D.L. 1983. "Hispanic Interaction with the Criminal Justice System in Texas: Experiences, Attitudes, and Perceptions." *Journal of Criminal Justice* 11, 211–227.

Carter, D.L. 1986. "Hispanic Police Officers' Perception of Discrimination." *Police Studies* 19(4), 204–210.

Carter, D.L. and Sapp, A.D. 1991. *Police Education and Minority Recruitment: The Impact of a College Requirement*. Washington, DC: Police Executive Research Forum.

Charles, M.T. 1982. "Women in Policing—The Physical Aspect." *Journal of Police Science and Administration* 10, 194–205.

Church, G.L. 1992. "The Fire This Time." *Newsweek* (1 May), p. 19–25.

Clancy, P. 1987. "Hispanic Population Rate Soars." *USA TODAY* (11 September), p. 1a.

Davis, J.A. 1984. "Perspectives of Policewomen in Texas and Oklahoma." *Journal of Police Science and Administration* 12(4), 395–403.

Dorschner, J. 1987. "The Dark Side of the Force." In Dunham, R.G. and Alpert, G.P. (eds.), *Critical Issues in Policing: Contemporary Readings*. Prospect Heights, IL: Waveland Press.

Felkenes, G.T. and Lasley, J.R. 1992. "Implications of Hiring Women Police Officers: Police Administrators' Concerns May Not Be Justified." *Policing and Society* 3(1), 41–50.

Fountain, J.W. 1991. "Minority Cops Making Gains in Suburbs." *Chicago Tribune* (20 October), sec. 2, pp. 1–2.

Fry, L. and Greenfield, S. 1980. "An Examination of Attitudinal Differences Between Policewomen and Policemen." *Journal of Applied Psychology* 65, 123–126.

Gaines, L.K., Kappeler, V.E., and Vaughn, J.B. 1994. *Policing in America*. Cincinnati: Anderson.

Garrison, C.G., Grant, N., and McCormick, K. 1988. "Utilization of Police Women." *Police Chief* (September), 32–72.

Gest, T. 1987. "A One-White, One-Black Quota for Promotions." *U.S. News and World Report* (March) 9, 8.

Grown, M.C. and Carlson, R.D. 1993. "Do Male Policemen Accept Women on Patrol Yet? Androgyny, Public Complaints, and Dad." *Journal of Police and Criminal Psychology* 9(1), 10–14.

Gup, T. 1988. "Racism in the Raw in Suburban Chicago." *Time* (17 October), pp. 25–26.

Hacker, A. 1992. *Two Nations: Black and White, Separate, Hostile, and Unequal*. New York: Ballantine Books.

Haynes, K.A. 1993. "How Good Are Women Cops?" *Ebony* (September), 64–68.

Homant, R.J. and Kennedy, D.B. 1985. "Police Perceptions of Spouse Abuse—A Comparison of Male and Female Officers." *Journal of Criminal Justice* 13, 29–47.

Horne, P. 1980. *Women in Law Enforcement*. Springfield, IL: Charles Thomas.

House, C.H. 1993. "The Changing Role of Women in Law Enforcement." *Police Chief* 60(10), 139–144.

Jackson, C. and Wallach, I. 1973. "Perceptions of the Police in a Black Community." In Snibbe, J.R. and Snibbe, H.M. (eds.), *The Urban Police in Transition*. Springfield, IL: Charles Thomas, 382–403.

Jacobs, J.B. and Cohen, J. 1978. "The Impact of Racial Integration on the Police." *Journal of*

Police Science and Administration 6(2), 179–183.

Johnson, W. 1992. "Breaking Ground Wasn't Always Easy." *Journal Star* (17 May), p. B5.

Journal Star. 1989. "Police Officers Named in Bias Suit" (15 December), p. 12.

Kanter, R. 1977. *Men and Women of the Corporation.* New York: Basic Books.

Kennedy, J.M. 1988. "Latino FBI Agents Bias Victims: Judge." *Journal Star* (1 October), p. A2.

Kerber, K.W., Andes, S.M., and Mittler, M.B. 1977. "Citizen Attitudes Regarding the Competence of Female Officers." *Journal of Police Science and Administration* 5(3), 337–347.

Koenig, E.J. 1978. "An Overview of Attitudes Toward Women in Law Enforcement." *Public Administration Review* 38, 267–275.

Kuykendall, J. and Burns, D. 1980. "The Black Police Officer: An Historical Perspective." *Journal of Contemporary Criminal Justice* 1(4), 103–113.

Langer, G. 1988. "Americans Say Racism Persists." *Journal Star* (8 August), p. 2.

Leinen, S. 1984. *Black Police, White Society.* New York: University Press.

Lin, T. 1987. "Chinese-American Police Officers in New York City." Unpublished master's thesis. Macomb, IL: Western Illinois University.

Linn, E. and Price, B.R. 1985. "The Evolving Role of Women in American Policing." In Blumberg, A.S. and Niederhoffer, E. (eds.), *The Ambivalent Force: Perspectives on the Police* 3 ed. New York: Holt, Rinehart & Winston, 69–80.

Maguire, K., Pastore, A.L., and Flanagan, T.J. 1992. *Bureau of Justice Statistics Sourcebook of Criminal Justice Statistics—1992.* Washington, DC: U.S. Government Printing Office.

Margolis, R. 1971. *Who Will Wear the Badge? A Study of Minority Recruitment Efforts in Protective Services.* Report of the United States Commission on Civil Rights. Washington, DC: U.S. Government Printing Office.

Martin, C. 1983. "Women Police and Stress." *Police Chief* 50, 107–109.

Martin, S.E. 1993. "Female Officers on the Move? A Status Report on Women in Policing." In Dunham, R. G. and Alpert, G. P. (eds.), *Critical Issues in Policing: Contemporary Issues.* Prospect Heights, IL: Waveland Press, 312–29.

Martin, S.E. 1978. "Sexual Politics in the Workplace: The Interactional World of Policemen." *Symbolic Interaction* 1, 44–60.

Martin, S. E. 1982. "Dilemma of Equal Versus Equitable Treatment: Structural Barriers to the Incorporation of Policewomen into Police Work." In Stuart, P. and Carter, M. (eds.), *Autonomy in Work and Society.* Beverly Hills, CA: Sage.

McDowell, J. 1992. "Are Women Better Cops?" *Time* (17 February), 70–72.

McGeorge, J. and Wolfe, J.A. 1976. "Comparison of Attitudes Between Men and Women Police Officers—A Preliminary Analysis." *Criminal Justice Review* 1, 21–33.

National Archive of Criminal Justice Data Bulletin. 1989. "National Survey of Law Enforcement Agencies, 1987." (Winter). Ann Arbor, MI: The University of Michigan.

Newsweek. 1988. "A Mixed Verdict on Howard Beach." (4 January), 24.

O'Connor, C. 1985. "Crime: An Equal-Opportunity Employer." *Newsweek* (30 December), 22.

Parker, L. 1989. "Miami Officer Convicted: Black Community Expresses Relief." *Journal Star* (8 December), 1.

Poole, E.D. and Pogrebin, M.R. 1988. "Factors Affecting the Decision to Remain in Policing: A Study of Women Officers." *Journal of Police Science and Administration* 16(1), 49–55.

President's Commission on Law Enforcement and the Administration of Justice. 1967. *Task Force Report: The Administration of Justice.* Washington, DC: U. S. Government Printing Office.

Rogers, C.J. 1987. "Women in Criminal Justice: Similar and Unique Obstacles to Their Acceptance in Law Enforcement and Corrections," cited in Balkin, 1988.

Sauls, J.G. 1992. "The Civil Rights Act of 1991: New Challenges for Employers." *FBI Law Enforcement Bulletin* (September), 25–32.

Schaefer, R.T. 1993. *Racial and Ethnic Groups*. 5 ed. New York: Harper Collins.

Sherman, L.J. 1975. "Evaluation of Policewomen on Patrol in a Suburban Police Department." *Journal of Police Science and Administration 3*, 434–438.

Sichel, J.L., Friedman, L.N., Quint, J.C. and Smith, M.E. 1978. *Women on Patrol—A Pilot Study of Police Performance in New York City*. New York: Vera Institute of Justice.

Sullivan, P.S. 1989. "Minority Officers: Current Issues." In Dunham, R. and Alpert, G. (eds.), *Critical Issues in Policing: Contemporary Readings*. Prospect Heights, IL: Waveland Press.

Swan, R.D. 1988. "The History of American Women Police." *Women Police 1988* 22(2), 10–13.

Walker, S. 1989. *Employment of Black and Hispanic Police Officers, 1983–1988*. Omaha, NE: Center for Applied Urban Research.

Wexler, J.G. and Logan, D. D. 1983. "Sources of Stress Among Women Police Officers." *Journal of Police Science and Administration* 11, 46–53.

Williams, L. 1988. "Police Officers Tell of Strains of Living as a 'Black in Blue.'" *The New York Times* (14 February), pp. 1, 26.

Winters, C.A. 1991. "Hispanics and Policing in Chicago and Cook County, Illinois." *Police Journal* 64(1), 71–76.

9

THE POLICE SUBCULTURE
AND THE PERSONAL COSTS
OF POLICE WORK

In Chapter 5 we focused on organizational and administrative aspects of policing, the formal structure, and the impact of police leaders. While these formal considerations are crucial to an understanding of the police role, there are two other contributing factors that must be considered in our attempt to understand policing as an occupation: the police subculture and the pressures and stresses of police work. While police administrators and the law specify the broad parameters within which officers operate, the police subculture tells them how to go about their tasks, how hard to work, what kinds of relationships to have with their fellow officers and other categories of people with whom they interact, and how they should feel about police administrators, judges, the law, and the requirements and restrictions they impose.

Combined, the effects of formal pressures and the pressures generated by the police subculture often lead police officers to experience a great deal of stress in their occupational, social, and family lives, resulting in cynicism, burnout, and retirement, as well as a host of physical and emotional ailments. Further, many officers, initially at least, fail to recognize the extent to which the police subculture and their chosen occupation affect the ways in which they view and act towards others.

According to Hernandez (1989: 85), "Unlike most other occupations . . . [the police] view of reality may be rejected by the very people they are trying to serve. . . . The result for the police is that they must function while juggling the two worlds of fact and fiction, each of which carries its own risks. They can't escape the reality because they deal with it every day, nor can they act without a constant awareness of the differing ways in which their client populations perceive both the world and the public."

Inciardi (1990: 227) indicates that police officers develop resources to deal with the isolation from the community that results from the job and the police socialization process. These police subcultural attributes include "protective, supportive, and shared attitudes, values, understandings and views of the world," which result in a "blue fraternity" or closed police society (Inciardi, 1990: 227).

The Police Subculture

According to Westley (1970), the police subculture is a crucial concept in the explanation of police behavior and attitudes. The subculture, in his view, characterizes the public as hostile, untrustworthy, and potentially violent; this outlook requires secrecy, mutual support, and unity on the part of the police. Manning (1977, 1979) suggests that the inherent uncertainty of police work combined with the need for information control leads to police teamwork, which in turn generates collective ties and mutual dependency.

More recently, Manning (1989: 362), reviewing twenty-five years of research on police cultures, concludes that researchers "grant the occupational culture a significant place in determining officer behavior."

Further, Manning (1989: 363) states that as a result of the uncertain nature of police work, "The police officer is *dependent* on other officers for assistance, advice, training, working knowledge, protection in case of threats from internal or external sources, and insulation against the public and periodic danger." Many police officers view themselves as teammates linked together by portable and car radios, part of a team that is no stronger than its weakest member. As members of the team, they feel a good deal of pressure to live up to the expectations of other team members.

Thus, police officers tend to socialize with other officers (not unlike members of other occupational groups) and come to realize (unlike members of many other occupational groups) that their identities as police officers sometimes make them socially unacceptable even when off duty. That is, in some circles at least, there is a kind of stigma attached to those who are perceived as being "too close" to police officers; police officers themselves are sometimes suspicious of the motives of nonpolice who become too friendly. Others see the police as pursuing their own interests (improving their salaries, for example) in cases in which money collected through traffic citations is returned to the police department. In some instances, the families of the officers get to know one another and a kind of mutual protection society develops, furthering the alienation and isolation from the public (Barker, Hunter, and Rush, 1994).

The police subculture, "blue fraternity," or "brotherhood" consists of the informal rules and regulations, tactics, and folklore passed on from one generation of police officers to another. It is both a result and a cause of police isolation from the larger society and police solidarity. Its influence begins early in the new officer's career when he or she is told by more experienced officers that the "training given in police academies is irrelevant to 'real' police work" (Bayley and Bittner, 1989: 87).

What is relevant, recruits are told, is the experience of senior officers who "know the ropes" "know how to get around things." Recruits are often told by officers with considerable experience to forget what they learned in the academy and in college and start learning real police work. Among the first lessons learned are that police officers share secrets among themselves. These secrets, especially when they deal with activities that are questionable in terms of ethics, legality, and departmental policy, are not to be divulged to others. Officers also learn that administrators often cannot be trusted, and that the police are at "war" with criminals and, sometimes, with other citizens in general. This emphasis on the police occupational subculture as unique results in many officers regarding themselves as members of a "blue minority" (Cox and Fitzgerald, 1991; Skolnick and Fyfe, 1993). "The general feeling among police officers is that the public is not to be trusted . . . that people are very finicky about supporting the police. People will say that they think police officers do a hard job, and they respect them. But if you're giving somebody a ticket, then suddenly you become the bad guy, and they think you're doing a lousy job and you're stupid" (Kunen, 1986: 127–128).

Thus officers tend to divide the world into "we" and "they," the former consisting of other police officers, the latter encompassing almost everybody else. To be sure, members of other occupational groups also develop their own subcultures and world views, but often not to the same extent as the police (Skolnick, 1966). "Set apart from the conventional world, the policeman experiences an exceptionally strong tendency to find his social identity within his occupational milieu" (Skolnick, 1966: 52). Skolnick goes on to indicate that some factors inherent in police work contribute to this tendency. Among these factors are danger, authority, and the need to appear efficient.

Danger, Authority, and Efficiency

While police work is not the most dangerous occupation, danger is always a possibility (see Highlight 9.1). Who knows when the traffic stop at midday will lead to an armed attack on the police officer involved? Who can predict which angry spouse involved in a domestic dispute will batter a police officer (or for that matter whether both spouses will)? Who knows when a sniper firing from a rooftop will direct his shots at the windshield of a patrol car? Under what circumstances will a mentally disordered person turn on an officer attempting to assist? Will drivers approaching an intersection heed the flashing lights and siren? Will minority group members organize, take to the streets, and single out police officers as targets? Does the fleeing youthful burglar have a firearm under his shirt? Danger is an ever-present possibility in policing and highly unpredictable except in certain types of situations.

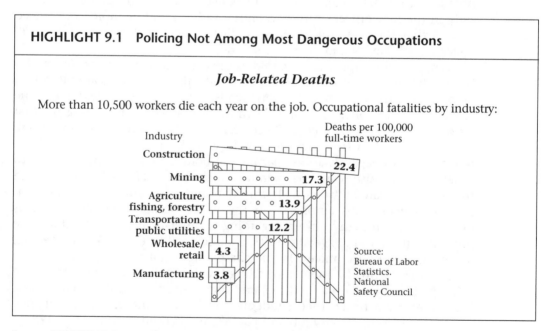

HIGHLIGHT 9.1   **Policing Not Among Most Dangerous Occupations**

Job-Related Deaths

More than 10,500 workers die each year on the job. Occupational fatalities by industry:

Industry — Deaths per 100,000 full-time workers

- Construction — 22.4
- Mining — 17.3
- Agriculture, fishing, forestry — 13.9
- Transportation/public utilities — 12.2
- Wholesale/retail — 4.3
- Manufacturing — 3.8

Source: Bureau of Labor Statistics. National Safety Council

Source: *USA TODAY*, Sept. 6, 1991: p. 1A.

In fact, because of the unpredictable nature of danger in policing, we train police officers to be suspicious of most if not all other citizens they encounter. We encourage them to treat other citizens encountered as "symbolic assailants," approach them in certain ways, notify headquarters of their whereabouts when making a stop, wait for a "cover" or backup car to arrive before proceeding in potentially dangerous cases, and so on (Skolnick, 1966; Barker, Hunter, and Rush, 1994). We teach police officers to assess others with whom they are involved in terms of their ability to physically "handle" those others if it becomes necessary and to be aware that in most instances their encounters with other citizens will be perceived as creating "trouble" for those citizens. We teach them that they work in an "alien" environment in which everyone knows who they are while they lack such information about most of the people with whom they interact (Rubinstein, 1973).

Additionally, of course, we tell police officers that as representatives of government, they have specific authority to intervene in a wide array of situations. We equip them with batons, side arms, handcuffs, portable radios, shotguns for their vehicles, mace, partners, backup officers, and uniforms to be sure that their image as authority figures is complete and unmistakable. We tell them that when dealing with a dispute in progress, their definition of the situation must prevail—they must "take charge" of the situation.

What we don't routinely tell them, but what they learn very quickly on the streets, is that other citizens frequently resent their intervention. We don't warn them that other citizens, when treated suspiciously by the police, may react with hostility, resentment, contempt, and occasionally physical violence; nor do we teach them routinely that certain segments of the population hate them or hold them in contempt simply because they wear the badge and uniform. When members of these groups challenge the authority of the police, based on their training, the police sometimes resort to threats or the use of force to impose their authority, raising the possibility of escalating the level of danger in the encounters. On those relatively rare occasions where the challenge to authority is prolonged or vicious, danger may become the foremost concern of all parties involved, and the capacity to use force, including deadly force in appropriate circumstances, becomes paramount (Bittner, 1970). Under these circumstances, the need for police solidarity and the feelings of isolation and alienation from other citizens become apparent.

At the same time, Skolnick (1966) argues, we expect the police to be efficient. The police themselves are concerned with at least giving the appearance of efficiency because performance evaluations and promotions often depend on it. Concerns with efficiency and the resulting pressures they produce have increased dramatically with the computerization of the police world and other technological advances. Simultaneously, taxpayers have begun to demand greater accountability for the costs involved in policing and more well-educated (and therefore more costly) police personnel. The resulting "do more with less" philosophy has led many police executives to emphasize even more the importance of efficient performance. "Citizens expect professional police behavior, respectful treatment, maintenance of human dignity, responsiveness, and a high value on human life. In addition, these increasingly sophisticated taxpayers also insist that the police achieve maximum effectiveness and efficiency in the use of their tax dollars" (Carey, 1994: 24).

However, the police subculture has established standards of acceptable performance for officers and resists raising these standards. Officers whose performances exceed these standards are often considered to be "rate-busters" and threats to those adhering to traditional expectations. For example, fueling the patrol car in some departments is an operation for which the officer is expected by the subculture to allot twenty to thirty minutes. Since the operation may actually take less than five minutes, administrators concerned about accountability, totaling the amount of time lost in this operation for, say, ten cars, recognize they are losing two to three hours of patrol time if they fail to take action to modify the fueling procedure. At the same time, however, officers concerned about accountability who wish to patrol an additional fifteen to twenty minutes and fuel the car in less time make those officers adhering to the twenty- to thirty-minute standard look bad and are under considerable pressure to conform to the established standard. Similar expectations and conflicts exist with respect to the number of drunk drivers and felons who can be processed in a shift, subpoenas that may be served, or prisoners who may be transported. Officers must make choices as to whose expectations are to be met and sometimes operate in a no win situation in which meeting one set of expectations automatically violates the other, leaving the officer under some stress no matter how he or she operates.

Sparrow, Moore, and Kennedy (1990: 51) argue that the police subculture creates a set of "truths" according to which officers are expected to live. Note that there is some basis in fact for each of these subcultural truths, and that each makes integrating the police and the citizens they serve more difficult. The "truths" are:

1. Police are the only real crime fighters.
2. No one understands the nature of police work except fellow officers.
3. Loyalty to colleagues counts more than anything else.
4. It is impossible to win the war on crime without bending the rules.
5. Other citizens are unsupportive and make unreasonable demands.
6. Patrol work is only for those who are not smart enough to get out of it.

The Police Personality: Myth or Reality?

Some have suggested that the impact of police work and the police subculture itself lead to the development of a distinctive police personality. Burbeck and Furnham (1985), in reviewing the literature on police attitudes, found that police officers (in comparison with the general population) place more emphasis on family security and sense of accomplishment and less on social equality. Further, experienced officers appear to deemphasize affective values.

Over the years, the literature on the police has characterized them as more authoritarian and prejudiced than other occupational groups. Authoritarian personalities tend to be conservative, rigid, punitive, and inflexible and emphasize authority and rules (Adorno et al., 1950). As Burbeck and Furnham (1985) have noted, studies do not support the contention that individuals possessing these traits seek out police work, thus the presence of the traits may be the result of occupational and subcultural pressures. In addition, it may be argued that the military background of large numbers of police personnel, particularly in the period between the Civil War and the middle of the twentieth century, may have been (and may still be, since some of these personnel are now chief executive officers in police agencies) a factor in authoritarianism (Hernandez, 1989).

Prejudice (in this case unfavorable attitudes toward a group or individual not based on experience or fact) appears to be more common among those with authoritarian traits. Prejudiced individuals tend to develop and adhere to stereotypes based on race, ethnicity, occupational group, and other factors. Police actions based on such stereotypes are discriminatory and clearly inappropriate in a democratic society. There is little doubt that many police officers have negative stereotypes of particular groups in the public, or that the police subculture creates, sustains, and supports such stereotypes (Van Maanen, 1978; Cray, 1972; Chevigny, 1969; Kirkham, 1977; Cox and Fitzgerald, 1991; Rudovsky, 1992). Since these stereotypes and prejudices are attitudes and cannot be directly observed, they are difficult, if not impossible, to eliminate among police officers or the general public. Discriminatory actions, however, are observable and steps to prevent such actions must be taken. The extent to which prejudices and stereotypes are translated into discriminatory action remains an empirical question, though there is no doubt that it sometimes happens.

Cynicism is yet another feature of the police officer's working personality addressed by students of the police. As defined by Niederhoffer (1967: 96), cynicism involves a loss of faith in people, enthusiasm for police work, and pride and integrity. Niederhoffer and others (Regoli and Poole, 1978) found that cynicism peaked in the seventh to tenth year of police service and the latter noted that the level of cynicism varies with the organizational style of the department and the type of department (urban or rural). Within different police subcultures, cynicism is thought to involve different issues including the public, police administration, courts, training and education, dedication to duty, and police solidarity (Regoli, 1976; Bouza, 1990).

Langworthy and Travis (1994: 354) note that cynicism is often found among officers who view themselves as combatants in a war. Such officers frequently believe that violence can occur at any moment, causing them to hold a negative image of the nature of humanity and to believe that only sheer force can maintain social order. Alpert and Dunham (1992: 94) conclude: "There is some evidence for the existence of a police working personality. Most of the evidence points to the influence of socialization and experiences after becoming a police officer as the main source of the unique traits."

In contrast, Terry (1989) reviews numerous studies that have found essentially no differences between police officers and those in other occupations with respect to either authoritarianism or prejudice, or that have found police officers to be intelligent, emotionally stable, and service oriented. Carpenter and Raza (1987: 16) report that police applicants differ from the general population in several positive ways: "They are more psychologically healthy than the normative population, as they are generally less depressed and anxious, and more assertive and interested in making and maintaining social contacts."

Terry (1989: 550) concedes that while some of the research on police personalities does appear to distinguish certain traits, no one has been able to "disentangle the effects of a person's socioeconomic background from the demands that police work and its subculture places upon individual officers." Lundman (1980: 74), summarizing police socialization practices at the end of the 1970s, noted that compared to the largely white, high school educated males of the recent past, more police recruits are college educated and members of minority groups. He found that quasi-military training is giving way to other, less rigid alternatives. "Some academies feature technical training with primary emphasis given to the maintenance of order under the rule of law. A minority of academies offer non-stress training featuring a condensed liberal arts curriculum. Some departments select 'coaches' for new officers in terms of their police skills and adherence to a 'softer' approach to policing. A possible effect of these slow and uneven changes is diversity in the working personalities of patrol officers" (Lundman, 1980: 74).

Changes during the past decade have followed the patterns discussed by Lundman and others (Post, 1992), and the number of departments and academies featuring such changes has clearly increased. As a result of these and other changes, it is difficult to say that there exists today a distinct police personality; research does not support the existence of a single dominant personality type among police officers. Yarmey (1990: 42) states: "There is no evidence for such a thing as a typical police personality showing a cluster of traits that is constant across time and space."

The Personal Costs of Police Work

In spite of the fact that there does not appear to be a cluster of personality traits that distinguish police officers from other occupational groups, there is no doubt that the nature of police work and the subculture in which it occurs create difficulties for officers, their families, and friends (see Highlight 9.2). The need to perform under stress is a concern in many professions; policing is probably not as stressful as some other occupations. However, as Trojanowicz (1980) indicates, it is easier to identify the factors that cause stress and strain in policing than it is to eliminate or substantially reduce them.

Bartol (1983) says that stress occurs when a stimulus leads to a response that does not lead to greater perceived or actual control over the stimulus. He lists as major causes of stress among police officers the following: inefficiency in the courts, court decisions, poor equipment, shift work, working conditions, eating habits, pay, boredom and inactivity, role conflict, and alienation from the public. To this list we might add excessive paperwork, red tape, lack of participation in decision making, and competition for promotion, among others.

Stratton (1978) has classified police stressors into four groups: external, internal, occupational, and individual. He has also identified some of the

HIGHLIGHT 9.2   "Attitude Change" Proves Lethal for Police

By Robert Davis USA TODAY

Family, friends and fellow officers will gather Tuesday to bury Washington, D.C.'s Jason White—one of 73 U.S. police officers gunned down in 1993.

At least 140 officers nationwide were killed in the line of duty last year. A final count will be available later this year.

"A major attitude change has occurred in this country toward law enforcement," says Dennis Martin, head of the National Association of Chiefs of Police, which released the statistics. "We see a lot of bitter attitudes toward police."

White was shot in the head Thursday night. Early medical reports indicate he was killed with controversial Black Talon bullets, which expand on impact. His partner survived a shot to her body armor.

She joins the ranks of more than 90,000 officers who annually survive various assaults.

Some experts note highly publicized examples of souring relations between police and the public, including:
• The videotaped beating of motorist Rodney King by Los Angeles police in 1991.
• Malice Green's 1992 beating death by Detroit police.
• Police officers charged with crimes, including 113 Washington, D.C., officers—out of 4,200—who were indicted or charged in 1993.

"That breaks down respect," Martin says. "There's a big wall up. It's them against us."

Both sides are shooting.

According to the FBI's latest figures, police killed 415 felons in the line of duty in 1992.

Overall, there were 23,760 homicides in 1992; while no tally is ready for 1993, at least 22 major U.S. cities have already reported homicide records.

"If I go into a back yard looking for a burglar and see a man with a gun, I don't know if it's the burglar or the homeowner hunting the burglar," says Lt. Jack Ballentine of the San Francisco Police Department.

194 gun deaths—and counting

One hour into the new year, a digital billboard on New York's Times Square began the grim task of counting the number of people killed by handguns in the USA in 1994.

Using federal statistics as a guide, the "deathclock" adds a new death every 14.8 minutes. Forty-eight hours after starting, the toll was at 194.

The clock also shows the number of guns in the USA—220 million and growing.

Investor broker, Robert Brennan, who helped the billboard's sponsor, Dehere Gun Fighters of America Inc., says he wants to install clocks in Los Angeles, Miami, Washington and other cities.

"They have a crisis and they get their gun out," Ballentine says. "They've had a few drinks and now they're going to make some decisions with this gun for the first time ever."

Martin says police officers are usually killed by white men ages 18 to 34 who have been drinking or using drugs.

"People are being desensitized by the movies and TV," he says. "They don't see the heartbreak, they just see Sylvester Stallone going around mowing people down. People don't see the human side."

Deaths of police officers in the line of duty

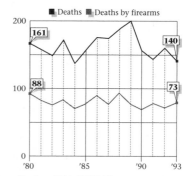

By Suzy Parker, *USA TODAY*

specific stressors occurring in police work as a result of these three categories: situations that require the officer to be in an alert state (autonomic nervous system response) whether or not action is taken; situations in which the officer is responsible for the lives of others; rotating shift assignments and the accompanying biological and social changes required. To these stressors others have added low self-esteem and constant exposure to the darker side of life. Geiger (1982) indicates that these sources of stress may be found in small and large police agencies. Bartol, Bergen, and Volckens (1992) found that, while stress was present among the officers they studied, it did not appear to affect job performance.

All occupations involve stress, and stress need not always be harmful. In fact, moderate stress appears to be positively related to productivity. Elimination of all stress is neither possible nor desirable. However, the effects of prolonged high levels of stress are clearly dysfunctional, producing both debilitating psychological and physical symptoms. In part, the damage caused by stress occurs because of the "General Adaptation Syndrome" identified by Selye (1974). In the first stage of this syndrome, the body prepares to fight stress by releasing hormones that lead to an increase in respiration and heartbeat. In the second stage the body attempts to resist the stressor and repair any damage that has occurred. If the stress continues long enough and cannot be successfully met through either flight or fight, the third stage, exhaustion, occurs. Repeated exposures to stressors that cannot be eliminated or modified by the organism eventually lead to stage three. Police officers experience such stressors repeatedly in the performance of their duties as well as during off-duty time (as when they are required to carry an off-duty weapon).

The inability to find a way to relieve stress may lead to burnout, which is characterized by emotional exhaustion and cynicism. Officers experiencing such stress sometimes turn to alcohol or other drugs, physical aggression, and even suicide in attempting to alleviate stress. In fact, these perceived solutions simply make the problem worse and increase the stress level of the officer. The literature on the police is replete with data on high rates of divorce (though there is conflicting research here), alcoholism, and suicide (Terry, 1981; Wagner and Brzeczek, 1983; Hill and Clawson, 1988; Josephson and Reiser, 1990; Swanson, Gaines, and Gore, 1991).

Perhaps an example of the incidents occurring in the first few hours of a police officer's tour of duty will help clarify the stressors to which officers are routinely subjected. Shortly after reporting to work the officer receives a call that another officer requires immediate assistance. The officer responding to the call for help turns on red lights and siren and drives as rapidly as possibly to reach his or her colleague. On the way, he or she is preparing for the possibility of a physical struggle or armed resistance and the physical changes described previously are taking place. The officer is tense and excited but also frightened. The fear experienced may have to do with anticipation about what will happen when he or she arrives at the scene but also has to do with what other drivers noting the red lights and siren—or failing to note them—will do. Will they yield at intersections? Will they pull off to the right? To the left? Will they stop in the middle of the street? Will they slow down or speed up? What will the chief say if the officer is involved in an accident?

Arriving at the scene, the officer finds the situation under control, a suspect in custody, and his or her colleague uninjured. As the officer gets back into the patrol car, another call comes from the dispatcher. This call involves an accident with serious injuries. The officer drives to the scene (with the same set of concerns about arriving safely as before), is the first emergency officer to arrive, and finds that several people have been seriously injured and an infant killed. After the accident has been "handled," the officer gets into his or her vehicle and is told to come to the station to meet with the chief. The officer's concerns on the way are somewhat different but perhaps equally stressful. For the next several hours and, in some cities, for the next several days, weeks, and years, these scenarios are repeated. The ups and downs of police work take their toll and the officer experiences repeated stress, tension, and perhaps burnout.

The literature on police stress is extensive and suggests that the interaction of personality and situational factors determines the amount and type of stress experienced by the individual. Fell, Richard, and Wallace (1980) examined police death certificates and concluded that they indicate a high rate of premature death due to stress-related factors. They also noted that the suicide rate among police officers is the third highest among 130 occupations. Wagner and Brzeczek (1983) found that Chicago police officers were five times as likely as other citizens of the city to be suicide victims, but their sample size was quite small (221 suicides). Josephson and Reiser (1990), however, found the rate of suicide among Los Angeles police officers to be about the same as the general population. The authors did find that the suicide rate among police officers was increasing but were unable to draw significant conclusions because the size of their sample was so small (14 suicides).

Storms, Penn, and Tenzell (1990) examined police officers' self-perceptions and compared them with police officers' perceptions of "the ideal" police officer. They found that the ideal officer was perceived as good, decisive, active, strong, fast, right (versus wrong), responsive, masculine, flexible, and considerate. Police officers perceived themselves as possessing most of these same characteristics but to a lesser degree than the ideal officer. The authors conclude that while officers perceive themselves as falling a little short of the ideal, they basically have positive self-images.

Spielberger, Westberry, Grier, and Greenfield (1981) indicate that organizational and administrative factors are as important in determining levels of police stress as are physical danger and emotional stress resulting from the police role. Stratton, Parker, and Snibbe (1984) studied the effects of shooting situations and documented psychological reactions ranging from sleep disturbances to anger. Violanti, Marshall, and Howe (1985) found that stress was an important factor in alcohol use among police officers. Burke and Deszca (1986) noted that older officers, with higher rank and more years of service, drank and smoked more and exercised less that their younger, less experienced, and lower-ranking colleagues. Pendergrass and Ostrove (1986) found that both male and female officers drank more alcohol than the general population and that female officers' drinking patterns resembled those of males. Violanti et al. (1986) found that police officers have significantly higher rates of death from cancer and suicide than the general population. O'Neil (1986) found that shift work is a source of stress among police officers who cannot maintain regular sleep patterns during days off, since adaptation to night work does not occur.

Stress and Police Families

Other studies have focused on the effects of police work on the police family. Maynard and Maynard (1982) found that police wives viewed inherent job demands, shift rotation, changing schedules, and promotional practices as sources of strain on police families. Carson (1987) found that marital difficulties sometimes result from police shootings and police use of excessive force. Hageman (1989) notes that while the family is often viewed as a stress reducer in other occupations, in policing the spouse often becomes identified as one of the stressors. Hageman also points out that while police divorce rates appear to be no higher than those in the general population, officers' perceptions of the impact of the job on their marriages often differs significantly from those of their spouses, indicating a potential for misunderstanding and distrust.

Blumberg and Niederhoffer (1985: 371), in discussing the police family, indicate "The police profession is a jealous mistress, intruding in intimate family relationships, disrupting the rhythms of married life. The danger of police work arouses fears for the safety of loved ones. The revolving schedule of a patrol officer's 'around-the-clock' tours of duty complicates family logistics. . . . Although wives adapt to the pressures of the occupation on family life, they, nevertheless, gripe about the injustices and inconsistencies. They resent the 'secret society' nature of police work that obstructs free-flowing communication between spouses. Paradoxically, although they are treated as aliens in the police world, their family lifestyle is scrutinized by a curious public."

The literature on the police contains discussions of the impact of policing on not only the primary marital relationship but on relationships between police parents and their children. The cycle of initial enthusiasm over the job leading to daily/nightly discussions of the workday between spouses, the hardening of the police spouse emotionally, and the alienation of the spouses has been vividly described by other writers as well (Doerner, 1985; Wambaugh, 1975).

Promotional Stress in Police Organizations

The announcement that promotional opportunities exist within a police department typically generates a good deal of stress among officers. This response should not be unexpected when we look at the hierarchical, paramilitary organizational structure of most police agencies. The organizational chart looks like a pyramid with very little room at the top, indicating that promotional opportunities occur only periodically and that one may have only a limited number of chances to be promoted in a twenty-year career. For those desiring to move up the rank ladder, every opportunity must be grabbed and pursued energetically. Yet, only a few individuals, sometimes only one individual, will be selected for advancement. How are these few selected?

In most departments, advancing through the ranks depends on success in passing both a written and oral examination and attainment and maintenance of high performance standards in the current rank. However, in many police agencies, the belief prevails that these assessments are not the only considerations. The belief prevails that officers who are "well-connected" at the upper levels of the department or in political circles have the edge. Some believe equally strongly that subjective elements play a major role in determining who gets promoted.

To some extent, current promotional procedures contribute to these concerns. For example, once the written test, performance evaluations, and oral examinations have been conducted and scored, the chief executive officer is often allowed to pick any of the top three candidates for the position. This practice raises questions as to the importance of the overall score attained on the three components of the testing procedure in determining promotability. If the tests are valid and reliable, why isn't the top scorer automatically given the position? Is the testing process followed because it is objective or to give the appearance of objectivity? Suppose that someone attains the highest score but is passed over for the position. Suppose that someone takes but fails the written examination. Suppose that someone takes the written examination whenever it is given, scores well on it and the other portions of the promotional process, but is never promoted? What if promotions are determined by race or gender, regardless of test scores, or worse, suppose test scores are altered so that only certain individuals are eligible for promotion? These and a host of other concerns relating to the promotional process make it a stressful event in many police departments (Schaefer, 1983).

Police Shootings as a Source of Stress

"Each year, some thirty thousand Americans die through the suicidal, homicidal, or accidental abuse of guns; many hundreds of thousands more are injured; many hundreds of thousands more are victimized by gun crime" (Wright, 1986: 1). The National Institute of Justice survey discussed by Wright, based on 1,800 convicted and incarcerated adult, male felons, indicated that 50 percent were "gun criminals" and another 11 percent were armed with other potentially deadly weapons. In 1993, a new gun death occurred every 14.8 minutes, and there were at least 220 million guns in the United States (Davis, 1994).

Although it is extremely difficult to predict future dangerous behavior, police officers must attempt to do so on a regular basis. Their failure to do so accurately may cost them their lives. Eighty-eight police officers were shot in the line of duty in 1980, sixty-seven were killed in the line of duty in 1989, and seventy-three lost their lives carrying out their duties in 1993 (Davis, 1994). Forty percent of the officers killed between 1980–1991 were in the process of apprehending or arresting suspects when killed, and 74 percent were "patrol officers," "deputy sheriffs," or "troopers" (Fridell and Pate, 1993: 578). Firearms continue to be the weapons most often used to slay police officers. Clearly, being shot or shooting someone else is a possibility for police officers, although the probability is low. The stress of actually being involved in a shooting, whether as shooter or victim, is very real.

Attempts to Combat Police Stress

Recognition of the fact that police work can exact a high toll in personal costs has led to numerous attempts to identify and deal with such stress. Many of the factors identified as related to police stress have been discussed previously. Let us look briefly here at some attempts to lessen the impact of these factors, keeping in mind our earlier statement that stress cannot be entirely eliminated and, unless it is prolonged and severe, serves some useful functions.

Farmer (1990: 210–215) has summarized various managerial attempts at dealing with police stress. These attempts are made to help police officers better manage the stress they encounter and include:

1. Design of programs and activities to increase officer participation in decision making and improve the quality of work life through enhanced communication/participation
2. Development of training programs in stress awareness
3. Establishment of specific police stress programs such as psychological services, health/nutrition programs, and exercise programs
4. Development of peer-counseling programs
5. Development of operational policies that are directed at reducing stress (shift assignments, scheduling, etc.)
6. Development of managerial skills that are people oriented
7. Improvement in understanding the nature of stress and coping alternatives through stress training
8. Use of relaxation and other stress-reducing techniques
9. Use of spouse/family orientation/involvement programs
10. Development of support groups
11. Implementation of total wellness (physical and emotional) programs

The movement toward community policing may also be important in the reduction of stress among police officers. If a good deal of the stress officers experience results from constant contact with the criminal elements in the community and from working in an environment in which the police are regarded as causing "trouble" for other citizens, then increasing contact with law-abiding citizens under positive circumstances should help alleviate stress. To some extent this gain may be offset by the additional problem-solving responsibilities placed on community policing officers, but if the administration accepts risks and occasional failures as part of the growing process in COP, this stress, too, can be reduced.

Dealing with Stress in Police Organizations

Based on the information provided in previous sections, it is clear that policing can be a stressful occupation. Whether it is more stressful than other occupations is debatable, but the real point is that efforts should be made to reduce stress in the interests of the officer, department, officer's family, and public served. Police officers often either fail to recognize the signs of stress or fail to seek help when they do recognize the symptoms. This may be due, in part, to the influence of the police subculture that holds that "real police officers" can handle their own problems and do not need the help of "shrinks," employee assistance programs, clergy, or other "outsiders" (Bouza, 1990).

Discrepancies between the official expectations of police administrators and unofficial expectations of the police subculture that create stress need to be confronted. Since both official and subcultural expectations will continue to play roles in policing, efforts must be made to reduce existing differences between the two. If stress is created and sustained by administrative policies that frustrate and befuddle officers, revisions need to be made.

As an example, we might look once again at police promotional practices. Promotions are recognized as being stressful, but unnecessary stress can be reduced. Promotional opportunities should induce healthy stress associated with preparation and enthusiasm for the testing process. However, the longer the process takes, the greater the amount of stress officers will experience. One way to reduce promotional stress is make the process as rapid as possible. Frankly, many departments do the opposite. The written examination is given and there is a time lag until the results are released. When the results are released, oral interviews are scheduled—often at the convenience of board members—over several days or even weeks. Then, the performance evaluations are completed, the scores tabulated, and an eligibility list posted. Sometime later the actual promotion is made.

While some time is required for each of these steps, where possible the waiting period for those participating in the promotional procedure or waiting for a new subordinate or supervisor to be appointed should be reduced as much as possible. Recognition and handling of problems such as these that increase stress levels enable us to be proactive rather than reactive in dealing with the problems.

Discussion Questions

1. What is the police subculture and in what ways does it conflict with the official mandates of police work?

2. Why is it so difficult for police officers to avoid getting caught up in the subculture? Give specific examples.

3. Is subcultural affiliation unique to the police? If not, should we be concerned about participation in and support of a subculture? If so, why?

4. Is policing a stressful occupation? Why and in what ways?

5. What are some of the major sources of police stress? How might some of these stresses be alleviated? Can they be eliminated?

6. What are the relationships among police stress, alcoholism, suicide, and family disruption?

7. How are police stress and the police subculture interrelated?

8. Discuss the ways in which community policing may help to reduce police stress. Can community policing also increase stress levels among officers? If so, in what ways?

References

Adorno, T.W. et al., 1950. *The Authoritarian Personality.* New York: Harper and Brothers.

Alpert, G.P. and Dunham, R.G. 1992. *Policing Urban America* 2 ed. Prospect Heights, IL: Waveland Press.

Barker, T., Hunter, R.D., and Rush, J.P. 1994. *Police Systems & Practices: An Introduction.* Englewood Cliffs, NJ: Prentice-Hall.

Bartol, C.R. 1983. *Psychology and American Law.* Belmont, CA: Wadsworth.

Bartol, C.R., Bergen, G.T., and Volckens, J.S. 1992. "Women in Small-Town Policing: Job Performance and Stress." *Criminal Justice and Behavior* 19(3), 240–260.

Bayley, D.H. and Bittner, E. 1989. "Learning the Skills of Policing." *Law and Contemporary Problems* 47, 35–59.

Bittner, E. 1970. *The Functions of the Police in Modern Society.* Chevy Chase, MD: National Institute of Mental Health.

Blumberg, A.S. and Niederhoffer, E. 1985. "The Police Family." In Blumberg, A.S. and Niederhoffer, E. (eds.), *The Ambivalent Force: Perspectives on the Police* 3 ed. New York: Holt, Rinehart & Winston, 371–372.

Bouza, A.V. 1990. *The Police Mystique: An Insider's Look at Cops, Crime, and the Criminal Justice System.* New York: Plenum.

Burbeck, E. and Furnham, A. 1985. "Police Officer Selection: A Critical Review of the Literature." *Journal of Police Science and Administration* 13(1), 58–69.

Burke, R., and Deszca, E. 1986. "Correlates of Psychological Burnout Phases Among Police Officers." *Human Relations* 39(6), 487–502.

Carey, L.R. 1994. "Community Policing for the Suburban Department." *Police Chief* 61(3), 24–26.

Carpenter, B. and Raza, S. 1987. "Personality Characteristics of Police Applicants: Comparisons Across Subgroups and Other Populations." *Journal of Police Science and Administration* 15(1), 10–17.

Carson, S. 1987. "Shooting, Death Trauma, and Excessive Force." In More, H. and Unsinger, P. (eds.), *Police Managerial Use of Psychology and Psychologists.* Springfield, IL: Thomas.

Chevigny, P. 1969. *Police Power: Police Abuses in New York City.* New York: Vintage Books.

Cox, S.M. and Fitzgerald, J.D. 1991. *Police In Community Relations: Critical Issues* 2 ed. Dubuque, IA: Wm. C. Brown.

Cray, E. 1972. *The Enemy in the Streets: Police Malpractice in America.* Garden City, NY: Anchor Books.

Davis, R. 1994. "'Attitude Change' Proves Lethal for Police." *USA TODAY* (3 January), p. 3A.

Doerner, W.G. 1985. "I'm Not the Man I Used to Be: Reflections on the Transition from Prof to Cop." In Blumberg, S. and Niederhoffer, E. (eds.), *The Ambivalent Force: Perspectives on the Police.* New York: Holt, Rinehart & Winston, 394–399.

Farmer, R.E. 1990. "Clinical and Managerial Implications of Stress Research on the Police." *Journal of Police Science and Administration* 17(3), 205–218.

Fell, R., Richard. W., and Wallace, W. 1980. "Psychological Job Stress and the Police Officer." *Journal of Police Science and Administration* 8(2), 139–144.

Fridell, L.A. and Pate, A.M. 1993. "Death on Patrol: Killings of American Law Enforcement Officers." In Dunham, R.G. and Alpert, G.P. (eds.) *Critical Issues in Policing: Contemporary Readings* 2 ed. Prospect Heights, IL: Waveland Press, 568–596.

Geiger, F. 1982. "Stress Reduction Techniques for the Chief of a Small Department." *Law and Order* 30(5), 56–63.

Hageman, M. J. 1989. "Family Life." In Bailey, W.G. (ed), *The Encyclopedia of Police Science.* New York: Garland Publishing, 187–190.

Hernandez, J., Jr. 1989. *The Custer Syndrome.* Salem, WI: Sheffield Publishing.

Hill, K.Q. and Clawson, M. 1988. "The Health Hazards of 'Street Level' Bureaucracy: Mortality Among the Police." *Journal of Police Science and Administration* 16, 243–248.

Inciardi, J.A. 1990. *Criminal Justice* 3 ed. San Diego: Harcourt Brace Jovanovich.

Josephson, R.L. and Reiser, M. 1990. "Officer Suicide in the Los Angeles Police Department: A Twelve-Year Follow-Up." *Journal of Police Science and Administration* 17, 227–229.

Kirkham, G. 1977. *Signal Zero.* New York: Ballantine.

Kunen, J.S. 1986. "Praised, Admired, Feared and Mistrusted, Cops Are Seen Not in True Colors, But Only Blue." *People Weekly* 26(17), 127–131.

Langworthy, R.H. and Travis, L.E. 1994. *Policing in America: A Balance of Forces.* New York: Macmillan.

Lundman, R.J. 1980. *Police and Policing: An Introduction.* New York: Holt, Rinehart & Winston.

Manning, P.K. 1977. *Police Work.* Cambridge, MA: M.I.T. Press.

Manning, P.K. 1979. "The Social Control of Police Work." In Holdaway, S. (ed), *British Police.* London: Edward Arnold.

Manning, P.K. 1989. "Occupational Culture." In Bailey, W. (ed.), *The Encyclopedia of Police Science.* New York: Garland, 360–364.

Maynard, P. and Maynard, N. 1982. "Stress in Police Families: Some Policy Implications." *Journal of Police Science and Administration* 10(3), 302–314.

Niederhoffer, A. 1967. *Behind the Shield: The Police in Urban Society.* Garden City, NY: Doubleday.

O'Neil, P. 1986. "Shift Work." In Reese, J. and Goldstein, H. (eds.), *Psychological Services for Law Enforcement.* Washington, DC: U.S. Government Printing Office.

Pendergrass, V. and Ostrove, N. 1986. "Correlates of Alcohol Use by Police Personnel." In Reese, J. and Goldstein, H. (eds.), *Psychological Services for Law Enforcement.* Washington, DC: U.S. Government Printing Office.

Post, G.M. 1992. "Police Recruits: Training Tomorrow's Workforce." *FBI Law Enforcement Bulletin* 61(3), 19–24.

Regoli, R.M. 1976. "An Empirical Assessment of Niederhoffer's Police Cynicism Scale." *Journal of Criminal Justice* 4(3), 231–241.

Regoli, R.M. and Poole, E.D. 1978. "Specifying Police Cynicism." *Journal of Police Science and Administration* 6(1), 98–104.

Rubinstein, J. 1973. *City Police.* New York: Farrar, Straus, and Giroux.

Rudovsky, D. 1992. "Police Abuse: Can the Violence be Contained?" *Harvard Civil Rights–Civil Liberties Law Review* 27(2), 467–501.

Schaefer, R.B. 1983. "The Stress of Police Promotion." *F.B.I. Law Enforcement Bulletin* 52(5), 3–6.

Selye, H. 1974. *Stress Without Distress*. Philadelphia: Lippincott.

Skolnick, J. 1966. *Justice Without Trial*. New York: John Wiley & Sons.

Skolnick, J.H. and Fyfe, J.J. 1993. *Above the Law: Police and the Excessive Use of Force*. New York: Free Press.

Sparrow, M.K., Moore, M.H., and Kennedy, D.M. 1990. *Beyond 911: A New Era for Policing*. New York: Basic Books.

Spielberger, C., Westberry, L., Grier, K., and Greenfield, G. 1981. *Police Stress Survey—Sources of Stress in Law Enforcement*. Tampa: University of South Florida Human Resources Institute.

Storms, L.H., Penn, N.F., and Tenzell, J.H. 1990. "Policemen's Perception of Real and Ideal Policemen." *Journal of Police Science and Administration* 17(1), 40–43.

Stratton, J.G. 1978. "Police Stress: Considerations and Suggestions." *The Police Chief* (May), 73–76.

Stratton, J.G., Parker, D., and Snibbe, J. 1984. "Post-Traumatic Stress–Study of Police Officers Involved in Shootings." *Psychological Reports* 55(1), 127–131.

Swanson, C., Gaines, L., and Gore, B. 1991. "Abuse of Anabolic Steroids." *Law Enforcement Bulletin* (August), 19–23.

Terry, W.C. 1989. "Police Stress: The Empirical Evidence." *Police Science and Administration* 9, 61–75.

Trojanowicz, R.C. 1980. *The Environment of the First-Line Police Supervisor*. Englewood Cliffs, NJ: Prentice-Hall.

Van Maanen, J. 1978. "The Asshole." In Van Maanen, J. and Manning, P.K. (eds.), *Policing: A View from the Street*. Santa Monica, CA: Goodyear, 221–238.

Violanti, J., Marshall, J., and Howe, B. 1985. "Stress, Coping, and Alcohol Use—The Police Connection." *Journal of Police Science and Administration* 13(2), 106–110.

Violanti, J., Vena, J., and Marshall, J. 1986. "Disease Risk and Mortality Among Police Officers—New Evidence and Contributing Factors." *Journal of Police Science and Administration* 14(11), 17–23.

Wagner, M. and Brzeczek, R.J. 1983. "Alcoholism and Suicide: A Fatal Connection." *FBI Law Enforcement Bulletin* (August), 8–15.

Wambaugh, J. 1975. *The Choirboys*. New York: Dell Publishing.

Westley, W. 1970. *Violence and the Police*. Cambridge, MA: M.I.T. Press.

Wright, J.D. 1986. "The Armed Criminal in America." *Research in Brief*. (November) National Institute of Justice. Washington, DC: U.S. Government Printing Office.

Yarmey, A.D. 1990. *Understanding Police and Police Work: Psychosocial Issues*. New York: New York University Press.

10

POLICE MISCONDUCT

Police misconduct is a complicated topic with a long history in the United States. Misconduct may be broadly divided into two categories—corruption and physical/emotional abuse—and may be either organizational or individual in nature. Both categories included numerous subcategories, the categories often overlap, and both are violations of the ethical standards of police officers. As we pointed out in Chapter 4, in a general sense, ethics refers to the moral obligations of humans to act in ways that are good and proper. Applied specifically to police officers, ethical conduct is especially important because of the authority granted officers and because of the difficulty of overseeing the daily behavior of police officers on the street.

The "police possess at least two capacities whose use raises special ethical problems. Police are entitled to use coercive force and to lie and deceive people in the course of their work. Moreover, as sociologist Egon Bittner reminds us, while 'few of us are constantly mindful of the saying, He that is without sin among you, let him cast the first stone . . . , only the police are explicitly required to forget it'" (Klockars, 1989: 427).

Additionally, of course, police performance has traditionally been subject to a good deal of moral controversy, partly because they deal with moral issues on a regular basis, partly because their behavior has sometimes offended the moral sensitivities of others. Finally, the police engage in discretionary behavior regularly, and other citizens must place a good deal of trust in their conduct with little assurance that their conduct is subject to adequate control (Klockars, 1989). Most ethical violations by the police fall under the general heading of conduct unbecoming a police officer and are investigated by other police officers. In light of the potential for police misconduct resulting from the periodic need to coerce or deceive the public, there is clearly a need for more attention to police ethics.

Police Corruption

> In 1894 the Lexow Commission, an investigative group appointed at the instigation of a coalition of concerned citizens and good government groups, closed its hearings into police corruption and ineffectiveness in New York City. It reported that corruption was systematic and pervasive, a condition that it attributed in large part to malfeasance, misfeasance and nonfeasance in the higher ranks. The next fifteen years found similar investigations and similar findings in almost every major American city (Bracey, 1989: 175).

"For cops as for anyone else, money works like an acid on integrity. Bribes from bootleggers made the 1920s a golden era for crooked police. Gambling syndicates in the 1950s were protected by a payoff system more elaborate than the Internal Revenue Service" (Lacayo, 1993: 43). In 1971, Frank Serpico brought to light police corruption in New York City, and the Knapp Commission investigation that followed uncovered widespread corruption among officers of all ranks. "In the 1980s Philadelphia saw more than thirty officers convicted of taking part in a scheme to extort money from [drug] dealers" (Lacayo, 1993: 43). A major corruption scandal "hit Miami in the mid-1980s, when about 10 percent of the city's police were either jailed, fired, or disciplined in connection with a scheme in which officers robbed and sometimes killed cocaine smugglers on the Miami River, then resold the drugs" (Lacayo, 1993: 44). "The Los Angeles County Sheriff's Department discharges approximately twenty officers a year, primarily as the result of misconduct" (Cooksey, 1991: 7). In 1993, twenty-two years after Serpico's disclosures in the same department, Michael Dowd and fifteen to twenty other New York City police officers led "A parade of dirty cops who dealt drugs and beat innocent people [which] has shocked the city during seven days of corruption hearings" (Frankel, 1993b: 3A). See Highlight 10.1 for more details.

HIGHLIGHT 10.1   "20 Years and It's Not Over," Serpico Says

By Lori Sharn USA TODAY

Frank Serpico, the cop who helped bring New York City police corruption to light 22 years ago, says new hearings into dirty dealings show "greed is the order of the day."

"It's 20 years and it's not over yet," Serpico said in a telephone interview Wednesday.

"You cannot have corruption in any police department or law enforcement agency unless you have it at the top."

Serpico has kept a low profile since his story was made into a book and then a 1973 movie, both titled *Serpico*.

He keeps an apartment in Brooklyn where he grew up, but he spends much of his time at a cabin in the New York countryside.

Former officer David Durk, who also testified before the Knapp Commission in 1971, continues to push for a clean police force.

But Serpico, 57, says he prefers to stay out of it, live simply and focus on self-healing and nutrition. Nevertheless, he says he has phoned Internal Affairs investigator Sgt. Joseph Trimboli—who testified before the Mollen Commission Tuesday—to offer him support. Serpico says he started laughing when Trimboli told him how top brass thwarted efforts to pursue corrupt cops.

"I have to laugh. It's the same thing," he says. "Rather than face the truth, they'd rather discredit someone who shows signs of integrity and the courage to talk about it."

After Serpico was shot in the head during a 1971 narcotics raid, he says he heard a "mighty voice" telling him "it's all a lie."

He says he has been searching for the truth for the last 20 years.

Stories at the time implied he was a marked man.

He spent the rest of the decade in Europe. Serpico says he was just frustrated with the system and looking for something better: "I found they're all the same.

"I'm working on self-change. I've done a lot of research on alternative healing. People would rather have a triple bypass than give up the garbage they're eating," he says.

Serpico doesn't lecture, but does work with others on nutritional issues.

He says he is not paid for this help, although he sometimes barters for things.

A 1981 paternity suit cost him part of his police pension. He gets $340 a month.

He says he has no regrets, but "my heart goes out to Joe Trimboli, because he knows . . . he's going to be left holding the bag."

Corruption occurs when a police officer acts in a manner that places his or her personal gain ahead of duty, resulting in the violation of police procedures, criminal law, or both (Lynch, 1989). "Corrupt acts contain three elements: (1) they are forbidden by some law, rule, regulation, or ethical standard; (2) they involve the misuse of the officer's position; and (3) they involve some actual or expected material reward or gain" (Barker and Carter, 1986: 3–4).

Police corruption is best viewed not as the aberrant behavior of individual officers, but as group behavior guided by contradictory sets of norms. It involves a number of specific patterns that can be analyzed in terms of several dimensions, including the acts and actors involved, the norms violated, the extent of peer group support, the degree of organization, and the police department's reaction. Barker and Roebuck (1974) used these dimensions to discuss eight different types of police corruption, which we will now summarize.

Types of Police Corruption

Corruption of authority involves officially unauthorized gains by police officers that do not violate the law. Included here are things such as taking free liquor or meals, free entertainment admissions, police "discounts," free sex, and other free services. While these gains typically violate departmental policies, they do not violate criminal statutes when offered voluntarily. In many cases, they are viewed as coming with the job and are overlooked by the department unless they become a matter of public concern. In other words, acceptance of gratuities is often condoned if not approved officially.

The difficulty with accepting such gratuities is that the officer never knows when the corruptor may expect or request special services or favors in return. This may, of course, never happen; however, if it does, it places the officer who has accepted the gratuities in a difficult position, although he or she may certainly refuse to grant the requests. In addition, it becomes difficult to draw a line between such gratuities and other types of corrupt activities in terms of monetary value and violation of ethical standards.

Such actions may also have a negative effect on the police image. For example, two police officers were recently witnessed during the lunch hour at a fast food chain. One officer was in uniform, the other in plain clothes. In front of a large number of lunch-hour customers, the uniformed officer was told by the person taking his order that he received a 50 percent discount on the price of his meal. This started some murmuring in the crowd. The second officer then informed the cashier that he, too, was a police officer, entitled to a 50 percent discount, and showed his badge to prove it. The cashier apologized, saying she hadn't recognized him as a police officer, and assured him that he would receive his discount. Needless to say, the muttering in the crowd became rather negative, with other patrons indicating that they now understood why so many police officers ate at the establishment in question.

Kickbacks constitute a second type of police corruption. Here, tow truck operators, lawyers, bondsmen, and others reward police officers who refer customers to them. The difficulties inherent in such referrals are obvious, but in some departments they, too, are condoned unless a public issue arises as a result.

A third type of corruption involves *opportunistic theft* from victims, crime scenes, and unprotected property. Such activity clearly violates both departmental norms and statutes.

Shakedowns involve police officers who accept bribes for not making an arrest or writing a citation. While the officer may not actively seek such bribes, he or she may indicate a willingness to consider "other alternatives" offered by guilty parties.

Some police officers engage in *protection of illegal activities* for profit. They accept payments or services from those engaged in gambling, prostitution, drug sales, pornography, code violations, and other activities in return for doing nothing about such activities and sometimes for creating obstacles to investigations of these activities. In order to protect the illegal behaviors, a good deal of organization is often required. It does little good for one officer to look the other way when gambling occurs if his or her replacement for days off and vacations or officers on other shifts fail to protect the parties involved.

The fix involves quashing prosecution following arrest or "taking care" of tickets for profit. Police actions in these cases may range from failure to show up in court when testimony is required to losing tickets to perjury.

Direct criminal activities include burglary, robbery, battery, intimidation, and other clearly criminal actions committed by officers. A good example involves the Miami Police Department in which "cops have been charged with murder, with shooting up a doper's house, with conspiring to sell police radios and badges, with big-time dope dealing. The elite Special Investigation Section opens its safe and finds $150,000 missing. In the back of the police compound, a simple bicycle padlock is clipped and several hundred pounds of marijuana is reported missing" (Dorschner, 1993: 254).

Finally, *internal payoffs* involve one police officer paying another (typically a superior officer) fees for assignments of particular types, promotions, days off, and so on.

While one type of corruption does not necessarily lead to another, where one finds more serious types of corruption, less serious types coexist. Consider, for example, a department that condones internal payoffs. If a supervisor attained his or her position by paying someone for it, it becomes difficult to deal with less serious forms of corruption among those supervised who may have knowledge of the way in which the promotion was obtained. In the long run, such a department is likely to be characterized by all other forms of corruption. In addition, services to the public are likely to be less efficient and effective than they might otherwise be, since promotions are not based on merit; less competent (or incompetent) people may become supervisors.

As Richardson (1974: 154) puts it, "Discipline may be especially weak since any action might lead to unpleasant publicity. If a large portion of a police department is implicated in such corrupt relations, no one can enforce the law against the police themselves. Officers outside the network of payoffs have to turn their backs on what goes on around them and deny publicly that any such activity exists. . . . Moreover, what is the effect on a young patrolman who learns that his colleagues and commanders are often more interested in profiting from the law than enforcing it?"

Frankel (1993b: 3A) reports that the same logic applies today. "Daniel Sullivan, former head of the [NYC] department's Internal Affairs division, testified that the message from the top brass to his investigators was simple: 'We shouldn't be so aggressive because the department doesn't want bad press. . . . Honest officers testified that their efforts to report and investigate corruption ran into resistance and retaliation."

The Background of Police Corruption

The history of U.S. municipal police is replete with examples and discussions of corruption. Reform movements have been initiated periodically to reduce or eliminate corruption but have largely failed to achieve their goals (see Highlight 10.2). The reform movement of the middle 1800s attempted to remove blatant, undesirable political influence from policing. The civil service reforms of the late 1800s sought the same goal and, though there were some successes, were bitterly opposed and circumvented by those wishing to retain undue influence over the police (Richardson, 1974; Johnson, 1981; Trojanowicz, 1992). Reforms in the early and middle 1900s emphasized the importance of professionalism as a means of reducing corruption of all types, and reform-oriented chiefs were appointed in many cities across the nation. However, the problem of corruption resurfaced, sometimes in departments previously marred and other times in departments previously untouched by scandal.

Some departments were, of course, built on foundations of corruption, with politicians requiring payments for positions or giving police positions away in return for political favors. Allegations of corruption still occur on a regular basis in many large departments as noted previously. Observations in recent years indicate that corruption of authority remains widespread in small and medium sized departments (under five hundred sworn personnel). Several of the other forms of corruption have been noted in these smaller departments as well.

It is difficult to estimate the proportion of police officers directly involved in corruption, but it is probably small. Still, the actual number of police officers involved nationwide is quite large and these officers attract a good deal of negative attention when their corruption is made public (see Highlight 10.2). While most police officers are not directly involved in corrupt activities, large numbers condone such activities by their failure to speak out or take action against them. These officers are referred to as "grass eaters" by the Knapp Commission; they passively accept the presence of corruption as a part of the police world (Knapp Commission, 1973). "Meat eaters" are those officers, typically far fewer in number, who actively seek out the opportunity for corrupt activities. Recognition that those officers who actively seek out corrupt activities are relatively few has led many police administrators to espouse

---

HIGHLIGHT 10.2 Police Corruption

All too frequently, the public's confidence in law enforcement is shaken by reports of officers falling victim to corruption. While no profession is untouched by corruption, its effect on law enforcement is especially damaging. As guardians of law and order in a free society, law enforcement officers must maintain a consistently high standard of integrity.

Combating crime claims many victims from the ranks of law enforcement. As criminals become more violent, increasing numbers of officers are being killed or injured in the line of duty. But increasing numbers of officers are also being lost to corruption. The lure of fast money associated with the drug trade and other temptations are creating new and potentially devastating problems for police departments and law enforcement managers across the country . . .

In order to combat corruption effectively, law enforcement managers must first acknowledge the potential for corruption and appreciate the devastating effects it can have on their agencies. The key elements of a corruption prevention strategy should integrate agency policy into recruitment, training, and thorough investigation of all alleged corruption.

While corruption has always been a factor in law enforcement, the need for effective corruption prevention strategies has never been stronger. Today's officers face more violent criminals and more potential temptations. Law enforcement must present a unified front against an increasingly sophisticated criminal element. It is important that managers provide today's officers with proper corruption prevention skills (Cooksey, 1991: 5–9).

Reprinted with permission from the *FBI Law Enforcement Bulletin,* 60(9), 5–9.

the "rotten apple" theory, which holds that while there are a few corrupt officers in policing, most officers are unaffected by corruption.

In fact, it is virtually impossible for a single corrupt officer to survive (other than in a one-person department). As we have seen, many of the forms of corruption require some degree of organizational support, at least in the sense that others within the organization turn their heads and refuse to confront the corrupt officer. This failure to take action against corrupt officers, even on the part of other officers who clearly dislike such activities, may be due in part to the police "code" or subculture discussed in the preceding chapter.

Some time ago, Stoddard (1968) discussed the informal code of silence that exists among police officers with respect to a variety of types of deviant behavior. He and others (Bouza, 1990; Frankel, 1993a) have indicated that such deviance is an "open secret" within the fraternity, but its existence is denied to those outside the group. Frankel (1993a: 1A) reports that for Bernie Cawley, a New York City police officer, it was "nothing to lie to grand juries, to steal drugs, weapons, and money, and to protect other cops doing the same thing." His fellow officer, Michael Dowd, testified "Cops don't want to turn in other cops. Cops don't want to be a rat" (Frankel, 1993b: 3A).

In some departments, officers who are "straight" are regarded as stupid for failing to take advantage of the benefits of corrupt activities, which have come to be defined as inherent in the job. When an officer decides to take action against corrupt colleagues, the fraternity may react violently and is very likely to ostracize the officer who has violated the code or broken faith with those in the subculture.

Police corruption has been recognized as a problem in this country for over one hundred years, and various reform movements and departmental programs to reduce or eliminate corruption have been attempted, as we shall see shortly. Why, then, does police corruption remain problematic? The answer seems to lie, in part at least, in the relationship between the police and the larger society. It has been said that the police are a reflection of the society/community they serve and this is never more true than with respect to police corruption. Simply put, police corruption could be stopped overnight if we decided we wanted to stop it. If other citizens stopped offering bribes, free services, and other gratuities and started reporting all police attempts to benefit in unauthorized fashion from their positions, it would be very difficult for corrupt police officers to survive. Such actions would, however, result in some degree of loss of control over police officers among those who desire such control.

To some extent, it appears that we want our police to be corrupt or at least corruptible. It gives us something to talk and write about, provides us with a sense that the police are not morally superior to others, and perhaps gives some of us a feeling of power over those who are recognized as having a good deal of power. Do we want our police to be totally honest and trustworthy, or would we prefer to believe that they will perhaps overlook at least minor violations as a result of the favors we have provided them? Are we satisfied regarding the police as morally superior because they routinely turn down opportunities to make thousands of dollars by accepting payoffs from drug dealers, gun runners, pimps, and those involved with other illegal activities? If the police adhere to high ethical standards, if they are basically citizens like ourselves, and if we would be tempted by opportunities to earn large sums of money by simply failing to enforce the law, are we less ethical or moral? Are we, too, convinced that corruption is inherent in the police role and that there is little we could do about it even if we wanted to?

Attempts to Control Police Corruption

"Management accountability is perhaps the most important, effective and most difficult proactive tool for preventing and detecting police corruption. This is not a program or a device, but rather a thorough rethinking of the meaning of supervision and management responsibility. The driving assumption underlying accountability is that commanders are responsible for all police activity that takes place on their command. At its simplest, a policy of accountability means that commanders may not plead ignorance and surprise when corruption is discovered in their areas" (Bracey, 1989: 176). Bracey goes on to indicate that while the accountability approach clearly can work, it can be carried to extremes by supervisors so concerned with protecting themselves from liability that they trivialize the process.

Trojanowicz (1992: 2) notes that supervisors can have an influence on corrupt activities, but they "must go the extra distance to ensure that the officers under their command treat people with respect and that they have not crossed the line. . . . The good news is that departments which have embraced Community Policing have taken an important step in fostering a climate where average citizens may well feel encouraged to share any such concerns or suspicions."

Other techniques used by management to detect corruption include the use of field associates, "turning" officers who have been found to be corrupt, and rotation of assignments. Field associates are those officers specially trained and sometimes recruited to obtain information on corrupt activities while performing normal police functions. This information is relayed to management without other officers knowing who the informants are, creating an atmosphere of suspicion among officers when the existence of the program is known. "Turning" involves offering leniency or immunity to corrupt officers who agree to provide information on other corrupt officers. Rotation of personnel across shifts and geographic assignments is a technique used to disrupt possible corruption by making permanent ties between officers and the citizens they police difficult. While this may have a positive impact on corruption, it disrupts the flow of information between officers and the citizens they police, may negatively impact on community relations, and makes community-oriented policing impossible (Bracey, 1989).

Another strategy that may be used to reduce corruption is recruitment. Recruiting police personnel of high moral character and providing training in ethics early in their careers would appear to be steps in the right direction (Lynch, 1989; Cooksey, 1991). If the department and subculture also foster an anticorruption attitude, promote on the basis of merit, and pay relatively well, the allure of corruption may be somewhat reduced. Internal affairs units and external review boards have also been used to help curb corruption by identifying and charging those involved.

It is difficult to assess the success of anticorruption programs. To some extent, police corruption may be related to economic conditions, but the relationship would appear to a curvilinear one. That is, when police and other wages are low, the temptation to accept dirty money may be great. Alternatively, as Lynch (1989: 166–167) indicates,

> *When the wages of sin are incredibly lucrative, as they are in so many instances today, the appeal of corruption is proportionately more alluring. . . . Let me suggest to you that given the potential for misuse of police power, the wonder is that police officers, who witness crime, inhumanity and degradation every day, do not lose their sense of integrity and do not violate their oath of office more frequently.*

After a twenty-two-month investigation into police corruption in New York City, the Commission to Investigate Allegations of Police Corruption (also known as the Mollen Commission) recommended the creation of a permanent, independent, outside agency with investigative and subpoena powers to oversee the department's anticorruption activities. The commission concluded that the department's ability to fight corruption had collapsed during the 1980s, allowing aggressive police officers to brutalize citizens, steal cash, and sell drugs with impunity. In addition, the commission recommended that the department require random, unannounced drug testing, require applicants to furnish tax returns and other financial records, and establish a system to reward honest officers who assist in rooting out corruption and other forms of misconduct (*Law Enforcement News*, 1994: 7).

In the long run, the only way to significantly reduce police corruption is to prosecute those involved to the fullest extent of the law, sending a clear message to the corrupt, uncorrupt, and corruptors that such action will be taken and that the consequences may be severe. Michael Dowd and another New York City police officer were receiving eight thousand dollars per week from one drug dealer, and Dowd used the proceeds of his corrupt activities for a red Corvette, four homes, and expensive vacations (Frankel, 1993b; Lacayo, 1993). Dowd was sentenced to fourteen years in federal prison in July of 1994 (Clark, 1994: 6).

While such actions in and of themselves may have a limited effect on corrupt police officers, when widely publicized they may alert the community to the fact that reform in the police department is required. While such reform is seldom sweeping enough to keep the problem from reemerging, it is possible to make it so. At a minimum, it disrupts the corrupt activities already in progress and alerts those involved that their activities are not secret and may result in official action.

It is essential that the issue of police corruption be addressed directly and openly. Otherwise, corruption can destroy the bond of trust between law enforcement and the public. Citizens expect law enforcement officers to perform their duties with a high standard of integrity. "When corruption occurs, citizen cooperation, on which law enforcement depends, can be jeopardized" (Cooksey, 1991: 8).

Physical and Emotional Abuse

Police misconduct is not limited to corrupt activities but includes perjury, emotional abuse/harassment, and physical abuse, including murder, as well. In some ways, perjury and other forms of unauthorized deception serve as links between corruption and other forms of misconduct. What is the difference, for example, between a police officer who perjures himself or herself in order to fix a ticket in return for payment from the defendant and one who perjures himself or herself in order to cover up the fact that he or she used physical force unnecessarily against a defendant? How does one draw the line between lying to informants and drug dealers and deceiving one's superiors? Once perjury and deception gain a foothold they tend to spread to other officers and to other types of situations until, in some cases, the entire justice system becomes a sham.

This is the case, for instance, when police officers perjure themselves in criminal cases in which the defendant is also perjuring himself or herself, the respective attorneys know that perjury is occurring, and the judge knows that none of the parties is being completely honest. The outcomes of such cases seem to depend on who told the most believable lie or the last lie. The overall impact is to increase the amount of suspicion and distrust of the justice system among all parties and this is certainly not the desired end product if we wish citizens to participate in and believe in the system.

Chevigny (1969), Cray (1972), Manning (1974), Skolnick (1966), and Roberg and Kuykendall (1993) among others have addressed the issue of police lying and all agree that the behavior, in some cases, becomes accepted as an inherent part of the job, similar to corruption. This acceptance is particularly relevant in cases in which police misconduct has occurred and the officers involved are trying to cover up the misconduct. Police officers who stop other citizens without probable cause, harass them, or use force unnecessarily must attempt to justify their actions or face relatively severe sanctions. Perhaps some examples will help illustrate the kind of behavior in question here.

The defendant, Ms. Stallworth, was parked illegally outside an elementary school in Cleveland, Ohio waiting to pick up her grandchild. Officer Currie asked her to move her vehicle. When she failed to move the vehicle, Officer Currie allegedly opened the car door, hit the woman in the mouth, and arrested her for failing to obey a lawful order and resisting arrest. Ms. Stallworth sued the city and Officer Currie. The jury concluded that the officer had used excessive force, and the city and the officer were both held liable (Stallworth v. City of Cleveland, 1990).

> *You bet I get (sex) once in awhile by some broad who I arrest. Lots of times you can just hint that if you are taken care of, you could forget about what they did (officer interview cited in Sapp, 1986: 88).*

> *Though 75 Miami police officers have been arrested since 1980, it is the seven who have been dubbed 'the Miami River Cops' who have been the focus of attention. They have been charged with big-time dope dealing, and three of them were charged with murder, which was altered to 'violating the civil rights' of the dead victims when the case was moved to federal court (Dorschner, 1993: 268).*

> *The national debate over the state's right to take life has been sidetracked, in a sense, on the issue of 'capital punishment,' or more precisely, execution after trial. Far more deadly in impact is the body of law permitting execution without trial through justified homicide by police officers. In 1976, for example, no one was executed and 233 persons were sentenced to death after trial, yet an estimated 590 persons were killed by police officers justifiably without trial. Even in the 1950s, when an average of seventy-two persons were executed after trial each year, the average number of police homicides was 240 per year, according to official statistics, and 480 a year according to one unofficial estimate. Since record keeping began in 1949, police actions have been by far the most frequent method with which our government has intentionally taken the lives of its own citizens (Sherman, 1980: 71).*

These examples are not intended as an indictment of the police, but as illustrations of the extent, nature and seriousness of the behavior included under the umbrella of police misconduct.

Emotional Abuse/Psychological Harassment by Police Officers

As indicated previously police officers, like those in other occupational groups, sometimes employ stereotypes and divide the world into "we" and "they" or insiders versus outsiders. Those who are perceived as outsiders are often labeled, and occasionally these labels are used openly to refer to the members of groups so designated. The use of racial slurs is but one example of the kind of harassment under consideration. Other special categories and labels are created for those belonging to particular deviant groups: drug dealers, homosexuals, prostitutes, and protestors. The creation of special categories and the ensuing labels are not unique to the police. However, as public servants who represent the authority of the government, the police are in a rather unique position when it comes to using the labels created.

First, the police are supposed to represent all citizens, regardless of race, creed, nationality, gender, or political beliefs. When they use dehumanizing terms or harass others, the impression may be that since they represent government, they are expressing the attitudes of those who govern; in fact, they may simply be expressing personal dislike, contempt, or hostility. Second, because of the fact that they represent governmental authority, they are very likely to be subject to harassment, name calling, and challenges themselves. When dehumanizing terms or deliberate attempts to harass or provoke the police occur, the possibility that the police will reciprocate in kind is heightened. Third, the occupational subculture legitimizes the use of labels behind squad room doors or among police officers, keeping these labels alive and meaningful. Fourth, few of those other citizens harassed or verbally abused are likely to report the abuse, which tends to reinforce the abusive behavior. Fifth, as an alternative to arrest, many of those harassed probably view the harassment as the lesser of two evils (homeless people, for instance, who are "escorted" to the city limits by police officers with a warning not to return).

Members of minority groups (both racial and behavioral), particularly in high crime areas, report that psychological/emotional abuse is a routine part of encounters with the police. The best available evidence also supports this contention. Although his study is now dated, Reiss (1968: 59–60) provides information concerning the incidence of police psychological mistreatment of other citizens. "What citizens object to and call 'police brutality' is really the judgment that they have not been treated with the full rights and dignity owing citizens in a democratic society. Any practice that degrades their status, that restricts their freedom, that annoys or harasses them, or that uses physical force is frequently seen as unnecessary and unwarranted. More often than not, they are probably right. . . . Members of minority groups and those seen as nonconformists, for whatever reasons, are the most likely targets of status degradation." Hacker (1992: 189), for example, notes that "Most black Americans can recall encounters [with the police] where they were treated with discourtesy, hostility, or worse. . . . And it would appear that at least a few police officers still move in circles where no censure attaches to using the word nigger.'"

It is clear, then, that what constitutes police brutality is at least in part a matter of definition, and that police definitions and those of other citizens may not always agree. What some segments of the public see as police harassment or brutality, the police are likely to view as aggressive policing, necessary for their survival on the streets as well as for maintaining some degree of order and crime control. Is a police officer in a high crime area where many residents are known to carry deadly weapons harassing a citizen when he or she approaches cautiously, pats the citizen down for weapons, appears suspicious, and has another officer back him or her up?

The answer depends, in part, on whether one is the police officer or the person being stopped, questioned, and searched, because while the latter knows whether or not he or she is a dangerous or criminal person, the officer typically does not. Obviously the way in which such encounters are carried out is important. Reiss (1968) notes that it is not always what the officer says, but how he or she says it that is degrading, and that whites, and racial or ethnic minority group members are also victims of psychological harassment. The conclusions drawn by Reiss are supported by the findings of the National Advisory Commission on Civil Disorders (1968), which concluded that foremost among the complaints of minority group members about the police were the use of improper forms of address (use of terms such as "boy," "nigger," first name when surname is appropriate) and stopping and questioning people with no apparent reason other than race or ethnicity.

The Tennessee Advisory Committee to the U.S. Civil Rights Commission (1978: 3) noted a decade later, in reviewing police conduct in Memphis, "A significant number of Memphians, notably the poor and members of the black community, express not only a lack of confidence in the Memphis Police Department but also outright fear and distrust."

Leinen (1984) indicates that the same basic complaints were voiced by members of the black community in New York City in the 1980s. A 1988 Media General Associated Press Poll found that 61 percent of blacks surveyed said minorities are not treated equally in the criminal justice system, while 68 percent said the society remains racist overall (Langer, 1988). A 1992 Time/CNN poll found that 50 percent of black respondents (compared to 18 percent of white respondents) felt that some or all police officers in their neighborhoods were prejudiced against blacks. Forty-eight percent of the black respondents felt they were at risk of being treated unfairly in police encounters compared to 23 percent of whites (Church, 1992). All of these findings and incidents—and others as well—imply that harassment and psychological brutality, if not actual physical brutality, continue to occur in police encounters with at least certain citizens.

Physical Brutality

In March of 1995, a New Orleans Police officer entered a restaurant, put a bullet in the head of the security guard, her sometimes police partner, and then executed the son and daughter of the immigrant owners. She failed to find a third sibling who later identified her as the killer (Gwynne, 1995: 45). In 1991, the world watched as a home-video tape of Los Angeles police officers beating Rodney King was repeated dozens of times on major network news programs. In 1993, two Detroit police officers were sentenced to prison for beating to death motorist Malice Green (Ferguson, 1993). Similar incidents occurred at the same time in New York City, Atlanta, Washington, DC, and Denver (Campbell, 1991).

Reiss (1971: 2) has observed that, "At law, the police in modern democracies such as the United States possess a virtual monopoly on the *legitimate* use of force over citizens." Bittner (1970) describes the capacity to use force as the core of the police role. Rubinstein (1973) discusses the police officer's body as his or her most important tool and the process by which police officers evaluate other citizens in terms of their physical ability to "handle" these other citizens should an encounter turn nasty. That the police have the capacity to use force is indicated by the baton, mace, and side arm they carry into every encounter, as well as by their sheer numbers in certain types of encounters. It should not be surprising, therefore, that the issue of misuse of force by the police should occasionally arise—especially if we recognize that we live in a society characterized by violence. Spouse abuse, child abuse, and drug-related street violence are common occurrences in our society; the police are routinely involved in dealing with all three. Since 1990, we have averaged over twenty-two thousand homicides annually, and several times that number are wounded, indicating the extent to which violence has become routine in the United States.

Physical brutality by the police involves the use of unnecessary or excessive force by the police. The Reiss (1968) study cited earlier, based on observations of the police in Chicago, Boston, and Washington, DC, led to the following conclusions:

1. Physical brutality occurs rarely (in less than 1 percent of the encounters observed), even in high crime areas.
2. Whites are twice as likely to be victims of police brutality as blacks.
3. White and black officers are about equally likely to misuse force.
4. Misuse of force is largely intraracial.
5. Physical brutality is most likely to involve male offenders who are also members of the lower social class.
6. Physical brutality is most likely to occur when a suspect openly defies, by word or deed, police authority.
7. Police supervisors who are aware of the misuse of force do little to prevent it.

Others (Chevigny, 1969; Cray, 1972) conclude that the police sometimes provoke other citizens to resist in order to create the need to use force. They then use force and cover their deeds by adding charges of resisting arrest or obstruction of justice to the original charge in an attempt to ensure that the alleged offender is found guilty of some violation. Chevigny refers to such proceedings as a pattern involving the use of force, arrest, and "cover charges."

As Highlight 10.3 indicates, there is no doubt that incidents of the type previously described continue to occur; however, it is difficult to judge whether they have increased or decreased in frequency in recent years, because there are no reliable data on which to base conclusions. Justice Department figures show some forty-eight thousand complaints against the police between 1985 and 1991. Of these, fifteen thousand were actually investigated, but only 2 percent of the cases resulted in charges against the police officers involved (Campbell, 1991).

Data for the years 1984 to 1990 show that New Orleans, Los Angeles County, Jefferson Parish, Louisiana and San Antonio received the highest average number of complaints annually (thirty-five, thirty-four, twenty-three, and twenty-one, respectively) (Nasser and Stewart, 1992). The city of Los Angeles alone paid out 8.1 million dollars in 1990 to victims of excessive force by police (Turque, 1991).

It is clear that the perception that such incidents occur is widespread in minority communities in cities of all sizes across the country. This perception becomes the reality for those involved, whether or not the perception is grounded in reality. The perception creates hostility and resentment on behalf of some citizens who view themselves as particularly likely to be victims of harassment and brutality, and on behalf of the police who view themselves as particularly likely to be harassed, challenged, and criticized by certain segments of the population. In spite of these misgivings on both sides, the vast majority of police encounters with other citizens continue to be without physical brutality on the part of either party.

Occasionally, however, suspicion, fear, resentment, and hostility escalate, resulting in physically violent encounters. In addition, of course, the police must be concerned about the possibility of violence that has nothing to do with harassment or social status but is based on felonious behavior. The possibility of physical violence always exists when the officer responds to calls involving domestic disputes, bar fights, robberies or burglaries in progress, bomb threats, street protests, gun running, and drug trafficking, to mention just a few. In a small proportion of these cases the end result will be the use of deadly force by one or more of the parties involved.

Deadly Force—A Two-Way Street

Deadly force is force capable of killing or likely to kill, it is the decision to shoot rather than the consequences of the shooting that define it (Fyfe, 1989: 133).

As might be expected, police use of deadly force in the United States most often involves the use of a firearm; however, data on the extent of its use are hard to find. The data available from the National Center for Health Statistics

---

HIGHLIGHT 10.3   Changing the Police: An Impossible Dream?

A.C. Germann

John Stuart Mill, many years ago, in his "Utilitarianism," put it thus:

"The entire history of social improvement has been a series of transitions, by which one custom or institution after another, from being a supposed primary necessity of social existence, has passed into the rank of a universally stigmatized injustice and tyranny."

Some observers of the current scene believe that the institution we call police, in some locales, epitomizes injustice and tyranny. Millions of people in 1991 and 1992, wherever TV satellites provide a video history of planetary events, witnessed a videotape depicting the cruel mistreatment of a human being by four unprofessional Los Angeles police officers.

It is an irrefutably and precisely recorded picture of the police brute in action, and of the assenting observer of brutality. The misbehavior videotaped and displayed to the world would be described by police professionals to each other as stupid, gross, brutal, insensitive, power-obsessed, and a genuine embarrassment to the city of Los Angeles, to the modern law enforcement community, and to the nation. Most citizens would agree with the assessments of those professional police.

The misbehavior videotaped and displayed to the world has been described both as an aberration and as accepted police practice. It is both an aberration in that independent videotapes of identifiable police brutality are a singular rarity, and an accepted police practice in that those who flee from brutal police are very often given immediate field punishment, and any injuries are explained falsely as the result of resisting arrest.

The videotaped horror represents but one small part of our current police-community relationship, yet is a very potent picture of the state of some self-titled "professional" law enforcement in this nation. The "have nots," those persons who don't have social respectability (read: not in the middle or upper-classes), those persons who don't have economic well-being (read: unable to earn the necessities of life), or those persons who don't have political power (read: cannot demand equal treatment without jeopardy) are most often the "torturables" who are consistently at the mercy of the brutes within criminal justice.

Brutal police officers are mirror images of those four depicted in the videotape, whose disgusting actions are tolerated, defended, justified and obviously accepted by the 13 other officers who stood by and watched, as interested observers, giving tacit approval to their colleagues. All who were present, including the supervisor, have the certain knowledge that to say or do anything indicating dissent or disapproval would be interpreted as "not supporting fellow officers" and would result in severe problems of acceptance by colleagues, assignment difficulties, probable negative performance ratings, damage to promotional potential, and ultimately, perhaps, career termination by personal choice or by shared department wish. Dissenters and whistle-blowers are, everywhere and always, in serious jeopardy.

At the present time, in any large police agency, too many officers have an unprofessional posture, but professional officers must become a conspicuous majority, for the health of the nation and for the well-being of all citizens, or a police state will soon become an odious reality in some larger American cities.

There are four major hurdles that must be dealt with, if ever and whenever large-scale changes are contemplated for any police agency: the rigidity of a hierarchical organi-

Continued

---

zation; the impact of socialization within the police subculture; the continuation of anachronistic policies and procedures, and the need for professional role models.

Hierarchical Rigidity

The police agency is a closed Civil Service system, with many ranks and very little room for independent thought, creative and imaginative initiatives, serious internal audit or reformation, or any elimination of anachronistic fiefdoms. Anyone who enters the system as a careerist, and who wishes good job assignment, promotional opportunity, an extended career and a pension, must walk in step with the organization, accept the customs and traditions of the service, and "sing the party line," so to speak. To do otherwise—to question or blow the whistle on immoral, illegal or flagrantly wasteful use of personnel, equipment or resources—is to seriously jeopardize one's career potential.

Police wrongdoing should never be seen as a matter of "a few bad apples in the barrel." It is the barrel that is tainted; the bad apples are created. The organizational environment, rigid and immobilized into protected fiefdoms, cannot change with the times, with modern challenges or with the needs of the moment, and cannot reform itself. Until it becomes an open, flexible, decentralized system, with all personnel and units working cooperatively, professionally and honorably to serve all of the citizens, and each other, with the highest motivation and with respect for the Constitution, any police agency will be a monstrous waste of public resources. It will have very little impact on crime, violence and disorder in the community. It will be no more than a public welfare program for the care, feeding, pleasure and lifetime support of large numbers of tenured, retired-on-the-job police personnel. The Civil Service system, while protecting police from gross political influence, often protects mediocrity, locks deadwood

into place with lifetime sinecures, and blocks the upward mobility of professionally oriented police change agents.

Subcultural Socialization

Wherever traditional police have ruled the roost, they have set the standards, and molded incoming recruits into identical mental sets— a mentality of "us versus them," with "them" being anyone without a badge. Slavish conformity to traditional values and practices is demanded of all personnel, and is the price of admission to the fraternity as an approved and accepted colleague.

There are far too many police whose values are selfish and individualistic, and who make the position work for them in many ways—free coffee, newspapers, meals, entertainment, clothes, transportation, cigarettes, foods, liquor, unnecessary overtime— a plethora of freebies that can lead all the way to theft of property, resale of drugs, and the skimming of expropriated drug money. Unprofessional police misuse their power and authority against anyone they choose and, particularly, against anyone who does not show deference. Such police plant false evidence, make illegal searches and seizures, engage in brutal verbal and physical abuse, manufacture probable cause, falsify official reports, and commit perjury on the witness stand. Such actions are repeated with regularity, impunity and immunity. All such actions are taken with obvious contempt for accepted standards of decency and integrity, and with an almost total insensitivity to the desires, needs or rights of the individual citizen or the community. Such actions are taken with indifference to the reputation of the agency, and to the damage inflicted upon the reputation of professional colleagues. All such actions are ignored, overlooked or condoned by traditionally programmed supervisors, middle managers, and top administrators.

Continued

Traditional internal discipline is more harsh and punitive with respect to violations of policy and procedure involving facilities and equipment than it is with respect to violations of human rights. Traditional internal discipline allows too many officers to resign in lieu of disciplinary action, instead of taking energetic action to fire and criminally prosecute badged felons. The traditional internal affairs disciplinary unit is often referred to as "the world's best washing machine, everything that goes in dirty comes out clean."

The traditional police academy seems to have as its goal the preparation of brutal hit-squad members, rather than community helpers and nonviolent conflict resolvers. Often the training is more oriented toward crime repression, subject control and weaponry than it is toward developing citizen involvement and participation with the police—jointly creating a more peaceful, safe and nurturing environment for all citizens.

The traditional police union or employee organization resists any and all attempts to eliminate unsavory customs and traditions, and any and all attempts to rid the department of officers who are very obviously misguided engines of destruction. The majority of traditional officers support their colleagues with a code of silence, coverup, and sophisticated political pressure that often results in the dismissal or resignation of professionally oriented administrators. Such a warped posture may include blackmail of the community power structure, for well-developed police intelligence files, complete with racy surveillance information, are a real threat to public representatives, and can be used to silence critics or influence administrative decisions.

Policy Anachronisms

Too many of our departments are mired in slavish devotion to anachronistic policies and procedures, with traditional leadership at the top level that tolerates, defends and smugly and arrogantly denies any and all evidence of misfeasance, malfeasance, or nonfeasance. The crude posture of many of our police Neanderthals (who often identify themselves as "professional") has made their police agencies objects of suspicion, derision, fear, hatred and contempt. This is particularly in evidence when their only response to crime and disorder is to get tougher—hire more police, make more arrests, pass tougher laws, set longer sentences, and build more jails and prisons—with never a word about the unfair treatment of human beings by government units, about the amelioration of ignorance, homelessness, unemployment, disease, poverty, racism, sexism, insane macho violence, or about the relationship of these realities to frustration, hatred, crime, violence and disorder.

There is a pressing need for revision of police priorities, so that primary attention is given to the prevention and control of violent predatory crime. The police traditionalist consistently calls for additional public resources—increased budgets for personnel, facilities and equipment—but never discusses the impotence of the police; the fact that most serious, major crime offenders are not convicted or punished, and that most serious, major crime offenders are not identified or charged. Thus the traditional police mislead the community in calling for ever-increasing resources to fight crime, while remaining ineffective in terms of really preventing crime. All professional policemen, in my personal judgment, would agree wholeheartedly, even if sadly and silently.

Professional Role Models

At the same time that there are so many horror stories of police excesses, there are police administrators, supervisors and officers who are very professional, very honorable, very truthful, and who are truly the unsung heroes of our age. These men and women act as role models for their agencies and for the community in which they serve. They see the police professional as a community

Continued

helper rather than as a fire-power-oriented lethal weapon, and as a person engaged in working closely with the people. They develop pride and trust in the department and in fellow professional officers. In short, all of their actions are in accord with human dignity, human rights and human values. People like these—professional, well educated, highly motivated, with keen minds, social sensitivity, strength of character, and the courage to tell the king that he is naked—are the pride of the American police service. They need to be encouraged, supported, and given the access to the authority and power that are needed for immediate implementation of necessary changes of policy and procedure.

Today, unfortunately, the role model for the traditional police department seems to be an administrator who believes that all problems of delinquency, crime and disorder can be solved with the energetic application of immediate massive force, and more of the same tired old protocols. We can expect more incidents, such as happened in Los Angeles. It is quite obvious that the administrative and legal structures of the city, county and department should be designed so that any appointed chief is controllable and answerable to all of the citizens he or she serves. They should be designed so that the chief serves not at his or her own personal pleasure, but at the pleasure of the appointing authority, and with the continuous full approval of community representatives. If the chief cannot or will not control brutal or venal conduct, or set policies and procedures that represent community values, he or she should be immediately replaced.

More Badged Brutes?

The moment of truth is at hand. Will American police continue to allow colleagues to act as a band of badged brutes, free to pursue an autocratic, immoral, lawless oppression of any person in whatever way they deem appropriate, or will American police undergo a forced metamorphosis wherein all members are controlled and retrained as professional community helpers, with mandated standards, to serve as protectors of all citizens working in mutual harmony to maintain a quality of life where violence is minimized and cooperation is maximized, and where the majority of police officers can be considered as valued and trusted members of the community?

The March 1, 1991, beating of Rodney King is not an aberration, but is an example of traditional posture and practice that goes on in all large police departments that do not have adequate leadership, training, supervision and control, and that do not have a philosophy and reputation of helping citizens, obeying the U.S. Constitution, and role-modeling nonviolent forms of persuasion. The impossible dream must become a reality even if achieving it means that many police officers must be remotivated and retrained, or, if necessary, disciplined, fired and/or prosecuted.

indicate that police shootings result in between 250 and 300 deaths annually, but some experts believe this figure to be very conservative (Fyfe, 1989). Data from the International Association of Chiefs of Police covering the fifty-seven largest departments in the United States between the years 1970 and 1983 indicate that these cities alone accounted for more than two hundred deaths each year (Matulia, 1985). According to FBI statistics, police killed 415 offenders in 1992 (Davis, 1994).

The police have traditionally had the authority to use force when someone's life is being threatened or to stop a fleeing felon. The fleeing felon rule, derived from common law, was finally challenged successfully in the case of

Tennessee v. Garner (1985). In that case, the police fatally wounded an unarmed teenage burglar fleeing from an unoccupied house. The Supreme Court ruled that the use of deadly force as a means of apprehending unarmed, nonviolent felons violated the Fourth Amendment right against unreasonable seizure. The ruling meant that some thirty-one states that employed the fleeing felon rule without modification were in violation of the Constitution.

Perhaps in part as a result of the Garner decision, the incidence of police killings has shown a downward trend over the past decade. In addition, many police departments had modified the fleeing felon rule prior to the Garner decision so that it applied only when the person fleeing represented clear and present danger to life or limb. Additionally, training in deescalating potentially deadly situations has increased dramatically in recent years. Keeping in mind the shortcomings of the data, what we know about police use of deadly force seems to support the following conclusions:

1. Younger officers appear to be more likely than older officers to become involved in shooting incidents.
2. The likelihood of police officers becoming involved in shooting incidents declines with years of service.
3. Race and gender of officers appear to be unrelated to the likelihood of police shootings.
4. Police use of deadly force appears to be positively correlated with the level of violence in the neighborhood in which the shooting occurs.
5. A disproportionate number of minority group members are victims of police killings (at least half of the victims are members of racial or ethnic minorities).
6. Police shootings occur disproportionately in high crime areas.
7. The decision to shoot is usually made within a matter of seconds.
8. Most police officers will not experience a shooting incident in their careers (Blumberg, 1986; Sherman, 1980; Dade County Grand Jury, 1982).

Based on the conclusions presented above, we might expect that police shootings are most likely to occur in situations (neighborhoods, incidents) in which the police suspect or are aware of the presence of weapons and in which they perceive a willingness on the part of the persons possessing them to use such weapons. These situations occur quite frequently. For example, there were 61,724 assaults on police officers reported in 1985, an increase of 550 percent over 1960 (FBI, 1960–1986). How much fear for their personal safety or for the safety of others leads to the use of deadly force is difficult to determine exactly, but it is undoubtedly a major factor. Such fear may be reality based or the result of inaccurate perceptions, but in either case it may cause the officer to use deadly force when it is unnecessary.

Of major concern is the fact that in some cases the maximum penalty to be handed down by the courts is imprisonment, leaving the police with greater power to execute than the courts, with no judicial review preceding the decision—which is, of course, often final. Such police killings have been termed "executions without trial" (Sherman, 1980).

As we have seen in this chapter and Chapter 9, deadly force is a two-way street. Police officers both use it and have it used against them. While the data indicate that the police are more likely to kill than be killed, we must keep in mind that it is the potential for killing that is the critical factor. Although there is no solid data on the subject, it seems logical that officers who fear that their own lives (or the lives of others) may be in danger would be more likely to consider the use of deadly force than those without such fears. These fears and the prediction of danger on which they are based are not evenly distributed geographically or situationally. Situations involving felonies in progress, riots, apprehension of felons known to have used a weapon in the commission of a crime, and geographical areas with known high violent crime rates would likely be regarded by any reasonable individual as potentially dangerous. Such situations clearly heighten the level of fear and preparedness among police officers, and one possible response is the use of force, including deadly force based more on the prediction of danger than the reality of the situation. While this response probably occurs infrequently, its importance as a factor in the use of deadly force cannot be overlooked. "There is a fine line you must walk to be a street cop on the West Side. A fine line balancing toughness and fairness. A sense of right and wrong without being judgmental. The willingness to listen without being suckered. The ability to talk without lecturing. To command respect without being brutal. And to be fearless without ever burning out" (Keegan, 1989).

Walking that fine line is difficult in areas where police officers know that fellow officers have been killed or seriously injured, and in situations where officers have been killed or injured very recently. Citizens have the right to expect that our police officers will be able to walk that line, and have the obligation to provide them with the tools necessary for action if the line must be crossed, as long as those involved in the encounters possess the potential for deadly force.

Further, we must recognize that mistakes in judgment will sometimes occur in such situations. We have the right, also, to expect that those responsible for police training and operations will do their utmost to minimize the likelihood of mistakes in judgment. While it may never be possible to eliminate all such mistakes, changes in the laws (such as those related to the Garner decision discussed previously) and thorough, proper training of police officers can go a long way toward achieving the goal. Enforceable gun control laws may also help in this regard.

This is not to suggest that gun control measures such as the Brady Bill should not be adopted, merely to indicate that no immediate decreases in the use of firearms by offenders are likely to result. The long-term impact of effective gun control legislation might indeed lessen the availability of weapons, reduce the level of perceived danger in some types of encounters, and result in fewer killings of and by the police.

Radelet (1989: 67) observes "Police in this country do a much better job than they did one, two, or three decades ago. This is a fair generalization, but there remain police agencies and locations facing situations appearing to turn the clock back to the 1960s, and in some cases showing little evidence of lessons learned from the past. Generally, police today deal with civil violence and disturbances in a more disciplined, restrained, sensitive, and professional manner."

The observation holds true with respect to police misconduct in general. While there have been improvements, the police are not perfect, as the incidents previously described clearly indicate. Still, through recruitment and retention of police officers who understand the importance of ethics and personal integrity and by providing officers with appropriate laws, training, resources, public support, and role models, we can minimize the likelihood of their misconduct. In a less-than-perfect world, that is perhaps the most we can hope for.

Discussion Questions

1. What are some of the more important ethical issues in policing? Should police recruits be taught ethics?

2. What constitutes police corruption? Can you cite examples of police corruption from your own experiences?

3. Why is corruption of authority (accepting gratuities such as free coffee, food, and so on) critical in understanding police corruption in general?

4. Does society desire or demand police who are incorruptible? Why or why not?

5. What is the relationship between internal corruption in police agencies and other forms of corruption?

6. How are police corruption, perjury, and use of force interrelated?

7. Why would a police officer perjure himself or herself? What is the effect of such perjury on the criminal justice network and other citizens in general?

8. Is psychological brutality an important form of police misconduct? Why and in what ways?

9. Discuss the relationship between police misuse of force and the fact that a number of police officers are killed each year.

10. Do you think police misconduct is as serious a problem now as it was a decade or so ago? Support your answer.

References

Barker, T. and Carter, D.L. 1986. *Police Deviance.* Cincinnati: Pilgrimage.

Baker, T. and Roebuck, J.B. 1974. *An Empirical Typology of Police Corruption: A Study in Organizational Deviance.* Springfield, IL: Charles C. Thomas.

Bittner, E. 1970. *The Functions of the Police in Modern Society.* Chevy Chase, MD: National Institute of Mental Health Center for Studies of Crime and Delinquency.

Blumberg, M. 1986. "Issues and Controversies with Respect to the Use of Deadly Force by the Police." in Barker, T. and Carter, D. (eds.), *Police Deviance*. Cincinnati: Pilgrimage, 232–244.

Bouza, A.V. 1990. *The Police Mystique: An Insider's Look at Cops, Crime, and the Criminal Justice System*. New York: Plenum.

Bracey, D.H. 1989. "Proactive Measures Against Police Corruption: Yesterday's Solutions, Today's Problems." *Police Studies* 12(24), 175–179.

Campbell, L.P. 1991. "Police Brutality Triggers Many Complaints, Little Data." *Chicago Tribune* (24 March), p. 10.

Chevigny, P. 1969. *Police Power: Police Abuses in New York City*. New York: Vintage Press.

Clark, J.R. 1994. "What Kind of Watchdog Is in Store for the NYPD?" *Law Enforcement News* 20(405), 1–6.

Church, G.J. 1992. "The Fire This Time." *Time* (11 May), 22–25.

Cooksey, O.E. 1991. "Corruption: A Continuing Challenge for Law Enforcement." *FBI Law Enforcement Bulletin* (September), 5–9.

Cray, E. 1972. *The Enemy in the Streets: Police Malpractice in America*. Garden City, NY: Anchor Books.

Dade County Grand Jury. 1982. "Police Use of Deadly Force: The Dade County Experience." In Barker, T. and Carter, D. (eds.), *Police Deviance*. Cincinnati: Pilgrimage, 171–187.

Davis, R. 1994. "'Attitude Change' Proves Lethal for Police." *USA TODAY* (3 January), p. 3A.

Dorschner, J. 1993. "The Dark Side of the Force." In Dunham, R.G. and Alpert, G.P. (eds.), *Critical Issues in Policing: Contemporary Readings*. Prospect Heights, IL: Waveland Press, 254–274.

Federal Bureau of Investigation. 1960–1986. *Uniform Crime Reports*. Washington, DC: U.S. Government Printing Office.

Ferguson, C. 1993. "Cops Get Long Terms for Beating." *USA TODAY* (13 October), p. 1A.

Frankel, B. 1993a. "'You'll be in the Fold' by Breaking Law." *USA TODAY* (30 September), p. 1A.

Frankel, B. 1993b. "For NYC Cops, License for Crime." *USA TODAY* (7 October), p. 3A.

Fyfe, J.J. 1989. "Deadly Force." In Bailey, W.G. (ed.), *The Encyclopedia of Police Science*. New York: Garland, 133–136.

Germann, A.C. 1993. "Changing the Police: An Impossible Dream?" *Law Enforcement News* 19(383), 6, 10.

Gwynne, S.C. 1995. "Cops and Robbers." *Time* (20 March), 45.

Johnson, D.R. 1981. *American Law Enforcement: A History*. St. Louis, MO: Forum Press.

Keegan, A. 1989. "Cronie." *The Chicago Tribune Magazine*. (27 August), pp. 10–16.

Klockars, C.B. 1989. "Police Ethics." In Bailey, W.G. (ed.), *The Encyclopedia of Police Science*. New York: Garland Press, 427–432.

Knapp Commission. 1973. *The Knapp Commission Report on Police Corruption*. New York: George Braziller.

Lacayo, R. 1993. "Cops and Robbers." *Time* (11 October), 43–44.

Langer, G. 1988. "Americans Say Racism Persists." *Journal Star* (8 August), p. 2.

Law Enforcement News. 1994. "Mollen Commission's Prescription for Reform." 20(405), 7.

Leinen, S. 1984. *Black Police—White Society*. New York: New York University Press.

Lynch, G.W. 1989. "Police Corruption from the United States Perspective." *Police Studies* 12(4), 165–170.

Manning, P.K. 1974. "Police Lying." *Urban Life* 3, 283–306.

Matulia, K.J. 1985. *A Balance of Forces* 2 ed. Gaithersburg, MD: International Association of Chiefs of Police.

Nasser, H.E. and Stewart, S.A. 1992. "S. Calif. Police on Alert after Mistrial in Shooting." *USA TODAY* (20 May), p. 3A.

National Advisory Commission on Civil Disorders. 1968. Washington, DC: U.S. Government Printing Office.

Radelet, L.A. 1989. "Community Relations." In Bailey, W.G. (ed.), *Encyclopedia of Police Science*. New York: Garland Press.

Reiss, A.J. 1968. "Police Brutality . . . Answers to Key Questions." In Lipsky, M. (ed.), *Police Encounters*. Chicago: Aldine.

Reiss, A.J. 1971. *The Police and the Public*. New Haven, CT: Yale University Press.

Richardson, J.F. 1974. *Urban Police in the United States*. Port Washington, NY: Kennikat Press.

Roberg, R.R. and Kuykendall, J. 1993. *Police in Society*. Belmont, CA: Wadsworth.

Rubinstein, J. 1973. *City Police*. New York: Farrar, Straus, and Giroux.

Sapp, A.D. 1986. "Sexual Misconduct and Sexual Harassment by Police Officers." In Barker, T. and Carter, D. (eds.), *Police Deviance*. Cincinnati: Pilgrimage, 83–95.

Sharn, L. 1993. "'Twenty Years and It's Not Over,' Serpico Says." *USA TODAY* (30 September), p. 2A.

Sherman, L.W. 1980. "Execution Without Trial: Police Homicide and the Constitution." *Vanderbilt Law Review* 33(71), 71–100.

Skolnick, J.H. 1966. *Justice Without Trial*. New York: John Wiley.

Stallworth v. City of Cleveland, 893 F. 2d 830 (1990).

Stoddard, E.R. 1968. "The Informal Code of Police Deviance: A Group Approach to 'Blue-Coat Crime.'" *Journal of Criminal Law Criminology and Police Science* 59 (June), 201–213.

Tennessee Advisory Committee to the U.S. Civil Rights Commission. 1978. *Civic Crisis—Civic Challenge: Police Community Relations in Memphis*. Washington, DC: U.S. Government Printing Office.

Tennessee v. Garner. 105 S. Ct. 1694 (1985).

Trojanowicz, R. 1992. "Preventing Individual and Systemic Corruption." *Footprints* 4(1), 1–3.

Turque, B. 1991. "Brutality on the Beat." *Newsweek* (25 March), 32–34.

11

POLICING IN A
MULTI-CULTURAL SETTING

It should be apparent from discussions in Chapters 1 and 2 that the police, whatever their perceived role, cannot be effective or efficient without public support. Without such support, they will be uninformed of most crimes, are likely to receive inadequate resources, will not be able to collect information needed to solve cases and apprehend offenders, and will be unsuccessful in recruiting quality employees. There is little doubt that, in democratic societies at least, community relations are the cornerstone of good policing. Burden (1992: 19) notes, "The police are—or should be—the protectors of a citizen's civil liberties and civil rights, as well as his life and property. They are, for example, the first line of defense for the First Amendment rights to assemble peaceably and speak freely. Few unpopular ideas would ever get a public hearing unless the police were on hand to ensure the speaker's safety and maintain order." If the police are to serve the community effectively and in a manner acceptable to citizens, there must be a reasonable working relationship between the two.

Developing such working relationships in a rapidly changing, multicultural society is difficult. Indications from the Bureau of Census are that the Asian population grew by as much as 105 percent between 1980 and 1990, and the Hispanic population increased by 53 percent (Stone, 1991). Most authorities agree that within one hundred years, people of color will be a numerical majority in the United States. Pomerville (1993: 30), for example, notes: "In the next few decades, the population will shift from a dominant Anglo-American society to a dominant multi-cultural majority of African-Americans, Asian-Americans, and Hispanic-Americans."

Some thirty-two million people over the age of four speak a language other than English at home, and about 2.9 million U.S. households are linguistically isolated: no one over the age of fourteen speaks English fluently (Stacey, 1993).

The elderly constitute an increasing proportion of our population. Gays and lesbians, the homeless, religious minorities, neo-Nazi skinheads, and refugees from Balkan countries, Central and South America, and island countries continue to seek asylum. Immigrants come to this country bringing "not only different languages, religious observances, dress, and lifestyles, but different views of the police. Some have come with very negative images of the police, having come from countries where the police are integrated with the military and police actions are not regulated by strong constitutional and human rights guarantees" (Scott, 1993: 26).

There are essentially two ways of attempting to develop good working relationships between the police and other citizens. The first, community policing, we have already discussed in some detail in preceding chapters. The second consists of police-community relations efforts. The two are not mutually exclusive, but they are not identical either, as Highlight 11.1 indicates.

The Nature of Police-Community Relations

As O'Brien (1978: 304) indicates, "The central position of the police in the community critically affects all sections of society. The multiple duties of the

---

HIGHLIGHT 11.1   Community Policing and Police-Community Relations Are Not the Same Thing

---

Comparison of Community Policing to Police-Community Relations

Community Policing

- Goal: Solve problems—improved relations with citizens is a welcome by-product
- Line Function: Regular contact of officer with citizens
- Citizens nominate problems and cooperate in setting police agenda
- Police accountability is insured by the citizens receiving the service
- Meaningful organizational change and departmental restructuring, ranging from officer selection to training, evaluation, and promotion
- A department-wide philosophy and acceptance
- Influence is from "the bottom up." Citizens receiving service help set priorities and influence police policy
- Officer is continually accessible, in person or by telephone recorder in a decentralized office
- Officer encourages citizens to solve many of their own problems and volunteer to assist neighbors
- Success is determined by the reduction in citizen fear, neighborhood disorder, and crime

Police-Community Relations

- Goal: Change attitudes and project positive image—improved relations with citizens is main focus
- Staff Function: Irregular contact of officer with citizens
- "Blue ribbon" committees identify the problems and "preach" to police
- Police accountability is insured by civilian review boards and formal police supervision
- Traditional organization stays intact with "new" programs periodically added, no fundamental organizational change
- Isolated acceptance often localized to PCR Unit
- Influence is from "the top down"—those who "know best" have input and make decisions
- Intermittent contact with the public because of city-wide responsibility; contact is made through central headquarters
- Citizens are encouraged to volunteer but are told to request and expect more government (including law enforcement) services
- Success is determined by traditional measures, i.e., crime rates and citizen satisfaction with the police (Trojanowicz, 1990: 6–11)

Reprinted with permission from the *FBI Law Enforcement Bulletin*, 59(10), 6–11.

police at all times and in all areas of the community dictate that they must influence the daily life of each citizen. . . . Unfortunately, in recent times there has been a rupture of mutual trust between the police and some segments of the community."

Actually, the "rupture of mutual trust" noted by O'Brien is not a recent occurrence, but has deep historical roots in U.S. policing. Conflict between the police and other citizens is rooted in the basic structure of U.S. society and the values on which it rests. This situation is shown in numerous discussions of police-community relations that are described, presumably unintentionally, in terms of police encounters with citizens. The language used here makes it appear that the police are not citizens and points to a dichotomy that has emerged in our society between the police and *other* citizens. In many respects the police have come to be viewed as adversaries not only by those involved in criminal activities, but by basically law-abiding citizens who occasionally violate speed limits, drive while intoxicated, or offer what they consider to be legitimate grievances without going through proper channels to obtain a permit.

Obviously, police officers are first and foremost citizens historically, traditionally, and legally. Yet, the language we use to describe things often indicates the way in which we view them; some tend to view the police as somehow distinct from "citizens." While the use of such terminology may not widen the gap between the police and other citizens, it does little to close the gap. Police encounters with other citizens are, at base, encounters between fellow citizens.

Also, when we are talking about police-community relations, we tend to think in terms of police encounters with the public. In fact, we are not dealing with one large homogeneous group called a public, but with many diverse publics. These publics are divided by factors such as geography, race, gender, age, social class, respect for law and order, and degree of law-abiding behavior (Cox and Wade, 1989: 11). These different publics have unique interests and concerns that separate them from one another in many ways. The police, as public servants, are to serve all these various publics; they organize in various ways to meet what they perceive to be the needs of the publics they serve. Since the expectations of members of these different publics are often dissimilar, providing effective service is often difficult, leading to many problems in policing. "Our communities are changing quickly—often too quickly for law enforcement to keep up. Failing to understand many of these changes, and still trying to conduct business as usual, we find that the tools and rules that worked before don't work now. For many seasoned officers, their main concern is to make it through each shift and go home in one piece. This only serves to reinforce a force-oriented culture that brings officers closer to each other and further from the community they serve" (Hennessy, 1993: 48).

In addition, members of the various publics are often apathetic about most issues involving the police but have very specific expectations when they or other members of their group require police services. The necessity of attempting to satisfy these different, sometimes conflicting, expectations should alert us that good police-community relations are not easy to achieve. In a large, industrialized, multiethnic society, based on values include democratic decision making, individual freedom, and tolerance for diversity, the need for social order and the demand for freedom will inevitably lead to conflict on some occasions (Cox and Fitzgerald, 1991).

To some extent, then, conflict between the police and other citizens is inevitable and perhaps even healthy within limits. However, when this conflict becomes extensive, or when certain groups are singled out for differential treatment by the police, the problem cannot be ignored. Solutions to conflicts of this type are not easily found and are not the sole responsibility of the police. Yet, we cannot easily force other citizens into classes on human or public relations, even though we recognize that successful programs in either of these areas require reciprocity. Therefore, the burden of trying to improve police-community relations often rests on the police.

Police-community relations are comprised of both human and public relations. The concept of human relations refers to everything we do to, for, and with other people. Included under this concept are things such as showing respect for one another, being sensitive to the problems of others, tolerating divergent points of view, and showing respect for human dignity. Public relations, from the police perspective, include all of the activities they engage in while attempting to develop and maintain a favorable public image (Cox and Fitzgerald, 1991). Let's examine each of these concepts as they relate to police encounters with other citizens.

Human Relations in Policing

With respect to police-community relations, humans relations in the millions of day-to-day encounters that take place are the foundation for community relations—good or bad. It is important to recognize that these encounters between individuals do not occur in a vacuum. When we encounter others, we often know (or think we know) a good deal about them even though we have never met them before. Thus, for example, we have preconceived notions about members of different racial or ethnic groups and about police officers. These preconceived notions or stereotypes are based on prior encounters, word of mouth, rumor, gossip, and/or information provided by the media. They may be quite accurate or almost totally inaccurate. Whichever is the case, we act in terms of these perceptions, at least until the encounter in which we are involved gives us additional or different information on which to base our actions.

Consider an encounter between a uniformed police officer and another citizen. The officer is easily identifiable because of the uniform, badge, nightstick, handcuffs, and gun; all of these items help identify his or her role in the encounter. The role that is, in part, defined by the "tools of the trade" includes the officer as an authority able to use force under certain circumstances to gain compliance with his or her wishes. This should indicate (and for the most part does appear to indicate) to other parties involved that the officer's definition of the situation will be the prevailing one; that is, that the officer is in control or will gain control.

In order for this definition of the situation to prevail, certain obligations must be fulfilled by the other party or parties to the encounter. These obligations include deferring to the officer's authority, treating the officer with some degree of respect, and complying with his or her directions. To do otherwise is to risk offending the officer, who may then resort to more drastic actions in light of what may be viewed as a challenge to his or her authority. Some officers are extremely sensitive to such challenges and the perceived loss of face that accompanies them. Such officers may feel compelled to respond quickly and forcefully to maintain their control. Obviously, such a response may lead to suspicion and hostility on behalf of the other party to the encounter, and the encounter may become nasty in short order.

Suspicions may increase when the two parties bring negative impressions of each other into the encounter, as sometimes occurs when the police and racial or ethnic minority group members interact. Such negative impressions also often exist when the police are called into a domestic violence situation in which they regard the offender with suspicion and the offender believes that police intervention into an essentially private matter is improper.

The extent to which encounters between the police and other citizens become problematic depends on a number of factors. These factors include the impressions brought to the encounter, the setting in which the encounter occurs (private or public, familiar or unfamiliar), the number and types of participants involved, the degree of control exercised by the participants, and what actually happens during the encounter. For example, the mere sight of a police officer puts some people "on guard." They drive more slowly and more carefully; if they are involved in illegal activities they may try to appear innocent, and they may treat other people more civilly. For their part, police officers are trained to be suspicious of others, especially when past experience or present knowledge leads them to believe an offense may be involved. Thus, the danger and difficulty of police encounters ranges from very great, as in a solo encounter with a known felon in the process of committing a felony in an isolated location, to very little, as in the case of locating a missing child lost in a shopping mall in which other participants are attempting to assist.

It is possible to exaggerate the difficulties involved in police encounters with other citizens. Most such encounters are civil, characterized by some degree of mutual concern, understanding, and respect (Reiss, 1968). Still, there is no denying that encounters between the police and some other citizens are more likely to be problematic than others. As we have seen, police-minority encounters in our society have been particularly problematic over the past quarter of a century and it is to these encounters that we now turn our attention.

Police-Minority Encounters

One of the most controversial areas of police-community relations in our society involves the police and racial or ethnic minority group members, particularly police interactions with blacks and Hispanics, though members of other racial and ethnic minorities are sometimes involved as well (see Highlight 11.2).

A minority group is comprised of individuals who are accorded unequal treatment from dominant group members in the form of discrimination; they are relatively easy to identify because of their physical or cultural characteristics that differ from those of the dominant group. Using this definition, the police themselves might well be considered as members of a minority since they are often victims of discrimination, are generally easy to identify, and have, as we have seen, some distinctive cultural characteristics (masculinity, authority, use of force, cynicism, etc.). One basic difference between police

HIGHLIGHT 11.2   Police-Minority Encounters

Lawyers Say Clients' Rights Were Violated

State Police Accused of Targeting Hispanics through Profile System

Four attorneys representing men facing drug charges in the LaSalle County area say their clients' constitutional rights were violated when they were stopped by Illinois State Police.

All the defendants are Hispanic or Hispanic-looking, said attorney Thomas McClintock. "I don't think it is coincidence."

McClintock said he believes the state police are using a profile system and specifically targeting Hispanics for drug searches.

The attorneys asked a judge to force the state police to turn over training materials and statistics from the State Police Drug Interdiction Program, also known as Operation Valkvrie.

However, Circuit Judge George C. Hupp ruled on June 14 he would not force police to turn over the Operation Valkvrie documents, and he also declined to review the materials in his chambers.

McClintock said the attorneys in the case still might be able to get the materials by filing a motion to suppress evidence during their clients' trials.

Assistant U.S. Attorney David Risley said he does not believe state police are using a profile system.

"Defense attorneys find it hard to believe that they (the police) are being successful without being dirty," Risley said. "They (defense attorneys) don't understand the program.

"Police put out a dragnet, and every single traffic stop, they are alert for the unordinary," he said.

"We train troopers not to profile because if they use a profiling system they'll miss many vehicles."

Even if police did use profiles to determine which vehicles to stop and search, "Courts say it doesn't matter what motive the police have for stopping a vehicle, as long as there is a violation of some sort," Risley said.

McClintock questioned the legitimacy of the violations for which the men were stopped.

"How many tickets do they (the police) issue for following too closely in a non-accidental situation or for going 3 miles an hour over the speed limit?" McClintock asked.

He said he also thinks the defendants were coerced into letting the police search their cars, and didn't realize they had the right to refuse.

"In order to voluntarily give up constitutional rights, you must knowingly and voluntarily do it," McClintock said. "The defendants did not know they would have had to be allowed to drive on" (Ferguson 1991: A7).

From Peoria (Ill.) *Journal Star*. Reprinted by permission.

officers and members of racial or ethnic minorities is that the former are voluntary members while the latter are not.

Traditional beliefs in our society hold that members of some racial or ethnic minorities are inferior to whites in some ways, even though scientific research indicates there is no basis for such beliefs. Since many police officers come from traditional backgrounds, it is not surprising to find that many agree that minority group members are inferior, especially when they police in areas with high crime rates that are inhabited principally by members of a minority who often view the police as intruders or members of an army of occupation (Baldwin, 1962; Hacker, 1992).

It is important to point out the difference between prejudice (a feeling about a person or persons based on faulty generalizations) and discrimination (which involves behavior that, in its negative form, excludes all members of a certain group from some rights, opportunities, or privileges [Schaefer, 1993]). We all have prejudices that may or may not result in discrimination. The existence of prejudice among police officers has been well documented; though we might hope to change these proclivities, there is little we can do in a direct fashion to alter peoples' feelings (Bayley and Mendelsohn, 1969; Schaefer, 1993).

When these feelings carry over into behavior (discrimination), however, serious problems result for both the police and minority group members. Thus, when police officers harass or abuse individuals because they are members of a minority or treat individuals as if they were above the law because they belong to another minority, community relations suffer. Harassment and abuse result in loss of face and human dignity and occasional physical injuries, and cannot be tolerated on the part of police officers. There is little doubt that members of many minorities, racial and ethnic as well as behavioral (alcoholics, homosexuals, prostitutes, drug addicts, etc.) believe that such harassment and abuse are commonly directed toward members of their groups. As a consequence, as well as for historical reasons, individuals belonging to these groups resent and are sometimes openly hostile toward the police. They often respond to police with harassment and verbal abuse. This response escalates the danger and hostility involved, while it ensures poor community relations. It is essential, then, to realize that prejudice and discrimination are not limited to the police. Therefore, the police alone cannot ensure good community relations.

It is equally important to recognize that many police officers who might not otherwise be involved in discriminatory practices fall victim to occupational discrimination. That is, even though an individual officer may not believe in acting in discriminatory fashion, his or her colleagues may exhibit such behavior. In order to be perceived as a part of the subculture we described earlier, these officers may emulate the behavior of their peers, thus harassing or abusing minority group members, not because they believe it is right, but because they wish to be perceived as members of the "in group."

Similarly, minority group members may not believe that harassing the police is appropriate behavior, but in the presence of other members of their group, may do so. Blacks in our society, for example, have historical reasons for disliking the police, whom they see as representatives of the establishment that made and keeps them second-class citizens.

As Sykes (1978: 395) pointed out, "In a democratic social order, the police are expected to be fair in their enforcement of the law and accountable to those who are policed. They are not to be an alien force imposed on a community, an autonomous body ruling by coercion, or agents of a tyrannical state, but servants of society maintaining a commonly accepted body of law in evenhanded fashion."

As we have pointed out elsewhere (Cox and Fitzgerald, 1991), however, the police in our society have often been an alien force when dealing with blacks and other minority group members. In contemporary society, the police expend a disproportionate amount of their resources in minority neighborhoods. Here again, conflicting points of view and the difficulty of finding solutions to police-minority relations problems are obvious. "Simply mixing culturally different people together does not resolve misunderstandings. Quite the contrary. Differences usually become more apparent and hostilities can actually increase during encounters between culturally diverse individuals" (Weaver, 1992: 2).

While minority group members regard the number of police in their neighborhoods as excessive and a form of harassment, the police are correct in arguing that some minority neighborhoods have high crime rates and therefore require police presence. While it may be argued that police presence contributes to high crime rates (the more police, the more crimes they discover), it is equally true that the number of victims and offenders found in such neighborhoods makes it difficult for the police to respond in any other fashion (Sykes, 1978). This fact, however, does not justify the use of discriminatory tactics in minority neighborhoods.

What *are* some of the forms of police discrimination in minority neighborhoods? The basic form of discrimination is psychological harassment based on the use of racial slurs and other attempts to embarrass or humiliate members of the minority group in question. Failure to use proper forms of address (use of first name rather than Mr. or Ms. and last name, for example) has been and remains a major complaint of minority group members (National Advisory Commission, 1968; Cox, 1984; Hacker, 1992). Failure to respond rapidly to calls in ghetto or barrio areas has also been an issue. Unreasonable use of stop-and-question and stop-and-frisk tactics further alarm minority group members. Finally, the relatively infrequent but totally unacceptable use of excessive force on the part of the police in dealing with members of minorities (or for that matter the dominant group) is of major concern (Reiss, 1970; Chavis and Williams, 1993). Such incidents become legend in minority neighborhoods and further the negative image of the police already present as a result of historical differences between the parties.

> *The patrol car in the ghetto or barrio may be perceived by blacks and Latinos as 'police harassment,' while the police may believe they are acting in the best interests of these minority groups by providing as many personnel as possible in those areas where citizens are most likely to commit and be victims of crime. . . . Alternatively, the young black or Latino males who use the slang and dress of their subcultures may be perceived by the police as challenging their authority. . . . The perception of all police as 'honky bastards' is no more accurate than the perception of all blacks as 'shiftless niggers.' Such negative stereotypes are clearly inaccurate, and their persistence makes sharing a definition of the situation, or mutual understanding difficult, if not impossible (Cox and Fitzgerald, 1991: 135).*

We should note that human relations problems involving the police and minority group members are definitely not a thing of the past. One national survey on racism in the United States found that 40 percent of those surveyed did not believe racial equality would occur within their lifetimes, 55 percent felt U.S. society is racist, 40 percent of white respondents felt minorities are treated unequally in the criminal justice system, and 61 percent of black respondents said minorities are not treated equally in the criminal justice system (Langer, 1988). Further, a 1992 survey revealed that only 29 percent of black respondents, and only 32 percent of other nonwhites rated the honesty and ethical standards of police officers as "very high" or "high." Additionally, only 38 percent of black respondents (compared to 68 percent of white respondents and 54 percent of Hispanic respondents) felt their local police treated people fairly. Forty-five percent of black respondents and 43 percent of other nonwhite respondents felt there was police brutality in their areas (compared with 33 percent of white respondents) (Maguire, Pastore, and Flanagan, 1993).

Police-minority problems are likely to increase in number for all of the reasons we have discussed unless steps are taken now to prevent this from occurring. Unless dramatic changes in the socioeconomic status of many minority group members occur, the number of encounters between them and the police will continue to increase, making resolution of some of the problematic aspects of such encounters even more important.

Police-Public Relations

Police-community relations are comprised of two components. The first of these, human relations, we have just discussed. The second component, public relations, consists of those efforts on behalf of the police to develop and present a favorable image. While it is true that community-relations programs are doomed to failure if the day-to-day human relations practices of participants are poor, publicizing the positive practices and programs of police departments can certainly affect the impression of the police in the minds of other citizens. The uniform of the officer, the symbol on the squad car, and the response of the dispatcher or receptionist at police headquarters all create an impression of the police and as such are all parts of police public-relations efforts. Police pamphlets, public speaking engagements, department-sponsored programs, news conferences, widely advertised training in cultural diversity, and many other activities also fall within the public relations domain.

Public relations involve two interdependent components. The first of these, policy, consists of decisions, statements, and plans made by management in an attempt to influence public opinion. The second component, practice, is the process of putting the policies into action (Nolte, 1979). In most police agencies, policies are formulated by the chief in consultation with his or her staff and those for whom the chief works (city manager, mayor, councilpersons), while putting the policies into operation is typically a task of rank-and-file officers. In Chapter 5 we discussed the importance to police personnel of good communications; it is especially important in the area of public relations. Policies formulated but not passed on, or formulated but not explained or understood, can hardly be expected to result in sound practice.

Similarly, policies developed without communication with those who will eventually be responsible for enforcement are often of little value. Policy and practice go together. Both must be present, and some coordination between the two is necessary if either is to be valuable. It is here that many police administrators fail at implementing good community-relations programs. Some administrators recognize the importance of policy making and appoint special community-relations officers or teams to create such policy. Some recognize the importance of human relations and emphasize to every officer the importance of encounters with other citizens. Far fewer recognize that policy making and practice are intimately intertwined, so that policy makers and those who implement the policies must be in constant communication to allow for feedback and evaluation on a routine basis.

Such feedback and evaluation should focus on measuring and evaluating public opinion concerning the police, developing and implementing policies to maintain favorable public opinion or changing it so that it becomes more positive, and then reevaluating policies, practices, and opinions (Nolte, 1979: 20). Public relations, then, are a process that is repeated over and over as conditions and opinions change. We should emphasize once again, police public-relations programs will lead to a favorable image only if they accurately reflect practices that are acceptable to the public. No amount of image building will convince citizens that they have a professional police department if the daily encounters between police and other citizens are conducted in unprofessional fashion.

Citizen Complaints

An important part of the process of evaluating police-community relations consists of soliciting, evaluating, and acting on citizen complaints. Good community relations require that citizens feel free to discuss their complaints about police officers or police behavior with appropriate authorities. Systematic efforts to determine the public's feelings toward police services should be an integral part of police management. Such efforts may be conducted by department personnel, university personnel, or private consultants and should attempt to establish a baseline of public opinion and then compare these opinions with those collected on a regular basis over time. A part of this process should include the development and publicizing of policies related to citizen complaints. Citizens should know who to contact and what to expect when they make such contact. Further, those complaining should be kept advised of the efforts made to investigate their complaint and of the final disposition of the complaint.

Many citizens who feel they have been abused or harassed by the police do not know how to make a complaint, or fear retaliation from the officer involved or his or her colleagues if they do complain. Public-relations messages indicating the desire of police administrators to know about such complaints, coupled with prompt, fair action when such complaints are received, can only help to improve community relations. While we can do a great deal to help improve the citizen complaint process, we should be aware that most citizens who have complaints about the police will probably never voice these complaints directly to the police (Homant, 1989). Similarly, we should note that some citizens who strongly support the police file complaints in the hope of helping the police improve, rather than with negative intent.

Police-Media Relations

Any police agency concerned about good community relations will want to develop a good working relationship with the media. Information presented on television, radio, or in newspapers is a major source of influence on public opinion. Police administrators today typically prefer to develop open, honest relationships with representatives of the media, although this has not always been the case. In the past, police administrators often had a policy requiring officers to tell media representatives only what they had to, thus engendering mutual suspicion and distrust.

In order to turn this relationship around, Davis (1978: 201) indicates, "It is very important that a police agency have an open media policy. A media policy should permit anyone in the department who has adequate knowledge of relevant information, from the lowest to the highest ranking person, to talk to the press." Mark (1977: 123) further emphasizes this point by stating, "There are two main ways in which public backing can be obtained or strengthened. The first is obviously by the adoption of a courteous and helpful attitude at all possible times by every member of the force (good human relations). The second, equally important, is by means of publicity given to the activities of the force in the press and on television and radio."

Since many citizens never have direct contact with the police, their view of the police is largely dependent on media presentations. These presentations include but are not limited to documentaries, news broadcasts, interviews with police personnel and those they serve, and police produced or assisted informational programs. They also include those television shows and movies that deal with police activities, many of which are highly misleading in their portrayals of violence, gun battles, and crime fighting as the major activities of the police. In such presentations the police often appear to be violent, sadistic, corrupt, and stupid, and their work appears to consist of going from one violent situation to another. To be sure, most viewers realize that there is no direct correspondence between what appears on the screen and what happens in reality. It is sometimes difficult, however, to separate fact from fiction and to correct inaccurate impressions.

By creating a positive public image, the police can benefit greatly. Cooperation and support on the part of the public can be encouraged in a number of ways. Police ride-along programs allow other citizens to observe the daily activities of the police. Open house days allow members of the public to view the internal workings of the police department from communications to investigations to incarceration. Walk-in centers provide the opportunity for neighborhood residents to discuss whatever is on their minds with citizen-oriented police officers. School liaison programs, drug resistance programs, and police athletic programs provide opportunities for youth to get to know police officers as individuals and vice versa. These and other public relations efforts on behalf of the police can improve community relations when accompanied by positive human-relations efforts.

Other Police Community-Relations Efforts

There are other things police administrators can do to improve the relationships between their departments and the communities they serve. We have discussed the recruitment and hiring of minority officers at length in Chapters 6 and 7. Clearly, the police department that represents the community it serves in terms of race and ethnicity has an initial advantage in community relations—particularly when segments of the community served fail to fully comprehend English or speak a different language altogether. It is difficult for Hispanics, for example, to believe that a police department with no Spanish-speaking officers is concerned about their well-being. If it is true that mutual trust and understanding are important components of police-community relations, the language barriers must be broken wherever possible. Training that familiarizes police officers with the cultural characteristics of the populations they serve, and courses that help those from different cultural and linguistic backgrounds understand the justice system in the United States (discussed next), are also both possible and important.

Programs aimed at specific minorities other than those based on race or ethnicity are also important. Police efforts to prevent crime against senior citizens, organize neighborhood watch groups, and help youth resist drugs or gang influence are widespread. School liaison programs in which police officers are assigned to the schools for the academic year and participate as counselors (and sometimes confidants) to youth are more and more common.

Police departments are also becoming more involved with training in the community-relations area. An example of the progress being made in this sector is the program developed in Clearwater, Florida. Prior to the commencement of training, both police officers and black city residents were surveyed to learn their impressions of one another. The results of this survey were used as the foundation for the training that followed, which involved exchanges between members of the black community and police officers concerning the issues brought forth by both groups. The training was conducted as a preventive measure, not a response to a crisis, and seems to have been perceived positively by all parties (Teagarden, 1988).

Yet another method of improving police community relations was developed by the Orange County Sheriff's Department. The basic tool used is a community feedback questionnaire designed to gather information about police behavior as perceived by victims and informants. The questionnaires along with cover letters from the sheriff are sent to about 10 percent of those who call the sheriff's department as victims or with information. The simple survey gives these individuals a chance to evaluate police performance. It also indicates that the department is interested enough in those served to care about what they think. The information collected is then passed on to the officers involved, providing direct feedback not only to that officer, but to the supervisory staff as well. The program represents a "valuable and inexpensive means of assessing community perceptions of department performance" (LaDucer, 1988: 224).

Public Opinion and the Police

Based on the material presented thus far it is clear that what the public think about their police is a critical determinant of police-citizen interaction. Over the years, numerous attempts have been made to assess public opinion concerning the police, and the results have been consistently favorable to the police, although opinions appear to vary by age, race (as we saw earlier in this chapter), residence, and other factors. Inquiries concerning public attitudes toward the police have been made as a part of the National Crime Survey (NCS) since 1972; the results have been consistently positive, indicating that over three-fourths of those surveyed rate police performance as either good or fair. In earlier studies, about two-thirds of those surveyed responded favorably to items concerning police performance (Ennis, 1967; Garofalo, 1977; Smith and Hawkins, 1973).

Although respondents rate the police favorably, whites are more likely to view the police favorably than nonwhites. Other studies indicate that crime victims and those who have been stopped by the police are more critical of the police and less willing to endorse police efforts in some areas than those who have not had such encounters (Ross, Snortum, and McKenna, 1982).

Overall, public support for the police has remained consistently high over the past two decades, and the level of support is consistently higher than is commonly believed by the police. We should be aware, however, that attitudes are difficult to measure, and the correlation between attitudes and behavior is certainly not one-to-one. An example of current attitudes toward the police can be seen in Table 11.1, which deals with attitudes toward honesty and ethicality of police officers over a fifteen-year period. As you can see, the attitudes expressed are consistent and relatively positive.

However, the police cannot rest on their laurels since, in spite of the positive findings, there are indications in most studies that room for improvement exists. Let us turn our attention to the roles of the police and the public, respectively, in making such improvement.

TABLE 11.1   Respondent's Ratings of the Honesty and Ethical Standards of Policemen Between 1977 and 1992

Respondents were asked to rate the honesty
and ethicality of policemen, among others

Honesty/Ethicality	1977	1981	1983	1985	1992
Very High	8%	8%	7%	10%	8%
High	29%	36%	34%	37%	34%
Average	50%	41%	45%	41%	42%
Low	9%	9%	7%	7%	10%
Very Low	1%	2%	3%	2%	4%

Adapted from: G. Gallup, Jr., The Gallup Report as it appears in *Sourcebook of Criminal Justice Statistics—1992*, 169.

The Police and Public in Community Relations

The Police Role in Police-Community Relations

In spite of the fact that the police sometimes feel separate from and in conflict with other citizens, they are nevertheless members of the community in which they serve. Both groups are controlled by the same government, both pay taxes to support the police and other public service agencies, the children of both groups attend the same schools, and both share in the fate of the community. By and large, the police are recruited from, hired by, and sworn to serve this same community. Further, the functions of the police are essential to the community but no more essential than the services provided by others. Good police-community relations depend on emphasizing this common community membership.

In order to indicate their willingness to participate as partners in the community, the police need to recognize and reflect the racial and ethnic composition of that community. Active efforts to recruit qualified minorities into policing are essential in this regard, as are promotions based strictly on merit. An all-white police department in an ethnically diverse community provides "proof" that the police are different in a very obvious way and raises suspicions that they may also be different in many other less obvious ways. A multiethnic police department will not be problem-free, but has a definite advantage in developing good community relations.

Innovative, regular training in human- and public-relations skills is an important requirement for police officers, as is training in cultural diversity. Cultural diversity/awareness programs are designed to familiarize police officers with people and customs different from those to which they are accustomed. Assigning a police officer to police a ghetto or barrio without such an introduction virtually guarantees community-relations problems. Programs designed to anticipate the types of crises that might arise in the community alert officers to the possibility that similar crises may occur and provide them with some structure and preparation should they occur.

Cultural Diversity/Awareness Training

Training in cultural diversity has become increasingly popular in the last five years. Such training typically focuses on improving communication skills, recognizing signs of prejudice and bias, understanding the perspectives of people of different backgrounds, and appreciating the benefits of diversity (Scott, 1993; Hennessy, 1993; Bickham and Rossett, 1993). Before being assigned to a beat, officers should receive orientation on the various groups residing in the area. Further, as police agencies themselves become more culturally diverse, internal problems may develop, so training should address derogatory language, racial and ethnic slurs, and ethnic jokes in the context of the police organization (Scott, 1993).

Bickham and Rossett (1993: 43) believe the outcomes of cultural diversity training should include:

1. Knowledge of cultures and groups present in the service area
2. Development of a positive, caring attitude toward cultural differences
3. Development of action plans that serve diverse communities

According to Himelfarb (1991: 53), the Royal Canadian Mounted Police identified six principles necessary for culturally sensitive policing. These include:

1. Respect for and sensitivity to diverse communities served
2. Broad-based multicultural strategy
3. Multicultural training
4. Training on a continuing basis (not just one or two courses)
5. Philosophy of policing that addresses multicultural issues and establishes operations to deal with these issues
6. Multicultural training and strategies developed in consultation with the ethnocultural communities served by the police

Training programs such as these require that police administrators recognize that community relations require effort on behalf of every individual officer and the police management team. The former determine the nature of human relations in daily encounters, the latter, in consultation with these officers and the various publics in the jurisdiction, determine and evaluate the policies to be implemented and their effectiveness in practice. As we have seen, community-policing efforts are intended to deal with these issues by empowering patrol officers and personalizing police efforts.

Police Responsiveness and Accountability

Two key terms for the police in community relations are responsiveness and accountability (Cox and Fitzgerald, 1991: 194–198). A responsive department provides appropriate services as promptly and competently as possible and refers cases not within their jurisdiction in the same fashion. Consequently, police administrators must recognize and convey to the public that it may be impossible or inappropriate for the police to respond to all citizen requests for service. Priorities may have to be established and differential response strategies developed in order to best allocate available resources. These tasks should be accomplished in partnership with the community, and the resulting policies and strategies should be communicated clearly to residents in order to prevent potentially negative reactions. The department must make it clear that requests for service on behalf of citizens are taken seriously and will be dealt with accordingly.

Accountability is the second key to police efforts to establish and maintain positive community relations. Police officers are employees of the community they serve. Like other employees, they are accountable to their employers for their actions. Accountability may be accomplished in a variety of ways, ranging from periodic reports to the public on police activities, to annual reports, to development and utilization of an internal affairs unit, to cooperation in developing a civilian review to hear complaints concerning the police. We can illustrate the two extremes of police concern with community relations by imagining what police departments at each end of a continuum might look like (see Table 11.2).

While few, if any, departments match these ideal types, all can be evaluated in terms of where they stand along the continuum of concern with community relations. Specifically the following concerns should be taken into account.

Police Administration

1. Recognize, attempt to assess, and meet the needs of diverse publics.
2. Emphasize training and indoctrination in community-relations skills.
3. Develop policies based on assessment and evaluations of officers' and other citizens' opinions.
4. Communicate policies effectively to publics and officers.
5. Provide for supervision of policy implementation.
6. Reevaluate periodically.
7. Form teams with members of diverse publics to assist in policy development.

Police Officers

1. Communicate concerns to public and administrators.
2. Implement policies.
3. Evaluate policies in practice.
4. Provide feedback to administrators.
5. Treat all citizens with respect and preserve human dignity.

The Role of the Community in Police-Community Relations

We have previously noted that the police are predominantly reactive rather than proactive. That is, the community in which they operate determines, in most instances, when the police act, about what they act, and on whom they act (Reiss, 1971). Thus, the community plays an important role in police-community

Table 11.2 Polarized Police Department Concern with Community Relations

Officer/Department Characteristics	Reactions to Encounters with Diverse Populations	Possible Consequences
Type 1		
Traditional, authoritarian structure	Uncertainty, anxiety, high fear/stress, suspicion, hostility, stereotypes, secret brutality	Ineffectiveness, psychological and/or physical
Homogeneous in terms of race, gender, lack of representativeness		
Minimal educational requirements		
Minimal prior contact with diverse publics		
Little emphasis on community relations in terms of training, assessment of public attitudes, evaluation of programs		
Strong subcultural "we-they" feelings		
Strict law enforcement orientation		
Forced participation in affirmative action and equal employment opportunity programs		
Unenlightened management		
Secret complaint investigations		
Type 2		
Participatory structure	Less uncertainty Less anxiety Less fear Less suspicion Less stress Less hostility Fewer stereotypes	Less psychological and physical brutality, better relations with diverse publics and more public cooperation, more professional conduct
Heterogeneous with respect to race, gender		
More representative of the publics served		
Higher educational/training requirements		
More contact with diverse publics		
Emphasis on assessment and evaluation of public attitudes		
Less subcultural closeness		
Strong service orientation		
Open complaint investigations		
More enlightened management		

relations. If the community does not do its part in building positive community relations, police-initiated programs cannot succeed (Cox and Fitzgerald, 1991).

In order to demonstrate their good faith in police-community relations, community residents and civic action can develop programs to support police efforts and recognize police performance. Neighborhood watch programs and "officer of the month" programs are two examples of community efforts to demonstrate support for the police. Willingness to serve as reserve or auxiliary officers also demonstrates support, as do joint programs to divert youth from drugs and delinquency. Providing the police with information concerning matters important to the community and being willing to serve as witnesses are other ways in which community residents can show appreciation for their police. While the police may be required to take the lead in developing community-relations efforts, the public is an important part of the team necessary for such efforts to produce the desired results, making the task of the police easier and the community a better place to live. "It is important for members of minority [all] communities to have continual, open dialogue with police officials in their various communities to deal with specific issues; indeed, this is critical to the success of policing" (Hennessy, 1993).

Discussion Questions

1. Trace the historical origins of some of the current problems in police-community relations.

2. What characteristics of a multiethnic, industrial, democratic society make police-community relations problematic?

3. Why are affirmative action and equal employment opportunity programs important to police-community relations?

4. What is the general perception of the police as reflected in public opinion surveys? What are some of the important factors in determining these perceptions?

5. List and discuss four specific steps the police can take to help improve community relations. Do the same thing for the public.

6. How are human relations and public relations different? How are they related to community relations?

7. What is the relationship between community policing and police-community relations?

References

Baldwin, J. 1962. *Nobody Knows My Name*. New York: Dell.

Bayley, D.H. and Mendelsohn, H. 1969. *Minorities and the Police*. New York: Free Press.

Bickham, T. and Rossett, A. 1993. "Diversity Training: Are We Doing the Thing Right?" *Police Chief* 60(11), 43–47.

Burden, O.P. 1992. "Peacekeeping and the 'Thin Blue Line.'" *Police Chief* (June), 19–28.

Chavis, B.F. and Williams, J.D. 1993. "Beyond the Rodney King Story: NAACP Report on Police Conduct and Community Relations." *NAACP News* 93(42).

Cox, S.M. 1984. "Race/Ethnic Relations and the Police: Current and Future Issues." *American Journal of the Police* 3(2), 169–183.

Cox, S.M. and Fitzgerald, J.D. 1991. *Police in Community Relations: Critical Issues* 2 ed. Dubuque, IA: Wm. C. Brown.

Cox, S.M. and Wade, J.E. 1989. *The Criminal Justice Network: An Introduction* 2 ed. Dubuque, IA: Wm. C. Brown.

Davis, E.M. 1978. *Staff One: A Perspective on Effective Police Management.* Englewood Cliffs, NJ: Prentice-Hall.

Ennis, P.H. 1967. *Criminal Victimization in the United States: A Report of a National Survey.* Washington, DC: U.S. Government Printing Office.

Ferguson, K. 1991. "Lawyers Say Clients' Rights Were Violated." *Journal Star: Peoria* (2 June), p. A7.

Gallup, G.I. 1993. "The Gallup Report" In Maguire, K., Pastore, A.L., and Flanagan, T.J. (eds.) *Bureau of Justice Statistics Sourcebook of Criminal Justice Statistics–1992.* Washington, DC: U.S. Government Printing Office, 169.

Garofalo, J. 1977. *The Police and Public Opinion: An Analysis of Victimization and Attitude Data from 13 American Cities.* Washington, DC: U.S. Government Printing Office.

Hacker, A. 1992. *Two Nations: Black and White, Separate, Hostile, Unequal.* New York: Ballantine Books.

Hennessy, S.M. 1993. "Achieving Cultural Competence." *Police Chief* (August), 46–54.

Himelfarb, F. 1991. "A Training Strategy for Policing in a Multicultural Society." *Police Chief* (November), 53–55.

Homant, R.J. 1989. "Citizen Attitudes and Complaints." In Bailey, W. G. (ed.), *The Encyclopedia of Police Science.* New York: Garland Press, 54–63.

LaDucer, D.W. 1988. "The Community Feedback Program." *The Police Chief* (July), 24.

Langer, G. 1988. "Americans Say Racism Persists." *Journal Star: Peoria* (8 August), p. 2.

Maguire, K., Pastore, A.L., and Flanagan, T.J. 1993. *Sourcebook of Criminal Justice Statistics—*

1992. The Hindelang Criminal Justice Research Center. U.S. Department of Justice. Washington, DC: U.S. Government Printing Office.

Mark, R. 1977. *Policing a Perplexed Society.* London: George Allen and Unwin Ltd.

National Advisory Commission on Civil Disorders (Kerner Commission). 1968. *Report.* New York: Bantam.

Nolte, L.W. 1979. *Fundamentals of Public Relations: Professional Guidelines, Concepts, and Integrations.* New York: Pergamon Press.

O'Brien, J.T. 1978. "Public Attitudes Toward the Police." *Journal of Police Science and Administration* 6(3), 303–310.

Pomerville, P.A. 1993. "Popular Myths About Cultural Awareness Training." *Police Chief* 60(11), 30–42.

Reiss, A.J. 1968. "Police Brutality—Answers to Key Questions." *Trans-action* 5(July–August), 15–16.

Reiss, A.J. 1970. *The Police and the Public.* New Haven, CT: Yale University Press.

Ross, R., Snortum, J.R., and McKenna, C. 1982. "Public Priorities and Police Policy in a Bicultural Community." *Police Studies* 5(1), 18–30.

Schaefer, R. T. 1993. *Racial and Ethnic Groups* 5 ed. New York: Harper Collins.

Scott, E.L. 1993. "Cultural Awareness Training." *Police Chief* 60(11), 26–28.

Smith, P.E. and Hawkins, R.O. 1973. "Victimization, Type of Citizen Contacts, and Attitude Toward the Police." *Law and Society Review* 8, 135–152.

Stacey, J. 1993. "Linguistic Diversity in the USA." *USA TODAY* (15 December), p. 9A.

Stone, A. 1991. "Asian Growth: 105% in 10 Years." *USA TODAY* (7 February), p. 11A.

Sykes, G. 1978. *Criminology.* New York: Harcourt Brace Jovanovich.

Teagarden, R.B. 1988. "Effective Community Relations Training." *The Police Chief* (November), 42–44.

Trojanowicz, R.C. 1990. "Community Policing is Not Police-Community Relations." *FBI Law Enforcement Bulletin* 59(10), 6–11.

Weaver, G. 1992. "Law Enforcement in a Culturally Diverse Society." *FBI Law Enforcement Bulletin* 61(9), 1–9.

12

THE FUTURE OF POLICING IN THE UNITED STATES

While it is risky to make projections for the future, it is clear that a vision of where one is going is an important part of getting there. The following discussion of the future of policing in this country is based on an analysis of current trends, projected demographic changes, and, in some instances, pure speculation.

The Public and Their Police

As we have shown, police strategies do not exist in a vacuum. They are shaped by legal and political attitudes and local resources. Still, there is room for change in these attitudes and resources, and change must be regarded as a critical ingredient in effective policing. New police strategies must be adopted to meet the changing needs of communities over time. "The two fundamental features of a new police strategy must be these: that the role of private citizens in the control of crime and maintenance of public order be established and encouraged, not derided and thwarted, and that the police become more active, accessible participants in community affairs. . . . The police must get out of their cars, and spend more time in public spaces such as parks and plazas, confronting and assisting citizens with their private troubles. This is mundane, prosaic work but it probably beats driving around in cars waiting for a radio call" (Moore and Kelling, 1983: 65).

> *We cannot simply continue with business as usual. Since most agencies are not equipped with crystal balls, true progress comes from trying something new, seeing if it works, making changes and trying it again. If the organization and its leaders are afraid to fail, stagnation quickly sets in (Bennett, 1993: 86).*
>
> *Imagine what would happen if a beat officer, during his or her first week on the beat, could be presented with an analysis of all the calls for service received from the area in the previous six months. And imagine he or she was then told that a significant performance measure would be the decrease in calls over the next six months. Naturally there would be occasional emergencies out of the beat officer's control. But the officer's attention would immediately be focused on repeat callers, sources of danger and anxiety in the community, and the identification and solution of underlying problems—exactly the commission a beat officer needs (Sparrow, Moore, and Kennedy, 1992: 228).*
>
> *The shift from time to turf is an absolute organizational necessity for the future of policing. Being shift-driven has had a destructive influence on the ability of the police to listen, relate to and effectively act on community-identified police problems (Couper and Lobitz, 1993: 16).*

Policing has come full circle. We are once again in the position of having to admit that the police cannot be all things to all people, and that the police can be effective only when they have widespread community support. This realization is not at all surprising when we realize that municipal police emerged as a result of citizen needs (the London Metropolitan Police are perhaps the most striking, but certainly not the only example). Citizens' needs, however, change at a sometimes frightening pace depending on economics, demographics, and social policies. In order to continue to meet the changing demands of citizens, police agencies must first have a realistic view of these needs and second, invite citizen input as to how best to meet them. A full partnership between the police and other citizens is necessary because the "police themselves are not to blame for the fact that crimes are so common, neighborhoods so frightened, and civility so fragile. And more police, with more technology, will not be enough to remove crime, calm neighborhoods, and promote civility" (William O. Douglas Institute, 1984: 9).

Assessing community needs on a continuing basis is the only way in which a realistic understanding of them can be attained. Assessment requires research efforts sponsored by the police.

Research and Planning as Police Functions

> In a society such as ours, there are bound to be different priorities placed on the police by different people who live in different communities. In addition, police officers are not all the same, do not have similar opinions or expectations, do not perform at the same level, and do not operate with the same style (Alpert and Dunham, 1993: 195).

How are the police to respond to these differing public priorities, in what ways will different types of officers respond, and what styles of policing are best suited to particular communities? These and other questions relating to areas such as crime and traffic management, level of satisfaction with supervisors, amount of perceived stress among officers, civil and criminal liability of police personnel, and dozens of other areas can best be addressed through the implementation of proper research and planning techniques.

In the research area, projects may be as simple as surveying community residents to determine their priorities, fears, satisfaction with police services, and perceptions of police misconduct, or as complex as attempting to measure the relationships among education, training, job performance, and supervisory evaluations. We might want to assess the impact of combined enforcement groups on drug trafficking or develop a profile of a specific type of offender. We might want to evaluate officer productivity in terms of certain criteria. All of these projects require a certain degree of expertise in research and, for that matter, a good deal of planning as well.

Police administrators could contract for such projects, but the potential for miscommunication in "hired hand" research is considerable, and research funds and grants are not always available for projects when they need to be completed (Fitzgerald and Cox, 1994: 7–10). Thus, greater reliance on "in-house" research and evaluation is desirable for a number of reasons. The conduct of in-house research requires that at least some staff members have the training and expertise necessary to design and implement scientific inquiries; the value and ease of conduct of such inquiries is increased considerably when an evaluation component is built into new initiatives from the start. "In order to understand the nature and current state of affairs in criminal justice, practitioners and students alike must be able to read and comprehend research reports and must know when and how to apply the results of such research. Many will also find it necessary or advantageous to conduct research themselves to do their jobs as effectively and efficiently as possible. . . . It is quite true that any in-depth study of research methods and statistical analysis would take years, but it is equally true that a student can achieve a basic understanding in a relatively short period of time. Complicated research designs and sophisticated statistical procedures do not necessarily result in better or more useful research, and often, useful insights can be gained through relatively simple research designs and elementary statistical analyses" (Fitzgerald and Cox, 1994: 2).

The number of police personnel with knowledge of basic research and statistical techniques is increasing as the number of college-educated officers increases and as the quality of college programs in criminal justice improves. Conducting such research requires considerable planning, both short and long range. For a variety of reasons, police administrators have regularly demonstrated their abilities to engage in the former, but rarely in the latter; a public service mentality characterized not only police chiefs but other chief executive officers in the public sector as well. This mentality was for years based on the premise that last year's budget plus 10 percent was a safe bet in most fiscal years. In the public sector, planning for no increases in funding, or for budgetary cutbacks, was unheard of and the assumptions appeared to be (1) that evaluation of programs was beyond the responsibility of the public sector executives, and (2) that fiscal responsibility was less important than in the private sector since funds, especially for emergency services, would always be made available.

As we have seen in the 1980s and early 1990s, several dramatic changes occurred in the public sector. First, "taxpayer revolts" made it clear that zero-based budgeting and budget cutbacks were not only possible but likely alternatives to the automatic 10 percent increase. Second, the demand for accountability in the public sector increased. The need for full-time fire departments was questioned in some small communities, public safety officers who would perform both police and fire fighting functions were hired in some areas, and police departments began to lose positions through attrition. Third, women and minorities were hired in greater numbers, and the issue of their performance on the job led to a number of evaluation studies. Fourth, the Kansas City Patrol study demonstrated the ability of police agencies to participate in the design and evaluation of responsible research. Fifth, the number of well-educated police officers (at all levels) increased, making possible the formation and utilization of research and planning units, along with other specialized units. Sixth, personal computers became available at reasonable cost, their capabilities were considerably improved, and police personnel became acquainted with them. Designing, implementing, and evaluating research within police departments is now a real possibility. Last, but not least, the National Institute of Justice, responding to the Justice Assistance Act of 1984, began to sponsor more evaluation and policy-related research, which, to be most efficiently conducted, required more long-term planning (Hagan, 1989: 379).

It appears unlikely that these trends will be reversed in the decade ahead. In fact, Sherman indicates that over the past twenty years the "difference in the willingness of police agencies to cooperate with research is astounding. The police are right out front with the medical community in doing the best possible kinds of research to evaluate what they're doing" (Sherman, 1990: 9). All of the factors previously outlined make it likely that research and planning will become increasingly important to and utilized by police administrators seeking to justify new programs and demonstrate the value of existing efforts.

Changing the Image of Patrol Officers

In spite of the specialization that is likely to continue to characterize police in the next century, patrol officers will remain the backbone of policing as a result of sheer numbers, frequency of contact with the public, and the shift to community policing. Patrol officers, as the eyes, ears, arms, and legs of the police organization, need to be competent, well informed, concerned, and self-confident. Yet, patrol officers of this century have often been those who could not progress to other specializations or supervisory roles. Many if not most young officers cannot wait to "put in their time" on patrol in order to be promoted to a supervisory position or transferred to the investigative division. College students in criminal justice programs frequently ask "Do I have to start as a patrol officer? Isn't there some way I can go directly into investigations or supervision?" To a great extent, those who remain in patrol are those who have been unsuccessful in demonstrating the qualities required for these other positions. When referring to a twenty-year veteran of the streets, it is not uncommon to hear "he's just a patrol officer" or "she's still on patrol." In fact, many veteran patrol officers think of themselves in these terms and some regard themselves as failures because of their inability to progress to "bigger and better things."

Patrol is seldom recognized as a specialization within police agencies, and being a member of the patrol division is somehow often less glamorous than being an investigator or a supervisor. Yet, extremely capable patrol officers are not all that common, and the function requires special skills if it is to be performed well. In short, those who perform the patrol function well are specialists in their own right and should be recognized and rewarded as such. They are specialists in handling whatever types of calls come their way and whatever types of encounters in which they become involved. Not everyone can perform these tasks well. However, we have seldom made the effort to recognize and reward those who perform well, and have in fact encouraged young officers to leave the patrol ranks as soon as possible.

This strategy makes little sense when we stop to consider that the reputation of any police agency depends greatly on the daily encounters between patrol personnel and other citizens. If we are truly interested in good community relations, we need to reward those officers who interact both frequently and civilly with other citizens. Some programs, such as the "dual career ladder system" and other progressive salary schedule systems, encourage productive officers to stay in patrol by rewarding their efforts monetarily. Such efforts need to be expanded if patrol personnel are to regard themselves and be regarded by the public positively. The importance of retaining competent patrol officers becomes increasingly apparent as community-oriented policing programs spread, officers become less isolated from the public, and cooperative efforts between the police and other citizens expand (Grossman and Doherty, 1994).

Expanding the Concepts of Community-Oriented and Problem-Oriented Policing

There is little doubt that the wave of the future in policing will involve expanded involvement of civilians in police work as employees in police agencies, members of advisory and planning groups, members of direct support groups (such as neighborhood watch and neighborhood patrol groups), and critics and reviewers of police activities. The message has finally become clear: the police cannot control crime or maintain order by themselves. The involvement of citizens other than police officers in crime prevention, apprehension of offenders, and order maintenance is absolutely essential. A partnership is required, but the partnership must be a real one. In the past, police partnerships with other citizens meant the police allowing these citizens to be minimally involved in police activities in which the police served as the experts, citizen input was sought in certain areas but denied in others, and policy making remained the exclusive right of the police.

> *The importance of citizen involvement in providing public safety and security cannot be overstated. Resources for crime control have dwindled over the years. At the same time public demand for police services has increased. While citizen involvement in community-police programs is no cure-all for the problems of crime and social disorder, it is essential for the maintenance of democratic values. Furthermore, law enforcement agencies can hardly continue to exclude the clients and producers of police service from the policies and decisions affecting the "quality of life" in American communities (Greene, 1989: 365).*

In keeping with the trend toward more community involvement in policing, we are likely to see increasing efforts on behalf of the police to improve citizen cooperation in high crime areas (see Highlight 12.1). While many of these areas have traditionally been "written off" by the police (as well as by the larger society) simply because they *are* high crime areas, the reality is that most of the people living in such areas are not criminals but victims. They continue to be victims because the streets and projects do not belong to them

---

HIGHLIGHT 12.1   Village to Implement Neighborhood Police Beat Program

---

In a giant step back to basics—back to the people being served, back to a more personal approach to police work—the Palatine Police Department is beginning a one year trial Neighborhood Police Beat program in an area roughly bounded by Rand Road, Dundee Road, Hicks Road and Carpenter Street.

Instead of the Village's 59 police officers rotating shifts in every area of the Village, the six officers who have asked to be part of the Neighborhood Police Beat program will be permanently assigned to the target area.

They will get to know the neighbors through attending homeowners association meetings, they will introduce themselves to the merchants on their beat, and they'll get acquainted with the local school principals and church pastors. Two initial proponents of this pilot program include Village President Rita Mullins and District 3 Trustee Dan Varroney. Both have called for increased neighborhood police patrols and had words of praise for the new program, saying that this effort represents just a beginning.

"The objective is to get closer to the people we serve," expained Police Chief Jerry Bratcher. "Instead of just responding to a call, writing a report, and being done with it, these Neighborhood Beat officers will follow up and become involved. Maybe they'll make an appointment to talk to the parents after the third call to the Police Department about loud parties while Mom and Dad are in Wisconsin on the weekends. Maybe they'll notice that a merchant could use better locks. Maybe they'll recognize a stray dog that belongs to someone on their beat. They'll bring continuity to the beat and have an interest in what happens there. They'll be accountable for what happens on their beat."

Bratcher describes the six officers who have volunteered to be part of this program as "bright, highly motivated well trained, and eager to get involved."

The officers—David Fanning, Brad Grossman, Dennis Langguth, Thomas Murphy, Alan Stoeckel, and Wayne Sunderlin—will have a team meeting every three weeks to look at traffic problems, crime, citizen concerns, and talk about anything of interest that has happened on the beat. This new system will give greater continuity, and will give the police officers and the people on the beat the chance to know each other and work together to solve problems.

"Our goal is to address concerns before they become problems," Bratcher said. "The people on this beat will get to know the officers on a personal basis. That makes it easier for a resident to call and talk over a concern or to relay some information. Communication can flow more freely on an informal basis. It is a lot easier to call and talk something over with an officer you know than to come in and file a formal complaint with someone you've never seen before."

District 3 Trustee Varroney expressed his enthusiasm for the program, and praised the fact that "we are working together to make our neighborhoods even safer than they are now."

The Neighborhood Police Beat program will be phased in in the target area during December and January. One important component of the program involves citizen satisfaction surveys that will be mailed to residents in the target area at the beginning of the program and at the end of the one year trial period.

"Hopefully, we'll see citizens feeling a greater sense of satisfaction with police services," Bratcher said. "We'll look at the before and after response to the surveys, evaluate the program, and decide if it's worth expanding to the rest of the Village after the one year pilot."

Continued

From *Palatine Newsletter*, Winter 1989: 1–2. Reprinted by permission.

Village President Rita Mullins voiced strong support from the Board of Trustees for the Neighborhood Police Beat program.

"The people have told us that they like the idea of having police officers permanently assigned to their area," Mullins said. "They'd like to be able to get to know the officers, and have the officers know them. They'd like to have police work become more pro-active than re-active.

"We will be watching this program with great interest. We hope it will be a great success."

As chief Jerry Bratcher puts the finishing touches on the program, he reflects on the common sense simplicity of it all:

"What we're really doing here is getting back to grass roots, getting closer to the people we serve. This pilot program represents a major departure from traditional police procedures, but it is really a basic, simple, fundamental notion. It is putting the officer closer to the people so he can be more responsive to their needs and concerns."

"We're looking forward to getting in closer touch with the citizens we serve."

but to gangs and other less well-organized but equally predatory criminals. The police patrol these areas and maintain a semblance of order, but the overwhelming evidence is that by themselves they have little impact on crime. In spite of gang crime units, gang intelligence, and the use of informants, the police cannot, nor are they ever likely to, obtain enough information to prevent crimes in these areas or apprehend the majority of offenders.

Preliminary evidence from community- and problem-oriented policing strategies suggests that their chief benefit may be in making area residents feel safer, although these strategies may have little direct effect on crime rates. However, if neighborhood residents feel safer, they may make greater use of the streets, which, over the long term, may make the streets less accessible to criminal elements. If well-planned, coordinated programs between the police and other citizens are initiated and implemented in such a way that more offenders are apprehended or fear being apprehended, the sense of public territoriality may reemerge even in high crime areas. Then, residents and the police together can take back the streets and projects from criminal elements. Such efforts will be successful, however, only when area residents are involved in the planning and implementation of policies and programs. Examples of the kinds of changes that can occur exist in several Chicago-area housing projects in which tenant management has been initiated and supported by residents and housing authorities.

Long-term solutions to the problems of high crime areas depend on the mutual respect and understanding of the police and neighborhood residents. Police officers who continue to serve (and be perceived) as soldiers of occupation in minority neighborhoods are unlikely to be effective in either crime control or order maintenance. They are very likely to continue to regard assignment to such areas as dangerous and unpleasant and to participate in perpetuating the isolation and alienation that exist for themselves and the citizens they police. This attitude increases the likelihood that what now appear to be separate incidents involving protests by citizens in the "underclass" against government policies and practices will once again become part of a nationwide protest, with the police as targets, unable to maintain order, prevent crime, or apprehend offenders. Only real partnerships between the police and other citizens in general—and citizens in high crime areas in particular—are likely to be successful in preventing the police from playing a major, undesirable, and unpleasant role in such protests. "Community-oriented policing does not transform police officers into social workers. It does, however, empower officers to connect individuals with problems to agencies that can help them. COP does involve a few extra minutes handling each call, but this time is well spent. Most importantly, community-oriented policing recognizes the value of the police and the community working together to reduce crime. A more involved community translates into a community more willing to cooperate with its police department" (Bobinsky, 1994: 19).

In spite of the enthusiasm for community policing, there is reason to be cautious. While the approach appears to make sense, evidence of success is sketchy at best. It may be because community-policing efforts are still in their infancy, but it may also be that the promise exceeds the practice. Can police officers help solve social problems that lead to crime more effectively than others who have tried before them? Will such attempts, even if successful, lead to reduction in crime and improvement in the quality of life? Only careful evaluation and assessment can provide answers to these questions (Joseph, 1994).

Changing the Image of the Police

Gender and Race

An important part of the community-oriented policing concept involves making the police as representative of the community as possible. Over the next few years we can expect to see continued research on police performance by gender and race. If the results of such research follow already established patterns, few if any significant differences in the performance of police officers will be accounted for by gender or race. The reasons for excluding women and minorities from policing will no longer be accepted, and the benefits of hiring police officers from culturally diverse backgrounds will become increasingly apparent.

Yet, there are some difficulties in changing the police image with respect to gender and race. Foremost among these problems are affirmative action programs based on consent decrees that lead to the hiring and promotion of unqualified women and minorities (Alpert and Dunham, 1993). Hiring and promoting police officers of either gender or any race simply to meet quotas and without regard to qualifications is detrimental to the officers hired, their police colleagues, the citizenry at large, and other members of the same gender or race for most of the same reasons that discrimination in terms of gender and race are detrimental. To avoid the negative consequences of discriminatory hiring of either variety in the future, race and gender of applicants should be considered only after the issue of proper qualification has been decided. This remains the intent of the Equal Employment Opportunity Act and the Americans with Disabilities Act; however, court-mandated programs have frequently contradicted this intent, resulting in lawsuits based on allegations of reverse discrimination, increasingly bitter feelings on behalf of qualified candidates and practitioners toward those unqualified recruits, serious difficulties for the department in terms of the performance of the latter, and poor service to the community in general.

Only when all new police recruits meet the same basic qualifications will there be any chance that race and gender will cease to be the controversial issues they have traditionally been in U.S. law enforcement (which simply reflects the larger society). Only if this happens will the difficulties in recruiting qualified women and minorities be eased, and the goal of a community-police partnership that includes all segments of the community be achieved.

Civilianization

In keeping with community-oriented policing efforts, increasing numbers of civilians are likely to become involved in policing as employees of police agencies and as volunteers. This trend is beneficial because it helps to break down barriers between the police and other citizens, often frees police officers to concentrate more of their time on matters for which they have been specifically trained, and fosters the belief that civilians play an important role in both order maintenance and law enforcement.

Accreditation

The image of the police is slowly being changed as a result of the incorporation of high standards of performance and conduct by many departments through the process of accreditation. A growing number of police agencies have demonstrated their desire to be considered among the best in the profession by undergoing the painstaking, lengthy process of accreditation by the Commission on Accreditation for Law Enforcement Agencies. Already more than two hundred police agencies have demonstrated their ability to comply with the majority of the more than nine hundred standards utilized by the commission and another five hundred are in the process (*Commission Update*, 1990). Agencies originally accredited five years ago are now applying for reaccreditation (see Highlight 12.2).

Many other agencies are doing self-evaluations to determine whether to pursue accreditation. Even for those who decide not to apply for accreditation, there is for the first time a set of standards available that allow police personnel to examine the extent to which they are operating according to the recognized standards of the profession. Some states have formed associations that help individual agencies prepare for accreditation, and this has fostered improved communications among agencies. Additionally, accreditation now requires the use of community surveys on a regular basis, thereby enhancing the police-community partnership and the use of research techniques by police personnel. The trend toward accreditation and the benefits that accompany it seem well established.

HIGHLIGHT 12.2   Accreditation and Reaccreditation

State Police Receive Recertification Award

SPRINGFIELD—The Illinois State Police organization has become the first state police agency in the nation to earn recertification from the Commission on the Accreditation of Law Enforcement Agencies (CALEA), Illinois State Police Director Terrance W. Gainer announced. "CALEA'S seal of approval means we have again met more than 800 state-of-the-art standards for police departments," Gainer said. "A team of objective professionals has examined how the state police measure up against volumes of demanding criteria, and we're proud to report to Illinois' citizens that we've passed their strictest tests."

Executive Director of CALEA, Ken H. Medeiros, congratulated the state police on earning reaccreditation. "Each of the agencies," he said, "that has been through the process has been willing to go the extra mile to prove to themselves, and to the citizens they serve, they are doing everything that is known at this time to provide the best in law enforcement."

Medeiros said CALEA's standards address four basic areas: policy and procedures; administration; operations; and support services. This means law enforcement agencies check themselves against universally recognized standards on everything from when and when not to shoot a gun to how records are kept. "The accreditation of any agency means it has outside, objective proof of professional excellence," he said.

"This has been a demanding process," said Gainer. "It's affected and involved virtually everyone in the agency, but it's been worth it. The process of meeting so many stringent standards has made us a better police agency." Gainer added the Illinois State Police was also the first state police department to receive accreditation from CALEA in 1986.

The Commission decided on the accreditation of reaccreditation of 18 law enforcement agencies at a conference held in Springfield, July 25–27.

From *Macomb Journal*. Reprinted by permission.

Lateral Entry

The concept of lateral entry (or movement from geographic location to enter employment in another area) has been around for some time but is still resisted by a majority of police agencies. Acceptance of the concept would allow police agencies to recruit personnel for various supervisory as well as line positions from other agencies and would allow officers from one department to apply for comparable positions in other departments. Presently most police officers wishing to transfer from one area or department to another have to start as entry-level officers even though they may have attained higher rank. While we are willing to accept lateral entry at the level of police chief, we have been far more hesitant to do so at other levels, limiting the pool of applicants for supervisory positions to those inside the department.

While this strategy protects insiders from competition from the outside, it is based on the assumption that there are always individuals qualified for promotion inside the department. This assumption does not always hold true. Further, refusal to accept lateral entry at mid-level positions deprives police departments of the pool of already-trained applicants seeking to leave their current positions or locations in search of better opportunities. While lateral entry may not become commonplace during the next decade, there is little doubt that its benefits outweigh the objections raised against it, and more and more police administrators, city managers, and personnel directors are likely to recognize this fact.

Training

Police personnel will have increasing opportunities to participate in training offered by a variety of training institutes. Among the more popular of these training groups are the Northwestern Traffic Institute, the Southern Police Institute, the Institute of Police Technology and Management, and the FBI National Academy, all of which offer courses ranging in length from a week to several months. Courses offered by these institutes cover topics ranging from traffic investigation to executive management. At California's Command College, future concerns of police officers and agencies are addressed. The college opened in 1984 and covers topics such as "Defining the Future," "Human Resource Management," and "Handling Conflict." Controversial topics and ideas are discussed and alternatives to traditional policing are outlined (Lieberman, 1990).

All training should be interrelated. The special skills learned at institutes such as those mentioned previously need to be updated on a continuing basis and shared with others through in-service training by those who have attended the institutes. Such sharing is both cost effective and rewarding to those who have received the training and should be encouraged on a widespread basis. In the past, the effects of training have infrequently been properly assessed by police agencies because of the assumptions that the information provided is understandable and absorbed. Increasingly, routine evaluations that include a pretest of attendees' knowledge of the material to be presented and a posttest of such knowledge are being employed. This trend should continue, since failure to evaluate training may lead to a waste of training resources.

A basic purpose of training is to keep police personnel up-to-date. As we have indicated throughout this book, in the 1960s and 1970s crime fighting and law enforcement were emphasized and many officers still view these aspects of the police role as the most important part of police work. Training courses dealing with survival techniques, patrol techniques, criminal investigation, use of force, and the law are among the most popular courses.

Successful intervention into the daily lives of citizens, however, requires negotiating skills. Communications skills (both verbal and nonverbal) and human/community/minority relations skills are emerging as among the most important assets of a competent, effective police officer.

One of the major purposes of future police training should be to make better communicators of the public servants responsible for maintaining order.

Courses dealing with both verbal and nonverbal communication should be required of all police personnel.

Education

> *As late as 1985 data were still being gathered which indicated that many in academia, for example advisors of undergraduate pre-law students, still perceived criminal justice education to be too heavily weighted toward technical and vocational training and too often taught by faculty which did not have the proper credentials (Broderick, 1987: 218).*

Shernock (1992) argues that many students seeking college degrees in criminal justice and law enforcement are only interested in being credentialed. Being credentialed does not lead to more professional behavior or change police perspectives toward their clients, and thus fails to fulfill the hope that college education will help police to understand and deal better with the human aspects of their work. To be effective, college education must not be associated simply with expectations for career advancement and pay increments, but must first become "a requirement for all who enter policing so that it does not become a source of differentiation within policing. In addition, police officials and educators must place less emphasis on mere college credits or a degree for police officers, and much more on receiving the kind of broad-based liberal arts education envisioned that Vollmer, the National Advisory Commission on Higher Education for Police Officers, and others have associated with professionalism" (Shernock, 1992: 88). The consensus appears to be that liberal arts curricula should be part of college/university criminal justice programs in the 1990s and beyond.

Police Leadership

As we have seen, the quality of leadership in police organizations has varied tremendously. Should leadership positions be filled by those with skills in communicating with and supervising personnel and other resources? Should they be filled by personnel with extensive street experience? Are policing skills or management skills more important? Answers to these questions are crucial in determining the criteria for promotion to leadership positions. The issue is further complicated by the fact that, at the level of the chief at least, political savvy and the ability to cooperate as an agency representative with respect to other public service agencies sometimes conflict with expectations of agency personnel.

Couper and Lobitz (1993) have identified a number of behaviors that they believe are essential for effective police leadership. The leader must create and nurture a vision of the future, and must live according to a set of values that can be shared with others. The leader must be a good listener, hire for the future, and be more concerned with "turf" (geographic areas) than with "time" (shifts or watches). Good leaders pay as much attention to perceptions as to reality, and they continually strive to improve the quality of their organizations. In order to bring about positive change within the organization, Couper and Lobitz (1993: 19) believe police leaders must develop:

1. A clear, shared vision of where the organization is going
2. A personal commitment to maintaining high standards
3. A system that empowers people to participate
4. A method that develops and rewards people
5. The ability to think and live in the long term.

Developing such leaders in policing has not been easy. Germann (1993: 10) indicates that the current role model for the traditional police department consists of an administrator who believes that all crime-related problems can be solved by the use of force. There are police leaders with a very different view, however. These leaders see police personnel as community helpers rather than as force-oriented lethal weapons. According to them, officers should be engaged in working closely with citizens and developing pride and trust in the department and in fellow professional officers. The actions of these officers show respect for human dignity, human rights, and human values. "People like these—professional, well educated, highly motivated, with keen minds, social sensitivity, strength of character, and the courage to tell the king he is naked—are the pride of the American police service. They need to be encouraged, supported, and given access to the authority and power that are needed for immediate implementation of necessary changes of policy and procedure" (Germann, 1993: 19).

Private and Contract Police

For a variety of reasons, we are likely to see a considerable increase in the use of private and contract police officers over the next several years. Policing in rural areas is becoming an increasingly expensive proposition. As standards for police officers improve, gangs and predatory criminals become more mobile and recognize that small city police are ill-prepared to deal with either swift hit-and-run crimes or more long-term invasions, and the technology of policing becomes more sophisticated and more costly, the willingness and ability of taxpayers to fund public services diminishes.

In many areas in the United States those living in townhouses, apartments, and condominiums have banded together to employ private protection agents. In numerous housing projects, largely independent police personnel are now responsible for security. "In some low-income housing projects here [Los Angeles], the U.S. Department of Housing and Urban Development pays for security guards to protect residents from gang warfare. New York City uses private guards to police schools. Miami hires rent-a-cops to patrol its metro-rail system. . . . In Kansas City, Missouri, police want to contract private companies to pick up twenty-two jobs done by the department. Already they've replaced civilian officers at school crossings and may soon be hired to respond to security alarm calls" (Nasser, 1993: 9A).

According to Cunningham, Strauchs, and VanMeter (1990), private security is a booming industry that employs some 1.6 million persons (as opposed to about 625,000 police officers) and is expected to expand to 1.8 million by the turn of the century. Cunningham, Strauchs, and VanMeter (1990: 266) conclude that, recently, the forging of cooperative crime- and fear-reduction ventures between the public and private sectors has progressed slowly. This indicates both a desire and a need for improved communication and cooperation between the police, private security, and business communities.

As Sherman (1990: 11) indicates, one problem with the hiring of private security officers to protect private space and property is a "disinvestment in public safety and the increased investment in private safety (which) raises issues of class, equality, and the increasing gap between the rich and the poor."

Another problem is the lack of regulation of the private security industry in terms of training and personnel selection (O'Leary, 1994: 23–24). There are currently a number of elected officials attempting to remedy this weakness by introducing bills calling for mandatory screening (criminal history and drug checks) and training (Nasser, 1993). The trend toward private security is likely to continue into the next century.

Technological Changes in Policing

No discussion of the future of policing would be complete without at least a brief look at the effect of advancing technology on the field. The computerized innovations of the past decade have left us on the threshold of challenging and sometimes controversial possibilities. In Illinois, for example, ALERTS (Area-wide Law Enforcement Radio Terminal System) allows police personnel using in-car computers to bypass radio dispatchers in order to retrieve vehicle, criminal history, warrant, and other police information directly (Illinois Criminal Justice Information Authority, 1989). Studies of the life cycles of insects (maggots in corpses) have provided new insights into crime victims' times of death. DNA fingerprinting and other forms of genetic testing, as well as the use of automated fingerprint identification and optical disk imaging, make it possible to solve crimes that were once thought to be unsolvable (Arkenau, 1990). "Clearly, advances in technology will affect intergovernmental relations and the whole of society, and will require a commitment from criminal justice practitioners to develop responsible information management policies appropriate for the decade ahead" (Ryder, 1990: vii).

The opportunities presented by "on-board" computers and instantaneous communication among police agencies at all levels and in diverse geographic areas are indeed exciting. Yet, the challenges of developing a criminal justice system in which information flows freely among agencies and at the same time reconciling the right to privacy with what police need to know will not be easily met. Nonetheless, the gap between technology available to industry and that available to the police will surely narrow, raising the possibility of an electronic 'Big Brother' society and the subsequent erosion of personal privacy rights (Gitenstein, 1990).

Clarifying the Police Role

The impact of the changes discussed in this chapter on the nature of the police role will be considerable. While economic circumstances will fluctuate with the times, doing more with less is likely to remain the rule of thumb for most police agencies. The role of the police as negotiators and educators should become increasingly clear in the decade ahead. Communication skills and the ability to resolve disputes through mediation without resorting to arbitration (arrest) have become increasingly important. The police cannot be all things to all people. Only by educating the public with respect to crime prevention and their rights and duties to help maintain order and enforce the law and understanding the needs of the police can we protect democratic values in a setting that encourages dissent while discouraging violence and destruction. Only through a meaningful partnership between the police and the public will we achieve this goal.

Discussion Questions

1. What is the role of community policing in the future of U.S. policing?

2. Discuss the current relationship between the private security industry and public policing. Is that relationship likely to change in the next few years? If so, in what ways?

3. What qualifications should we look for in tomorrow's police leaders?

4. Will the emphases on police education and training remain the same in the years to come? If not, what changes do you anticipate?

5. Discuss some technological changes that are likely to have a major impact on policing for the rest of this century.

6. What do you see as the future for accreditation? Lateral entry?

References

Alpert, G.P. and Dunham, R.G. 1993. *Policing Urban America* 2 ed. Prospect Heights, IL: Waveland Press.

Arkenau, D.L. 1990. "Records Management in the 1990s." *FBI Law Enforcement Bulletin* 59(6), 16–18.

Bennett, C.W. 1993. "The Last Taboo of Community Policing." *Police Chief* 60(8), 86.

Bobinsky, R. 1994. "Reflections on Community-Oriented Policing." *FBI Law Enforcement Bulletin* 63(3), 15–19.

Broderick, J.J. 1987. *Police in a Time of Change.* Prospect Heights, IL: Waveland Press.

Commission Update. 1990. Commission on Accreditation for Law Enforcement Agencies XLIII (March).

Couper, D. and Lobitz, S. 1993. "Leadership for Change: A National Agenda." *Police Chief* 60(12), 15–19.

Cunningham, W.C., Strauchs, J.J., and Van-Meter, C.W. 1990. *The Hallcrest Report II: Private Security Trends 1970–2000.* Boston: Butterworth-Heinemann.

Fitzgerald, J.D. and Cox, S.M. 1994. *Research Methods in Criminal Justice: An Introduction* 2 ed. Chicago: Nelson-Hall.

Germann, A.C. 1993. "Changing the Police: An Impossible Dream?" *Law Enforcement News* 19(383), 6, 10.

Gitenstein, M.H. 1990. "Integrating Technology and Human Values Through Responsible Law and Policy." *Criminal Justice in the 1990s: The Future of Information Management.* Proceedings of a BJS/SEARCH Conference. U.S. Department of Justice (April), 51–53.

Greene, J.R. 1989. "Police and Community Relations: Where Have We Been and Where Are We Going?" In Dunham, R.G. and Alpert, G.P. (eds.), *Critical Issues in Law Enforcement: Contemporary Readings.* Prospect Heights, IL: Waveland Press, 349–368.

Grossman, I. and Doherty, J. 1994. "On Troubled Waters: Promotion and Advancement in the 1990s." *FBI Law Enforcement Bulletin* 63(4), 10–14.

Hagan, F.E. 1989. *Research Methods in Criminal Justice and Criminology.* 2 ed. New York: Macmillan.

Illinois Criminal Justice Information Authority. 1989. "ALERTS In-Car Terminals: Providing Fast, Accurate, and Complete Police Information." *The Compiler* (Fall), 1–5.

Joseph, T.M. 1994. "Walking the Minefields Of Community-Oriented Policing." *FBI Law Enforcement Bulletin* 63(9), 8–12.

Lieberman, P. 1990. "Facing the Future." *Police* 14(1), 44–71.

Macomb Journal. 1991. "State Police Receive Recertification Award." (18 August), p. 2A.

Moore, M. and Kelling, G. 1983. "To Serve and Protect: Learning from Police History." *The Public Interest* 70, 49–65.

Nasser, H.E. 1993. "Private Security Has Become Police Backup." *USA TODAY* (21 December), p. 9A.

O'Leary, D. 1994. "Reflections on Police Privatization." *FBI Law Enforcement Bulletin* 63(9), 21–25.

Ryder, J. 1990. "Introduction." *Criminal Justice in the 1990s: The Future of Information Management.* Proceedings of a BJS/SEARCH Conference. U.S. Department of Justice (April).

Sapp, A.D. and Carter, D. 1988. "Factors in the Choice of an Educational Institution and Police Executive College Degree Preferences." *ACJS Today* 7(2), 1.

Sapp, A.D., Carter, D., and Stephens, D. 1989. "Police Chiefs: CJ Curricula Inconsistent with Contemporary Police Needs." *ACJS Today* 7(4), 1, 5.

Sherman, L.T. 1990. "LEN Interview: Lawrence Sherman." *Law Enforcement News* (31 March), pp. 9–12.

Shernock, S.K. 1992. "The Effects of College Education on Professional Attitudes Among Police." *Journal of Criminal Justice Education* 3(1), 71–92.

Sparrow, M.K., Moore, M.H., and Kennedy, D.M. 1992. *Beyond 911: A New Era For Policing.* New York: Basic Books.

William O. Douglas Institute. 1984. *The Future of Policing.* Seattle: The William O. Douglas Institute.

Appendix ☐

JOB DESCRIPTIONS FOR OFFICERS: QUINCY, ILLINOIS, POLICE DEPARTMENT

Quincy Police Department
Policy and Procedure Manual

Job Analysis

Position Title:	Chief of Police
Division:	Department Head
Immediate Supervisor:	Mayor of the City of Quincy
Employees Supervised:	4
Span of Control:	Ultimate responsibility for all departmental employees
Probationary Period:	Appointed by the Board of Fire and Police Commissioners
Status:	Sworn officer—exempt

I. Duties, Responsibilities, and Tasks:
A. Assumes duties as the active head of the department.
B. Assigns personnel for duty in its several divisions, details members to special duties, and assigns officers to special assignments.
C. Has charge and custody of all property pertaining to the department.
D. Supervises all members of the department and assumes responsibility for its proper management and conduct.
E. Formulates all rules and policies governing the activities of the department.

Reprinted by Permission of Quincy, IL Police Department

F. Formulates and sets forth all work practices and procedures to be followed by members of the department and takes necessary steps to improve police operations.

G. Through subordinate officers, supervises the overall operations of the department.

H. Maintains ultimate authority and accountability for all fiscal matters and financial operations of the department.

I. Assumes responsibility for the control of departmental expenditures, the preparation of the fiscal reports and annual budget documents, and the direction of departmental accounting practices.

J. Maintains a planning and research unit and directs the overall departmental planning and research function.

K. Evaluates the performance of subordinate personnel according to established procedures.

L. Assures departmental cooperation with federal, state, and municipal agencies in matters concerning the police department.

M. Provides fair, equitable, and effective discipline within the department in a manner consistent with existing laws and ordinances and departmental rules and regulations.

N. Sets goals and objectives for the department and its divisions and watches and monitors the progress of subordinate personnel in attaining same.

O. Represents the department at public and private gatherings to explain and elaborate on its activities and functions and to establish positive public relations.

P. Designates two Deputy Chiefs who serve at his or her pleasure.

Q. Protects the interests of subordinates insofar as is consistent with the goals, policies, and rules of the department.

R. Performs and/or directs such other duties as may be required by applicable laws and ordinances or as directed by higher authority.

S. Maintains or causes to be maintained police records of incidents occurring within the corporate limits of the city and any other records required by law.

T. Sets the example for other members of the department by abiding by all departmental rules and policies, accepting job responsibilities, and by avoiding any and all acts which might be construed as compromising one's integrity.

U. Performs the duties of a police officer when required.

V. Serves as a member of the Quincy Traffic Commission, the Quincy Area Safety Council, and the Quincy/Adams County 911 Governing Board.

W. Serves as ex officio harbor master of the city.

X. Supervises the administration of the Quincy Auxiliary Police Program.

Y. Serves as custodian of all lost, abandoned, or stolen property recovered in the city.

II. Supervisory Status:

As department head, the Chief of Police shall supervise all members of the department in accordance with applicable laws and departmental rules and regulations.

III. *Qualifications and Selection Criteria:*

A. A thorough knowledge of the principles and practices of all phases of the police function.
B. A formal education and the appropriate degree consistent with the specific requirement of the appointing authority.
C. Attendance and graduation from recognized police service schools as required by the appointing authority.
D. Extensive administrative skills.
E. The ability to deal tactfully and formally with the public and subordinate officers.
F. An extremely high degree of responsibility.
G. The ability to maintain a high degree of discipline and morale in the department.
H. The ability to supervise the work of a number of subordinates performing a variety of tasks related to police operations.
I. The ability to establish and maintain effective working relationships with other city officials, state and federal authorities, civic leaders, the media, and the general public.
J. The ability to provide effective leadership for and to maintain harmonious relationships within the department.
K. The ability to prepare and effectively present written and oral informational material relating to the activities of the department.

Nothing in this Section shall be construed as limiting the authority of the Chief of Police, and/or a Superior Officer, from assigning such functions or responsibilities as are necessary to establish and maintain maximum departmental efficiency and effectiveness.

Job Analysis

Position Title:	Patrol Section Commander
Division:	Operations
Immediate Supervisor:	Deputy Chief of Operations
Employees Supervised:	3
Span of Control:	78
Probationary Period:	Appointed to position by Chief of Police
Status:	Sworn officer—permanent rank of Captain

I. *Duties, Responsibilities, and Tasks:*

A. Supervises, coordinates, and organizes the patrol forces of the Quincy Police Department in a manner which will utilize patrol personnel in the most effective way.
B. Supervises the patrol section through the Watch Commanders.
C. Requires that patrol supervisors, both Lieutenants and Sergeants, assume the responsibility for supervision and leadership of their subordinate officers.
D. Maintains all patrol section records, such as shift personnel files, compensatory time files, and shift schedules.

E. Coordinates the activities of the Quincy Auxiliary Police within the framework of department operations.

F. Coordinates the investigation of complaints made against the patrol section in accordance with department procedures.

G. Coordinates patrol coverage of special events and assists the Deputy Chief of Operations in planning for such special events with regards to patrol personnel.

H. Performs planning and research duties within the Patrol Section's area of responsibility to identify specific crime problems and areas and initiates and coordinates special programs by which the patrol force can more effectively respond to these problems.

I. Coordinates training of patrol personnel with the Training and Crime Prevention Officer.

J. Represents the department at public and private gatherings to explain and elaborate on its activities and functions and/or establish positive public relations.

K. Supervises the patrol Lieutenants.

L. Evaluates the performance of subordinate personnel in accordance with established procedures.

M. Protects the interests of subordinate officers insofar as is consistent with the goals, policies, and rules of the department.

N. Sets an example for other members of the department by abiding by all departmental rules and policies, accepting job responsibilities, and by avoiding all acts which might be construed as compromising one's integrity.

O. Serves as Watch Commander when necessary.

P. Performs and/or directs such other duties as may be required by applicable laws and ordinances or as directed by higher authority.

Q. Performs the duties of a police officer when required.

R. Mediates complaints concerning parking tickets issued by sworn officers of the department.

S. Participates in the process of setting goals and objectives for the Patrol Section and monitors the performance of subordinate personnel in the attainment of same.

T. Reviews and updates the department's Hazmat and Disaster Plan, annually, or more often if circumstances dictate.

U. Assumes responsibility for supervising the treatment of juveniles taken into custody by sworn officers under his or her command based on applicable departmental policies and procedures.

II. Supervisory Status:

A. The Patrol Section Commander is a supervisor.

III. Duties, Responsibilities, and Tasks:

A. As granted by applicable laws and ordinances and/or as provided by departmental rules and regulations, the Patrol Section Commander has the authority to:

1. Direct the activities and work of subordinate officers and employees.

2. Discipline subordinate officers and employees.
3. Evaluate the performance of subordinates.
4. Relieve subordinate personnel from duty.

IV. Qualifications and Selection Criteria:
A. A sworn member of the Quincy Police Department with the permanent commissioned rank of Captain.
B. A thorough knowledge of patrol and investigative procedures, in addition to a considerable knowledge of all phases of police administration.
C. The ability to direct subordinate supervisors in an efficient and harmonious manner.
D. A thorough knowledge of progressive police management procedures, methods, and techniques.
E. A thorough knowledge of the policies, rules, orders, and procedures of the department.
F. The ability to deal courteously with the public.
G. An extensive knowledge of state laws and local ordinances relating to criminal and traffic matters.
H. The ability to analyze complex police problems and situations and to adopt quick, effective, and reasonable courses of action with due regard to surrounding hazards and circumstances.
I. The professional ability and desire to work toward the accomplishment of the goals of the department and to make substantial contributions toward the realization of these goals.

Nothing in this Section shall be construed as limiting the authority of the Chief of Police, and/or a Superior Officer, from assigning such functions or responsibilities as are necessary to establish and maintain maximum departmental efficiency and effectiveness.

Job Analysis

Position Title: Investigative Section Commander
Division: Operations
Immediate Supervisor: Deputy Chief of Operations
Employees Supervised: 3
Span of Control: 14
Probationary Period: Appointed to the position by Chief of Police
Status: Sworn officer—permanent rank of Lieutenant

I. Duties, Responsibilities, and Tasks:
A. Administers the Investigative Section of the department and assists the Deputy Chief of Operations in coordinating its functions with those of the other sections and divisions of the department.
B. Supervises and coordinates the functions of the Criminal Investigation Unit and the Youth Investigation Unit.

C. Periodically reviews progress on investigations to ensure proper follow-up.

D. Assumes responsibility for the management, control, and use of the investigative funds as directed by the Chief of Police.

E. Performs planning and research duties within the Investigative Section's areas of responsibility as are necessary to address specific problems or as assigned by the Deputy Chief of Operations.

F. Maintains current property control inventories of equipment, property, and supplies assigned to the Investigative Section. Assumes responsibility for the operational readiness, distribution, issuance, and accountability of all applicable property, equipment, and/or supplies within the section.

G. Requires that all personnel under his or her supervision maintain cordial relationships with other members of the department to facilitate an adequate flow of information on criminal and juvenile matters.

H. Establishes sources of intelligence and information regarding criminal matters.

I. Establishes and maintains a good working relationship with the courts and the Office of the State's Attorney.

J. Supervises the maintenance of the evidence room to ensure the proper preservation and disposition of physical evidence.

K. Keeps informed of crime trends in the city and surrounding communities.

L. Participates in the process of setting goals and objectives for the Investigative Section and monitors the performance of subordinate personnel in the attainment of same.

M. Evaluates the performance of subordinate personnel according to established procedure.

N. Establishes and maintains a liaison with the Investigative Divisions of departments in surrounding communities and counties, and with state and federal agencies, in order to facilitate an exchange of information on criminal matters of mutual interest.

O. Assumes responsibility for all investigative section records and files and requires that all reports by subordinates be prepared in a complete, accurate, and prompt fashion.

P. Directs and supervises his subordinates in the collection, identification, and preservation of evidence and sees that the chain of custody of evidence is established to ensure its proper presentation in court.

Q. Maintains good relations with the public and the media.

R. Protects the interests of subordinate personnel insofar as is consistent with the goals, policies, and rules of the department.

S. Sets an example for other members of the department by abiding by all departmental rules and policies, accepting job responsibilities, and by avoiding any and all acts which might be construed as compromising one's integrity.

T. Performs such other duties as may be required by applicable laws and ordinances or as directed by higher authority.

U. Performs the duties of a police officer when required.

V. Assumes responsibility for supervising the treatment of juveniles taken into custody by sworn officers under his or her command based on applicable departmental policies and procedures.

II. Supervisory Status:

A. The Investigative Section Commander is a Supervisor.

B. As granted by applicable laws and ordinances and/or as provided by departmental rules and regulations, the Investigative Section Commander has the authority to:

1. Direct the activities and work of subordinate officers and employees.
2. Discipline subordinate officers and employees.
3. Evaluate the performance of subordinates.
4. Relieve subordinate personnel from duty.

III. Qualifications and Selection Criteria:

A. A sworn member of the Quincy Police Department with the permanent commissioned rank of Lieutenant.

B. The ability to accept responsibility, supervise subordinates, accomplish work requirements and to ensure compatibility between personnel of the Investigative Section and those of other sections and police departments.

C. A thorough knowledge of state laws and city ordinances relating to criminal and juvenile matters.

D. A thorough knowledge of investigative techniques, crime scene procedures, evidentiary procedures, and techniques of interrogation.

Job Analysis

Position Title:	Watch Commander
Division:	Operations
Immediate Supervisor:	Patrol Section Commander
Employees Supervised:	2
Span of Control:	15—actual number varies according to scheduling
Probationary Period:	Appointed to the position by Chief of Police
Status:	Sworn officer—permanent rank of Lieutenant

I. Duties, Responsibilities, and Tasks:

A. Commands and administers a patrol shift within the Operations Division.

B. Keeps informed of conditions within the city which are of concern to the department and makes any tactical decisions necessary to provide a proper and effective police response to problems which occur.

C. Keeps informed of conditions within the department and maintains lines of communications to his superior and subordinate officers, keeping them informed on pertinent matters.

D. Delegates authority to subordinate officers to ensure that the patrol shift maintains a high level of performance.

E. Supervises and monitors subordinate officers to ensure the efficient operation of the shift and compliance with all departmental policies, rules, orders, and procedures.

F. Promptly corrects all observed mistakes by subordinate officers assigned to his or her shift.

G. Motivates, trains, instructs, and counsels officers under his or her command, giving particular attention to probationary officers.

H. Recommends departmental personnel who display excellence of performance for commendation.

I. Insists that all personnel under his or her command be familiar with, and adhere to, the policies, rules, orders, and procedures of the department.

J. Enforces discipline among the personnel under his or her command and takes appropriate action when violations are noted.

K. Makes reports of disciplinary problems, along with recommendations, and forwards them through the chain of command.

L. Evaluates the performance of subordinate personnel according to established procedure.

M. Reviews the case reports and other work done by officers to ensure that all duties are completed properly.

N. Assumes responsibility for properly preparing, transmitting, and filing all reports, forms, and records pertaining to his or her command.

O. Reviews individual officer's activity reports and counsels those officers who demonstrate substandard levels of activity.

P. Requires that all subordinate officers maintain cordial relations with personnel from other units, sections, and divisions of the department to ensure a proper flow of information.

Q. Makes work assignments for personnel under his or her command and requires that those work assignments be completed in compliance with the established policies, rules, orders, and procedures of the department.

R. Assumes responsibility for informing the Chief of Police, the Deputy Chief of Operations, and the Patrol Section Commander of the facts and circumstances pertaining to any crime of great magnitude or importance or matter of serious departmental concern and is responsible for supervising such investigation until relieved by competent authority as specified by department policies and procedures.

S. Assumes responsibility for holding a daily roll call for all personnel assigned to his/her shift. Such roll call shall include the reading of any pertinent information from the daily log (wanteds, stolen vehicles, major incidents, etc.) and the exchange of any other information necessary to the efficient operation of the shift.

T. Ensures that meaningful roll call training is presented to officers under his or her command.

U. Performs the duties of a police officer when required.

V. Assumes responsibility for supervising the treatment of juveniles taken into custody by sworn officers under his or her command based on applicable departmental policies and procedures.

W. Protects the interests of subordinate officers insofar as is consistent with the policies, rules, orders, and procedures of the department.

X. Performs planning and research duties within the patrol operations area of responsibility as are necessary to address a specific requirement or as may be assigned by the Patrol Section Commander by the Deputy Chief of Operations and/or the Chief of Police.

Y. Assumes responsibility for accepting bail from persons charged with bailable offenses and shall complete all required forms.

Z. Ensures that the activities of his or her shift and other pertinent information are entered on the daily log.

AA. Participates in the process of setting goals for the shift and monitors the performance of subordinate personnel in the attainment of same.

AB. Inspects the appearance and equipment of officers under his or her command and insists that all equipment and uniforms be maintained and worn properly.

AC. Performs and/or directs such other duties as may be required by applicable laws and ordinances or as directed by a higher authority.

AD. Sets an example for other members of the department by abiding by all departmental rules and policies, accepting job responsibilities, and by avoiding all acts which might be construed as compromising one's integrity.

II. Supervisory Status:

A. The Watch Commander is a supervisor.

B. As granted by applicable laws and ordinances and/or as provided by departmental rules and regulations, the Watch Commander has the authority to:
   1. Direct the activities and work of subordinate officers and employees.
   2. Discipline subordinate officers and employees.
   3. Evaluate the performance of subordinates.
   4. Relieve subordinate personnel from duty.

III. Qualifications and Selection Criteria:

A. A sworn officer of the Quincy Police Department with the permanent commissioned rank of Lieutenant.

B. Ability to accept responsibility and supervise subordinates and to administer the patrol shift which he or she commands.

C. An extensive knowledge of state laws and local ordinances relating to criminal and traffic matters.

D. A thorough knowledge of the policies, rules, orders, and procedures of the department.

E. A knowledge of the methods of criminal investigation.

F. The ability to deal with the public in a courteous manner.
G. The ability to analyze complex police problems and situations and to adapt quick, effective, and reasonable courses of action with due regard to surrounding hazards and circumstances.
H. The ability to command the respect of subordinate officers and to establish and maintain effective working relationships among the personnel in his or her watch.
I. A thorough familiarity with progressive police management procedures, methods, and techniques.
J. The professional ability and desire to work toward the accomplishment of the goals of the department and to make substantial contributions toward the realization of these goals.

Nothing in this Section shall be construed as limiting the authority of the Chief of Police, and/or a Superior Officer, from assigning such functions or responsibilities as are necessary to establish and maintain maximum departmental efficiency and effectiveness.

Job Analysis

Position Title:	Patrol Sergeant
Division:	Operations
Immediate Supervisor:	Watch Commander
Employees Supervised:	Approximately 13—varies according to scheduling
Span of Control:	Approximately 13
Probationary Period:	Appointed to the position by Chief of Police
Status:	Sworn officer—permanent rank of Sergeant

I. Duties, Responsibilities, and Tasks:
A. In the absence of the Watch Commander, performs the duties of the Watch Commander.
B. Keeps informed of conditions within the city which are of concern to the department and makes any tactical decisions necessary to provide a proper and effective police response to problems which occur.
C. Keeps informed of conditions within the department and maintains lines of communication to his or her superior and subordinate officers, keeping them informed of pertinent matters.
D. With the authority delegated to him or her by the Watch Commander, makes work assignments to subordinate officers and requires that these work assignments be completed in compliance with the established policies, rules, orders, and procedures of the department.
E. Conducts direct field supervision and monitoring of subordinate officers to ensure the efficient operation of the shift and compliance with departmental policies, rules, orders, and procedures.
F. Motivates, trains, instructs, and counsels subordinate personnel, giving particular attention to probationary officers.

G. Promptly corrects all observed mistakes by subordinate officers.

H. Enforces discipline among personnel under his or her command and takes appropriate action when violations are noted.

I. Makes reports of disciplinary problems, along with recommendations to the Watch Commander.

J. Recommends department personnel who display excellence of performance for commendation.

K. Evaluates the performance of subordinate personnel according to established procedures.

L. Inspects the appearance and equipment of officers under his or her command and insists that all equipment and uniforms be maintained and worn properly.

M. Inspects squad cars and the equipment therein.

N. Conducts roll call and roll call training.

O. Supervises Quincy Auxiliary Police personnel who are working during the shift's tour of duty.

P. Responds to the scene of police emergencies, major crimes, and disasters, and ensures that adequate personnel and equipment are on hand to deal with the incident. Takes command, if necessary, of the scene and directs the efforts of all personnel until the problem is resolved or he/she is relieved by competent authority as specified by departmental policies and procedures.

Q. Maintains such records as may be required to carry out departmental requirements.

R. Ensures that officers assigned to street duty remain on the street unless circumstances dictate otherwise.

S. Supervises, in a staff capacity, members of other sections of the department on street duty in the absence of their own supervising officer.

T. Requires that subordinates give special attention to areas where crimes are frequently committed and where criminals may congregate.

U. Requires that subordinates promptly investigate crimes, traffic violations, and unusual occurrences which occur in their beats and take appropriate action.

V. Maintains a courteous and professional attitude when dealing with the public.

W. Protects the interests of subordinate officers insofar as is consistent with departmental policies, rules, orders, and procedures.

X. Performs and/or directs such other duties as may be required by applicable laws or ordinances.

Y. Set an example for other members of the department by abiding by all policies and rules, accepting job responsibilities, and by avoiding all acts which might be construed as compromising one's integrity.

Z. Performs the duties of a police officer when required.

AA. Assumes responsibility for supervising the treatment of juveniles taken into custody by sworn officers under his/her command based on applicable departmental policies and procedures.

II. Supervisory Status:

A. The Patrol Sergeant is a supervisor.

B. As granted by applicable laws and ordinances and/or as provided by departmental rules and regulations, the Patrol Sergeant has the authority to:
  1. Direct the activities and work of subordinate officers and employees.
  2. Discipline subordinate officers and employees.
  3. Evaluate the performance of subordinates.
  4. Relieve subordinate personnel from duty.

III. Qualifications and Selection Criteria:

A. A sworn member of the Quincy Police Department with the permanent commissioned rank of Sergeant.

B. The ability to accept responsibility and supervise subordinates.

C. A thorough knowledge of the policies, rules, orders, and procedures of the department.

D. An extensive knowledge of state laws and local ordinances relating to traffic and criminal matters.

E. A knowledge of modern criminal investigation techniques.

F. The ability to deal with the public in a courteous manner.

G. The ability to analyze complex police procedures and situations, and to adopt quick, effective, and reasonable courses of action with due regard to surrounding hazards and circumstances.

H. The ability to command respect of subordinate officers, and to establish and maintain effective working relationships among the personnel in his or her watch.

Nothing in this Section shall be construed as limiting the authority of the Chief of Police, and/or a Superior Officer, from assigning such functions or responsibilities as are necessary to establish and maintain maximum departmental efficiency and effectiveness.

Job Analysis

Position Title:	Investigative Sergeant
Division:	Operations
Immediate Supervisor:	Investigative Section Commander
Employees Supervised:	Criminal Specialist—6
	Youth Specialist—5
Span of Control:	Criminal Specialist—6
	Youth Specialist—5
Probationary Period:	Appointed to the position by Chief of Police
Status:	Sworn officer—permanent rank of Sergeant

I. Duties, Responsibilities, and Tasks:

A. General:
  1. Keeps informed of crime trends in the city and surrounding areas.
  2. Reviews all reports of subordinate personnel.

3. Delegates job assignments and monitors individual officer's work to ensure effective performance by all personnel, correcting deficiencies where observed.
4. Encourages and requires that all personnel under his or her supervision maintain cordial relationships with other members of the department to facilitate an adequate flow of information on investigative and intelligence matters.
5. Evaluates the performance of subordinate personnel according to an established procedure.
6. Maintains such files and records as may be required to carry out departmental requirements.
7. Takes command, if necessary, of the scene of major crimes and directs and supervises the efforts of all personnel involved until the problem is resolved or until he/she is relieved by competent authority.
8. Assumes responsibility for the ongoing training of subordinate officers.
9. Performs the duties of Investigative Section Commander when assigned to do so by proper authority.
10. Performs the duties of Investigator as needed.
11. Protects the interest of subordinate officers insofar as is consistent with departmental rules, policies, order, and procedures.
12. Sets an example for other members of the department by abiding by all departmental rules and policies, by accepting job responsibilities, and by avoiding any and all acts which might be construed as compromising one's integrity.
13. Performs such other duties as may be required by state laws, local ordinance, or as directed by higher authority.

B. Criminal Specialist:
   1. Directly supervises the activities of the Criminal Investigators.
   2. Keeps informed of current laws and court decisions regarding criminal investigation and procedure.
   3. Establishes sources of intelligence information regarding criminal activity.
   4. Performs the duties of Youth Specialist when required or when assigned to do so by proper authority.
   5. Establishes and maintains positive working relationships with the office of State Attorney and other entities involved in the prosecution of criminals.

C. Youth Specialist:
   1. Directly supervises the activities of the Youth Investigators and Liaison Officers.
   2. Keeps informed of current laws and court decisions regarding juvenile investigation and procedure.
   3. Establishes and maintains sources of intelligence information regarding delinquent juvenile activity and the activity of those who might harm children.
   4. Assumes responsibility for establishing and maintaining a positive working relationship with the various agencies or institutions which

provide service to the youth of the community. This includes, but is not limited to: the Department of Children and Family Services; Family Service Agency; public and private school systems; other law enforcement agencies; probation and juvenile prosecutors.
  5. Performs the duties of Criminal Specialist as required or when assigned to do so by proper authority.

II. Supervisory Status:
  A. The Investigative Sergeant is a supervisor.
  B. As granted by applicable laws and ordinances and/or as provided by departmental rules and regulations, the Investigative Sergeant has the authority to:
   1. Direct the activities and work of subordinate officers and employees.
   2. Discipline subordinate officers and employees.
   3. Evaluate the performance of subordinates.
   4. Relieve subordinate personnel from duty.

III. Qualifications and Selection Criteria:
  A. A sworn member of the Quincy Police Department with the permanent commissioned rank of Sergeant.
  B. The ability to accept responsibility, supervise subordinates, accomplish work requirements, and ensure compatibility between personnel of the Investigations Section and those of other units and departments.
  C. A thorough knowledge of court procedures.
  D. An extensive knowledge of investigative techniques, crime scene procedures, evidentiary procedures, and techniques of interrogation.
  E. The ability and willingness to deal with youth and their families in another than traditional law enforcement manner.

Nothing in this Section shall be construed as limiting the authority of the Chief of Police, and/or a Superior Officer, from assigning such functions or responsibilities as are necessary to establish and maintain maximum departmental efficiency and effectiveness.

Job Analysis

Position Title:	Patrol Officer
Division:	Operations
Immediate Supervisor:	Patrol Sergeant
Employees Supervised:	DNA
Span of Control:	DNA
Probationary Period:	Eighteen Months
Status:	Sworn Officer—permanent rank of Patrol Officer

I. Duties, Responsibilities, and Tasks:
  A. Preserves the public peace.
  B. Prevents crime.

C. Detects and arrests violators of the law.

D. Protects life and property.

E. Enforces all criminal and traffic laws of the State of Illinois and the ordinances of the City of Quincy.

F. Patrols an assigned area of the city and checks buildings to ensure that they are in a safe condition and that no forced entries have occurred.

G. Investigates suspicious or unusual incidents occurring during his or her tour of duty and conducts preliminary investigations of all actual crimes which he or she discovers or is assigned to investigate.

H. Submits written reports to supervisors of activities on assigned shift.

I. Apprehends and arrests suspects for felony or misdemeanor offenses in accordance with city ordinances and state statutes, collects evidence, and interviews any possible witness that may be used in a court hearing.

J. Investigates complaints of a noncriminal nature; i.e., family disputes, missing persons, and injured subjects, and assesses each individual case to determine appropriate action.

K. Establishes sources of intelligence and information.

L. Conducts traffic accident investigations, completes required forms including the identification of all passengers, vehicles, witnesses, location, injuries, date, and time, and issues citations where appropriate and consistent with departmental procedure.

M. Enforces traffic and parking regulations through visual and radar patrol.

N. Assists in the maintenance of traffic control for efficient flow through the city; issues warnings or citations to violators.

O. Observes and searches the scene of a crime for physical evidence. Collects, photographs, and/or preserves evidence found for possible use in future legal proceedings.

P. Completes special investigations when assigned.

Q. Serves as an escort when assigned.

R. Provides traffic and/or crowd control at special events.

S. Furnishes assistance and information to citizens and motorists.

T. Completes follow-up investigations of criminal and misdemeanor offenses and ordinance violations as required or as assigned by higher authority.

U. Notifies headquarters when fires are observed and responds when dispatched to fires or fire alarms.

V. Completes all required records and reports of activities.

W. Serves as a witness in court cases and is responsible for obeying all lawful subpoenas.

X. Performs specialized assignments as may be assigned by the Chief of Police or other competent authority. Examples of specialized assignments include, but are not limited to: Breath Test Operator, Field Training Officer, Range Officer, etc.

Y. Requests specialized assistance—as may be required—to handle specific problems encountered, i.e. Evidence Technician, Criminal Investigator, Youth Investigator, etc.

Z. Responsible for attending daily roll call, unless otherwise engaged in police duties, and for recording all appropriate information relayed by the Patrol Sergeant or Watch Commander.

AA. Serves subpoenas and summonses as required.

AB. Attends training sessions and departmental meetings as may be required.

AC. Maintains a courteous and professional demeanor when interacting with members of the public.

AD. Establishes and maintains a rapport with all members and segments of the community to enhance the police image and instill a respect for law and order.

AE. Reports any circumstances which may present a public safety hazard and/or takes appropriate measures to reduce or remove such hazards.

AF. Observes parks, schools, and other places where children may gather for the purpose of investigating suspicious persons or activities that might be of danger to children.

AG. Notifies dispatch of location and reason for being out of service, of location of vehicle stops and vehicle information, and of all requests for police service.

AH. Answers and executes all orders from dispatchers as if they were a direct order from a superior officer.

AI. Remains obedient and responsible to all verbal and written orders issued by superiors and to all work assignments transmitted to him or her by authorized persons.

AJ. Performs such other duties as may be required by state law, city ordinances, and departmental rule, or as may be assigned by a superior officer.

II. Qualifications and Selection Criteria:

A. Appointment to the rank of Patrol Officer by the Board of Fire and Police Commission.

B. Requires knowledge, skill and mental development equivalent to the completion of four years of high school as demonstrated by a diploma from a high school or equivalent certification (G.E.D.).

C. Requires certification by the Illinois Local Governmental Law Enforcement Officers Training Board within six months of the date of initial employment or as soon as practicable.

D. Requires working knowledge of the geography of the city and location of important buildings.

E. Requires working knowledge of first aid principles and skill in its application.

F. Requires ability to analyze situations and to adopt a quick, effective and reasonable course of action.

G. Requires ability to use good discretion.

H. Requires ability to deal courteously, but firmly with the public.

I. Requires ability to speak clearly and give precise and understandable directions.

J. Requires skill in the use and care of firearms.

K. Requires physical strength and ability sufficient to meet police duty requirements.

L. Requires ability to understand and follow oral and written instructions.

M. Requires the ability to prepare clear and comprehensive written and typed reports.

N. Requires ability to establish and maintain effective relationships with staff, fellow workers, and the general public.

O. Requires working knowledge of pertinent federal and state laws and municipal ordinances.

Nothing in this Section shall be construed as limiting the authority of the Chief of Police, and/or a Superior Officer from assigning such functions or responsibilities as are necessary to establish and maintain maximum departmental efficiency and effectiveness.

Job Analysis

Position Title:	Investigator
Division:	Operations
Immediate Supervisor:	Investigative Sergeant
Employees Supervised:	DNA
Span of Control:	DNA
Probationary Period:	Appointed to the position by Chief of Police
Status:	Sworn officer—permanent rank of Patrol Officer

I. Duties, Responsibilities, and Tasks:

A. General:

1. Enforces state laws and local ordinances and makes arrests when necessary.
2. Conducts crime scene searches and gathers, documents, and preserves physical evidence.
3. Operates specialized equipment as required.
4. Establishes sources of intelligence and information.
5. Prepares cases and presents evidence in court.
6. Establishes and maintains cordial relationships with other members of the department to facilitate an adequate flow of information and intelligence.
7. Fingerprints and photographs persons as may be required.
8. Completes and forwards such forms, reports, and records as may be required.
9. Performs such other duties as may be required by State law, city ordinance, or departmental rule, or assigned by a superior officer.
10. Performs the duties of a Police Officer as required.
11. All investigators are hereby designated as juvenile officers as is required in Chapter 37 of the Illinois Revised Statutes.

B. Criminal Investigator:

1. Initially investigates and/or continues investigation of major criminal complaints or other such special investigations as assigned by the Investigative Section Commander or Investigative Sergeant.

2. Questions and obtains statements from suspects, victims, witnesses, and other interested parties.
3. Serves as and performs the duties of Evidence Technician when so assigned.
4. Cooperates with the patrol section in criminal investigations and gives assistance when requested.
5. Cooperates and assists with agencies as requested in the investigation of criminal matters and maintains a good working relationship with said agencies to expedite the flow of intelligence and information.
6. Conducts background investigation of applicants for police officer and city license holder, i.e. taxi license, liquor license, special police officer, second hand store, etc.
7. Performs duties of Youth Investigator as necessary or when assigned to do so by competent authority.
C. Youth Investigator:
1. Initially investigates and/or continues investigation of police matters involving juveniles.
2. Investigates various incidents of criminal and juvenile conduct including but not limited to: child abuse; neglect; dependency and addiction; sexual abuse and exploitation of children; missing and/or runaway children; minors requiring authoritative intervention.
3. Prepares and delivers speeches and/or presentations on juvenile-related matters and other matters to civic, school and special interest groups as assigned.
4. Provides preventive patrol in the vicinity of places frequented by youths, such as fast food restaurants, schools, parks, bowling alleys, malls, etc.
5. Utilizes all remedies and/or options available to him or her through the Juvenile Court Act (IRS Chapter 37) to satisfactorily deal with juvenile matters and to divert youth from the juvenile court system.
6. Establishes and maintains cordial relationships with schools, other groups, agencies, and institutions that might be of assistance to the department in juvenile matters.
7. Performs the duties of Criminal Investigator as necessary or when assigned to do so by competent authority.

II. Qualifications and Selection Criteria:
A. General:
1. A Sworn member of the Quincy Police Department with the permanent commissioned rank of Patrol Officer.
2. Meets or exceeds the qualification and selection criteria for the position of Patrol Officer.
3. A general knowledge of investigative procedure, techniques of interrogation, crime scene procedures, evidentiary procedures, and the use of specialized equipment required by the job.

B. Criminal Investigator:
1. Must have extensive knowledge of State laws and local ordinances relating to criminal matters.
2. Must have extensive knowledge of court procedures.
3. Must have initiative and be willing to accept responsibility.

C. Youth Investigator:
1. Must have extensive knowledge of State laws and local ordinances specifically relating to juvenile matters.
2. Must have extensive knowledge of juvenile court procedures.
3. Must have the ability to deal with juveniles in other than a traditional law enforcement role.
4. Must have the desire and attitude required to aid youths and their families and to assist with community-related problems.
5. Must have the ability to speak to groups of citizens and present a professional image.

Nothing in this Section shall be construed as limiting the authority of the Chief of Police, and/or a Superior Officer, from assigning such functions or responsibilities as are necessary to establish and maintain maximum departmental efficiency and effectiveness.

NAME INDEX

SUBJECT INDEX